AFTER DEATH

Suches,

I hope the words written by Léon Dennis can help you understand why sometimes things happen in our lives. Reading his book helped me a lot, because it opened my mind to understand that we are immortal spirists, and, consequently, we need to be aware in being a better human begin day after day.

I really hope his book can help you as well, in your life and decisions that need to be made.

I hope you can enjoy these new concepts. With affection

Dele nfl

AFTER DEATH

*Being a Treatise on Spiritual Philosophy, offering a Scientific and Rational Solution of the Problems of Life and Death.
Nature and Destiny of Human Beings.
The Successive Lives.*

Semper ascendens

Léon Denis

After Death
Translation copyright © 2017 by
United States Spiritist Council (Jussara Korngold)

All rights reserved. No part of this publication may be reproduced, stored in or introduced into a retrieval system, or transmitted, in any form, or by any means (electronic, mechanical, photocopying, recording or otherwise) without the prior written permission of the publisher, except in the case of brief quotations and if the source and publisher are mentioned.
United States Spiritist Council
http://www.spiritit.us
Email: info@spiritist.us
Original Title: Après La Mort – Léon Denis

ISBN: 0998648108
ISBN: 9780998648101
Library of Congress Control Number: 2017932059
United States Spiritist Council

Translation: George G. Fleurot (1909) and Jussara Korngold (2017)
French Editing: Jussara Korngold (2017)
This version was edited and revised utilizing the French original (Nouvelle Edition conforme a L'Edition Originale - Union Spirite Française et Francophone)

Cover design: Mauro de Souza Rodrigues

Main entry under title:
After Death
1. Religious Philosophy 2. Spiritist Doctrine 3. Christianity I. Denis, Léon
Manufactured in the United States of America

*To The Great and Noble Spirits
Who Have Revealed to Me
The August Mysteries of Destiny,
Whose Teachings Have Strengthened Within Me The
Sentiment of Justice, The Love of Wisdom, and of Duty;
Whose Voices Have Banished My Doubts
and Appeased My Cares;
Whose Generous Souls Have Sustained Me in My Struggles;
Comforted Me in the Hour of Trial;
Who Have Elevated My Thoughts
To the Level of Those Luminous Heights
Where Truths Sits Enthroned;
I Dedicate These Pages.*

Table of Contents

Foreword · xi
Introduction · xiii

First Part Beliefs and Unbeliefs

1 Religion and the Secret Doctrine · · · · · · · · · · · · · · · · · · 3
2 India · 13
3 Egypt · 26
4 Greece · 33
5 Gaul · 44
6 Christianity · 54
7 Materialism and Positivism · 77
8 The Moral Crisis · 89

Second Part The Great Problems

9 The Universe and God · 103
10 The Immortal Spirit · 122
11 The Plurality of Lives · 127
12 The Purpose of Life · 132
13 Trial and Death · 136
14 Objections · 141

Third Part The Invisible World

15 Nature and Science · 149
16 Matter and Force – The Sole Principle of All Things · · · · · 152
17 The Fluids – Magnetism · 155
18 Spiritist Phenomena · 160
19 Scientific Testimony · 163
20 Spiritism in France · 177
21 The Perispirit or Fluidic Body · · · · · · · · · · · · · · · · · · · 185
22 The Mediums · 190
23 The Evolution of the Soul and of the Perispirit · · · · · · · · · 196
24 Ethical and Philosophical Consequences · · · · · · · · · · · · 198
25 Spiritism and Science · 200
26 The Dangers of Spiritism · 203
27 Charlatanism and Venality · 207
28 The Utility of Psychological Research · · · · · · · · · · · · · · 210

Fourth Part The Hereafter

29 Know Thyself · 215
30 The Last Hour · 217
31 The Judgment · 221
32 The Will and the Fluids · 225
33 The Life of Space · 231
34 Errant Souls · 235
35 The Higher Life · 237
36 Inferior Spirits · 248
37 Hell and its Demons · 254
38 The Action of the Human Being over Unhappy Spirits · · · 256
39 Justice, Solidarity, Responsibility · · · · · · · · · · · · · · · · · 259
40 Providence and Free-Will · 264
41 Reincarnation · 268

Fifth Part The Straight Way

42 The Moral Life 275
43 Duty 279
44 Faith, Hope and Consolation 283
45 Pride, Wealth and Poverty 288
46 Selfishness 294
47 Charity 299
48 Patience and Goodness 306
49 Love 310
50 Resignation in Adversity 314
51 Prayer 325
52 Work, Sobriety and Continence 333
53 Study 338
54 Education 342
55 Social Problems 345
56 The Moral Law 351

    Recapitulation 353
    Conclusion 357
    Biography of Léon Denis 363

Foreword

Léon Denis first encountered Spiritism when he was eighteen years old. He was passing a bookstore in Tours, France, his home town, when he saw a book that caught his attention at the window: The Spirits' Book by Allan Kardec. Living on a meager salary at the time, it was an extravagance for him to purchase such a relatively expensive book for his means. Nevertheless, the young Léon Denis decided to invest his money on that book. His difficulties did not end there, he would face yet another obstacle: his mother's censorship of the books he was allowed to read, so he had to hide it from her. Interestingly, as life would have it, she would eventually find that book later, read it and become a spiritist.

In his adult life, Léon Denis would be invited to follow a political career as a direct result of his oratory and rhetoric, which had already granted him the status of a famous and very respected speaker. He would go on to become Deputy of Tourane, France; nevertheless, upon heeding the advice of the spirits, he would leave his political career in order to dedicate himself exclusively to the dissemination of Spiritism. Tourane's loss and an immense gain for Spiritist history. Today, we can only but express our heartfelt gratitude to his extraordinary spirit and to the outstanding contribution he brought to the Spiritist Doctrine.

Among his works, After Death is one of the most important books of classic Spiritist literature. In his poetic prose, a style that we find in his other books, Léon Denis wrote, "As a writer, Kardec is both admirably clear and extremely logical." One could certainly state the same about Monsieur Denis, who wrote with both his mind and heart. It is therefore not surprising that After Death has been translated into several languages and that it continues to elate people all over the world...

Jussara Korngold
New York, NY, February 2017

Introduction

I have seen, half buried in their winding-sheets of sand or stone, the famous cities of a bygone day; Carthage, of the white promontories; the Greek towns of Sicily; the Roman Campaign with its broken aqueducts and gaping tombs, and also those ancient cities of the dead, that lie so still, wrapped in their twenty centuries of slumber beneath Vesuvius' ashes. I have seen the last vestiges of ancient towns that teemed, of yore, like ant hills with human life - today but forsaken ruins, simmering in loneliness beneath the ardent rays of Eastern sun.

I have evoked the multitudes that populate these cities with their busy life. At my call they have parade before me with passions that consumed them: their hatreds, their loves, their fleeting ambitions, their triumphs and their reverses; all to be blown away like a puff of smoke by the breath of time. Beholding which I said to myself: this then is what becomes of great nations, of giant capitals - a few heaped stones, a few dreary mounds, a few stones carvings meagerly sheltered by a sparse vegetation through which the night wind moans. Of these, history has kept a record telling of their existence, of their passing greatness, of their final fall - until the earth has buried all. But, besides these, how many others are there whose very names are unknown? How many towns, how many races, how many civilizations lie forever engulfed beneath the glittering waste of waters that overspreads submerged continents!

And I asked myself, whence this unrest that torments the peoples of the earth: wherefore these countless generations that succeed one another like the sand beds that the tide so constantly brings to overlay those that were before? Why this work, the struggle, the sufferings, if all is to end in the grave? The centuries, those brief instants of eternity, have witnessed the passing of nations and of kingdoms, and nothing has remained: the Sphinx has devoured all.

Where then is the individual bound? Is it to nothingness or towards some light unknown? Nature, smiling and eternal, frame with garlands of beauty the crumbling remains of fallen empires. In it nothing dies but to be born again. Its evolutions are presided over by profound laws and immutable order. Can it be that the individual and his other works are alone destined to nothingness, to oblivion?

The impression wrought by the contemplation of dead cities I have again experimented, more acutely, in the presence of the cold remains of some dear one who had shared my life.

One, beloved, is about to die! While, as with a heavy heart you bend over him, even as you look, upon his features the shadows of the hereafter slowly spread. The inner light now casts but a pale and trembling flicker: so, it weakens still, and then goes out. And now, all that in him attested life: the sparkling eye, the mouth that smiled, the limbs that so freely moved, all is glazed, silence, and motionless. On that funereal couch there lies but a corpse outstretched. Where is the person who has not pondered this mystery; who, during the final vigil, alone in solemn communication with death, has not asked oneself how it would be with him? This problem concerns us all, for we must, each one of us, submit to the law. It behooves us to know whether, at that hour, everything is verily at an end, whether death signifies but annihilation's gloomy rest; or whether it is, on the contrary, the portal to a new realm of sensation.

But problems everywhere arise. Over the world's vast area, some thinkers claim, suffering holds sovereign sway; everywhere the goad of need and pain urges on the frantic round, the terrible saturnalia of life and death. From every quarter arises the despairing cry of some human being, speeding over the dark roadway that leads to the unknown: to such, life spells but a perpetual struggle-glory, wealth, beauty, talent, the royalties of a day. Death passes and in passing gleans these glittering flowers and leaves the withered stalks behind. Death is the question mark that unceasingly confronts us; the great first question upon which hang other questions without end, the study of which has been the preoccupation and the despair of the ages, and to whose solution so many philosophies have been dedicated.

Despite all these efforts, night still enshrouds us. Our own epoch struggles in darkness and in emptiness, vainly seeking a remedy for its woes. Material progress is immense, but in the midst of the wealth accumulated by civilization one may still perish from want and privation. The human being is neither happier nor better, his heavy labors are no longer lightened by a high ideal, nor is he heartened by any clear conception of his destiny: hence his backslidings, his excesses, and his rebellion. Vanished is the faith of the past; materialism and skepticism have stepped into its place, their breath has fanned the devouring flame of human passions, desires and appetites, and social revolutions lowers upon us!

At times, tormented alike by the spectacle that this world presents and by the uncertainty of the hereafter, the human being raises his eyes heavenward in search of the truth. He silently questions nature and his own soul; he demands of science its secrets, of religion its enthusiasm. But nature is sealed and the answers of priest and scientist alike satisfy neither his heart nor his mind. There is, however, a solution to these problems: one greater, wiser, more rational and more comforting than any of the creeds and philosophies of the day can offer, and this solution rests upon the strongest possible foundation - upon the testimony of the senses, and upon experience.

At a time when materialism has reached its apex, and has sown broadcast the creed of negation, there arises a new belief, based upon fact, which offers to the mind a refuge wherein thought may finally master the eternal laws of justice and progress. An efflorescence of ideas, long believed to be dead but which were but slumbering, bursts forth, heralding a renascence both intellectual and moral. Doctrines that were marrow of past civilizations now reappear broader and greater: manifold phenomena, long disdained, but whose importance some scientists are beginning to realize, at last supply a basis for demonstration and for certitude. The practice of magnetism, hypnotism, suggestion, still more, the physical researches of men like Crookes, Wallace, Lodge, Myers, Aksakof, Paul Gibier, A. de Rochas, etc., furnish new data towards the solution of the great problem. Horizons roll back and forms of life appear in regions where one no longer thought to seek them. From out of these discoveries, there is born a conception of the world and of life, a knowledge of the superior laws, an assurance of universal justice and order well calculated to awaken in the heart of the individual, together with a firmer and more enlightened faith in his destiny, a profound feeling of his duties and a real attachment for his fellow-beings. These are indeed truths well calculated to transform the face of the world!

Such is the doctrine that we extend to all those in search of the truth, whatsoever their class or belief. Many books have already been filled with this faith, but we have nevertheless deemed it wise in these pages to recapitulate its principal facts under another form, both for the use of those who are tired of living as blind individuals, without self-knowledge, and for those who, having ceased to be satisfied with what a material and wholly superficial civilization can give, crave a nobler purpose. Above all, it is for you, sons and daughters of the people! For you, workers whose path is stony, whose life is hard, whose skies are forbidding, and to whom more bitter seem the winds of adversity: it is for you that this book was written. It would not supply you with all the scientific explanation, as the human brain would not be able to absorb it, but it can be a further step to a true enlightenment.

In proving to you that life is neither an irony of fate nor the stupid outcome of chance, but that, on the contrary, it is the product of a law, both just and equitable, in throwing open to you the radiant vistas of the future, it will furnish you with a nobler incentive for your actions, it will cause a ray of hope to shine in the darkness of your uncertainty; it will lighten the burden of your trials and will teach you to be unafraid when death draws night. Open it with confidence and read it without misgivings, for it proceeds from one who strives above all for your welfare.

Many, perhaps, will reject our conclusions and but a few will accept them. Be this as it may! We care not for success, one motive alone inspires us: the respect and the love we bear truth. A single ambition actuates us; we would like that when this worn figment returns to earth, our immortal spirit might exclaim: My stay here below will not have been barren if I have helped to mitigate one single sorrow, to enlighten one single mind in quest of the truth, to uplift one downcast and fainting spirit.

First Part
Beliefs and Unbeliefs

1

Religion and the Secret Doctrine

In looking backwards over this world's past, in recalling its vanished religions, its shaken faiths, one is overcome by dizziness at the mere sight of the sinuous trail described by human thought. Slow indeed has been its advance. In the beginning, thought found its favorite haunts in the gloomy crypts of India, in Egypt's subterranean temples; the catacombs of Rome; later, it lingered in the dim twilight of great cathedrals. Strangely did it seem to prosper in obscure places, in the heavy atmosphere of the monastery and in the stillness of cloisters, rather than in the broad daylight of open spaces, an in a word, in the study of nature.

A cursory survey, a superficial glance, over the beliefs and superstitions of the past inevitably conduce to doubt. But if one perseveres and lifts the dazzling outer veil which is interposed between the great hidden mysteries within and the gaze of the public without; if one but penetrates into the inner sanctuaries of religious conception, then will one find himself in the presence of a momentous revelation. The showy outer shell, and the pomp of ceremony, were designed to impress the masses. Behind these veils the ancient religions wore a very different aspect; they presented a grave and lofty character that was both scientific and philosophic.

Their teaching was dual: public and superficial, hidden and inner, the latter being solely revealed to the initiated. This inner teaching has been but lately reconstructed by dint of patient labor and many discoveries of inscriptions[1], which have dissipated the doubt and confusion that reigned where religion was involved. With light, harmony has ensued. It has been proved that all the religions of the past were interconnected, that they all were based upon one single doctrine, that this doctrine was handed down from century to century by a lengthy line of thinkers and sages.

We are now aware that all the great religions had two sides: the one hidden, the other apparent; the one revealing the spirit, the other exhibiting its form or letter. But beneath their material symbolism there lurks a profound meaning. The Brahmanism of India, the Hermetism of Egypt, the Polytheism of Greece, and Christianity itself at its origin, all present this dual character. To judge of them by their outer or vulgar side would be as fair as to appraise the moral character of a man by his clothes. In order to understand them one must burrow into the inner thought that inspired and justified their existence; at the heart of these myths and dogmas one must seek the generating principle which lent them force and life. And there lies the unique, the superior, the immutable doctrine of which human creeds are but the imperfect and transitory presentment, contrived to fit epoch and circumstance.

In our day we have arrived at a purely materialistic and superficial conception of the universe. Modern science has limited its research to the accumulation of the greatest possible quantity of facts, and from these it has deduced laws. The results are, to be sure, astounding, but by this method, the knowledge of first causes and higher principles will remain forever inaccessible: and

---

[1] See Max Muller's "*Essays on the History of Religions;*" St. Yves d'Alveydre's "*La Mission des Juifs;*" Ed. Schuré's « *Les Grands Initiés.* »

also that of the secondary causes. The unseen domain of life is too vast for our feeble senses to grasp; yet out of it proceeds those causes of which we can perceive but the effects.

Antiquity saw and reasoned quite otherwise. The wise men of East and those of Greece did not scorn to study nature; but it was, before all, in the study of the soul and of its innate forces that they sought the everlasting principles. To them the soul was like a book, in which all the laws and all the facts are recorded in mysterious characters. By the concentration of their faculties, by a profound self-scrutiny, they strove to uplift themselves to the causeless Cause, to that First Principle whence all beings proceed. From the innate laws of the intellect they deduced nature's order and harmony, and the study of the soul yielded them an inkling into the problems of life.

They pictured the soul, that supreme vehicle of knowledge, as placed between the two worlds of the visible and the occult, the material and the spiritual, observing and studying them both is the supreme instrument of knowledge. According to the soul's greater or less degree of perfection and purity, it reflected more or less clearly the rays of the divine light. Not only do reason and conscience guide our acts and decisions, but also they are likewise the surest means to the acquirement and comprehension of the truth.

To such researches the initiated consecrated their lives; for in those days a short span of hasty and ill-digested study was not thought, as it is now, sufficient to equip one for the inevitable struggles and duties of life. Adepts were chosen, and from childhood prepared for their destined career; then, very gradually were they led up the slopes of those intellectual eminences, from which life may be surveyed and comprehended. The principles of the secret science were imparted to them, as befitted their intellectual and moral capacity. The initiation was in itself an entire remolding of character, and awakening of dormant faculties. No adept was allowed to participate in the great mysteries - that is, in the revelation of superior law - until he had conquered the flame of passion and the lust of desire, and was capable of concentrating the impulses of his nature upon that which is Good and Beautiful. Then only was he allowed some power over nature, and was it given to him to communicate with the occult forces of the universe.

The evidences of history as regards Apollonius of Tyana and Simon the Mage, as well the so-called "miraculous" acts performed by Moses and the Christ, leave no room for doubt on this point. The initiated, indeed, possessed the secret of fluidic and magnetic forces: a realm most unfamiliar to modern scientists, to whom all somnambulistic and psychical phenomena appear inexplicable, and which they vainly struggle to reconcile with their own preconceived theories.[2] This domain had been thoroughly explored and mastered by the science of the eastern sanctuaries. From it they had derived a power, which was incomprehensible to the masses, but of which the phenomena of Spiritism can easily suggest a solution.

Through psychological experimentation contemporary science has at last attained the threshold of this occult world known to the ancients. So far science has not dared to cross it openly, but the day is close when it will be obliged to do so by the very force of things and by the example of a few daring people. Then will it discover nothing that is supernatural; but, quite the contrary, an unknown side of nature, a manifestation of subtle forces, a new aspect of life that fills the infinite.

If from the domain of facts we would pass to that of causes, we must first recapitulate the secret doctrine in its essential features.

---

2 See Ochorowitz, "*La Suggestion Mentale.*"

According to it, life is but the evolution through time and space of the one permanent fact, the soul, of which matter is but the inferior expression, the changing form. The Being of beings, the Source of all life is God: at once triple and unique, essence, substance and life, in whom all nature is summarized. Hence arose Trinitarian deism, which has passed, in garbled form, from India and Egypt into Christianity, which latter has made three persons out of the three elements of the Supreme Being. The human soul, part of the great soul, is immortal. It progresses and ascends towards its author through numerous existences, alternately terrestrial and spiritual, and through constant improvement. Through bodily incarnation, it constitutes the human being whose ternary nature, body, perispirit and soul, is a microcosm, or small world, a reduced image of the macrocosm, or Great Whole. Therefore it is that we earnestly seek in quiet introspection, through the cultivation of our latent faculties of reason and conscience, we will find God in the very depths of our being. Universal life has two phases: involution, or the descent of the spirit into matter, and evolution, or its gradual ascent through the chain of lives, to the divine Unity.

A whole ramification of sciences was affixed to this central philosophy: such as the science of numbers, or sacred mathematics, theogony, cosmogony, psychology and physics. In these the inductive and experimental methods were combined, and each counterbalanced the other so as to form a perfect unity: a great whole of harmonious proportions.

This teaching revealed to thought abysms of such depths that ill-prepared minds might well be dazed by them; so it was reserved for the strong. If weak spirits are disturbed or maddened by a glimpse of the infinite, the strong are thereby strengthened and broadened. They derive, from the knowledge of the higher laws, an enlightened confidence in the future and a sure reliance in adversity. Such knowledge begets indulgence towards the weak and all those who, victims of their own ignorance and passions are still struggling in the lower circles of life. It instills tolerance for all beliefs: the initiated know how to unite and pray with all men. They worshipped Brahma in India, Osiris at Memphis, Jupiter at Olympus; they worshipped them as the pale images of that Supreme Power which governs all souls and all worlds. Thus true religion transcends all creeds and condemns none.

The teaching of the sanctuaries formed people, truly remarkable for the elevation of their views, and the greatness of their achievements: and *élite* of thinkers and of people of action, whose names blazon history's pages. From their ranks have risen the great reformers, founders of religions and indefatigable tillers of the mind: Krishna, Zoroaster, Hermes, Moses, Pythagoras, Plato, Jesus, all who have aimed at bringing the sublime truths to which they owed their own elevation, within the comprehension of the people. To the winds they cast the seeds that mature the soul; everywhere they preached the moral law, that immutable, omnipresent and ever consistent law.

Disciples, however, have not always been able to preserve intact their master's heritage. The masters gone, their teachings have been marred and rendered almost unrecognizable by successive alterations. The average individual is little apt to perceive the things of the spirit, and thus religions soon lost their primitive purity and simplicity. The truths they bring were veiled under the details of a gross and material interpretation.

To impress the imagination of the faithful symbols were too freely used, and before long the original thought was buried and forgotten beneath the rubbish of overlying symbolism.

Truth is comparable to the dewdrop trembling at the tip of a branch; so long as it remains suspended on high it glistens like a pure diamond in the light, but as soon as it touches the ground than it is mingled with all its impurities. Thus, all that comes to us from above is besmirched by earthly contact.

Even into the heart of the sanctuary has the individual brought his evil passions, his covetousness and his moral ailments; and thus in every religion is error, that world founding, mingled with truth, the Divine Offspring.

One wonders at times if religion is really necessary. Religion,[3] rightly understood, is a bond uniting the human beings to one another, and by the same thought uniting them to the supreme principle of all things.

There dwells in the soul an innate sentiment that inclines it towards an ideal perfection with which righteousness and justice are identified. Were but this noblest of sentiments enlightened by science, strengthened by reason and grounded upon liberty of conscience, then would it be the very mainspring of high and generous deeds: but tarnished, falsified, materialized and manipulated by theocracy, it has but too frequently been the tool of selfish domination.

Religion is both necessary and indestructible; it is based upon the very nature of the human being, whose highest aspirations it crystallizes and expresses. Religion is likewise the expression of eternal law, in which essential it resembles philosophy, out of whose theory it evolves practice, whose inertia it quickens into life.

If religion is ever again to exercise a salutary influence and become a lever of progress and elevation, it must divest itself of the coats it has assumed with the passing centuries. It is not the spirit

---

3 From the Latin *religare*; French, *relier*; to unite, to bind together.

that is amiss, but the obscure myths, the outer garb of materialistic semblances which must be discarded: there must be no confusion of things so different.

True religion is not an external manifestation: it is a sentiment, and in the heart of the human being stands the true temple of God. True religion cannot be circumscribed by narrow rules and rites. It requires neither ritual nor imagery; it occupies itself little with pretense or ceremonious worship; It does not judge the dogmas other than through the influence that they may exert upon the perfectioning of the societies; it embraces all faiths and all creeds; but transcending them all it bids them not to forget that Truth is greater than all else.

All individuals were not destined to attain intellectual eminence, hence the need for indulgence and good will. If it be our duty to point out to the better endowed minds those vulgar sides of religion, so that they may avoid them: we must at the same time guard against offending the sorrowful and humble spirits to whom the comprehension of abstract notions would be impossible, and who derive strength and comfort their simple faith.

But when all is said and done, one cannot but realize that the ranks of the faithful are growing daily thinner. The idea of God that once seemed so simple and so grand has been distorted by the fear of hell and has thus lost power. Some people, finding the infinite beyond them, have thought it necessary to adjust and reduce to their own stature all that they have sought to conceive, and so they have brought God down to their own level, attributing to Him their passions and weakness: they have shrinking nature and the universe, decomposing truth's golden ray into many-hued deviations through the prism of their ignorance.

The clear notions of natural religion have been woefully obscured; fiction and fantasy have generated error, and, petrified by dogma, error has reared itself like a huge barrier in the highroad of progress. Those who constituted themselves its guardians have obscured the light, and the darkness in which they shrouded their fellow-beings has likewise overcome them, both inwardly, and outwardly. Religion's pure meaning has been blurred by dogma, and caste interests have perverted moral sense. Out of this an avalanche of superstition, of idolatrous practices, has accumulated, the sight of which has driven many to unbelief.

However, the reaction is imminent. The religious creeds, swaddled in their dogmas, like mummies in their cloths, at a time when everything around them evolves and progresses, remain stifled by their earthly ligaments and each day grow feebler. They have lost almost all hold on social life and morality, and are doomed to perish; only, like everything else, religion dies but to be born again. Human being's own ideal of truth changes and expands with the epoch in which he lives. For this reason those creeds which are but the temporal manifestations and partial reflections of Eternal Truth must be modified as soon as their work is done, and as soon as they no longer satisfy humanity's progress and requirements. As humanity advances it requires new conceptions and higher ideals: these it finds in the discoveries of science and in the growing intuitions of thought.

We have reached a time in the history of the world when the aged religions sink back upon their foundations, when a philosophical and moral renascence is preparing. Material and intellectual progress demand a similar moral progress. In the depths of the souls of people a tumult of inspiration is seething, striving to take shape, ready to spring into life. Sentiment and reason, mighty twin forces, imperishable as the human spirit whose attributes they are, hitherto hostile, setting society on end, discord, confusion and hatred wherever they meet - incline at last to an understanding. To become scientific, religion must discard its dogmatic and sacerdotal character, and science must move away from pure materialism if it would be enlightened by a ray of the divine light. A new doctrine will arise: idealistic in tendency, positive and experimental in method, based on incontrovertible facts. Schools of thought that appear diametrically divergent: philosophies, inimical and contradictory, such as spiritualism and naturalism, will find a common ground. This new doctrine, a grand synthesis, will include and conciliate all the many conceptions of the human beings.

It will be a resurrection of that same secret doctrine of the past, but with this difference: it will now be broader and within the reach of all, it will herald the dawn of a natural religion, simple and pure. Through a new and earnest craving for righteousness, religion itself will be translated into action; its holocaust will be the sacrifice of our passions and the cultivation of our minds. Superior, final and universal shall be this religion of the future: all ephemeral and conflicting creeds, but too long a source of strife and division, will low into its broad bosom as rivers lose themselves in the sea.

2

India

We have asserted that the secret doctrine was to be found at the base of all great religions and in the sacred writings of all nations. But whence does it come, and where lies its source? What manner of men were they who first conceived and then transcribed it? The most ancient writings are those inscribed in the heavens: [4] the stellar worlds which softly radiate throughout the quiet night are the eternal and divine scriptures which Dupuis had in mind. The human beings doubtless consulted these long before they had learnt to write, but the Vedas are the first books to which the great doctrine was entrusted. They are the mold in which was cast India's primitive religion: a patriarchal religion, simple as the life of a person without desires, breathing an atmosphere both strong and serene, amid the splendid Eastern nature.

The Vedic hymns are equal in grandeur and moral elevation to the noblest lyrics that have ever been written. They worship Agni, the fire, symbol of the Eternal Masculine, or creative, spirit; Sômâ, the fluid of the sacrifice, symbol of the Eternal Feminine, Soul of the World, ethereal substance. In their perfect union these two essential principles of the universe constitute the Supreme Being, Zyaus, or God.

---
4 The signs of the Zodiac.

The supreme One immolates and divides himself to produce universal life. Thus do the world and its creatures, issued from God, return to God through ceaseless evolution. Out of this proceeds the theory of the fall and of the re-ascension of souls, which later we find in the western world.

The sacrifice of fire illustrates the Vedic belief. At dawn of day the head of the family, who was both father and priest, kindled the sacred flame upon the earthen altar; with it ascended, into the azure vault, a prayer, an invocation from all to the One living power, hidden by nature's transparent veil.

During the consummation of the sacrifice, according to the Vedas, the Asouras, or superior spirits, and the Pitris, souls of the ancestors, surround the participants and unite with them in prayer. From this we see that the belief in spirits already existed in the world's early ages.

The Vedas assert the immortality of the soul and its reincarnation.

"In man there is an immortal part. This it is, O Agni, that thou must warm with thy rays and influence by thy fire. Whence proceeds the soul? Some come to us and go back again; others go back and again return."

The Vedas are monotheistic: the allegories which abound in every page barely conceal the image of the great first cause whose name was held so sacred that to speak it was to incur the penalty of death. As to the Devas, or secondary divinities, they personified the inferior auxiliaries of the divine Being; they represented the forces of nature and its ethical quality. Out of the teaching of the Vedas flowed the entire organization of primitive society: the respect for woman, ancestor-worship, electoral and patriarchal power.

In the Vedic epoch, the "rishis," or anchorites, spent their days in retreat, in the solitudes of the great woods or on the banks of lakes and rivers. Interpreters of the occult science, of the secret doctrine of the Vedas, they already possessed those mysterious powers which have been transmitted from century to century, and which we still find in the "fakirs" and the "yogis." From this hermit fraternity arose the creative thought, the first great impulse that makes of Brahmanism the greatest of all theocracies.

Krishna brought up by the ascetics in the heart of the great cedar forests that grow beneath the Himalayas' snowy peaks, was the inspirer of the Hindu faith. His noble figure looms in history as the first of religious reformers, the first divine missionary. He renewed the Vedic doctrines, basing them upon the conception of the Trinity, upon that of the immortal soul and its successive births. Having sealed his work with his blood, he departed from Earth, bequeathing to his country that conception of the universe and of life, that high ideal upon which India has rested these thousand of years.

This doctrine, under many appellations, has spread throughout the world with the numerous migrations that have proceeded out of the high regions of India, the sacred land which is not only the mother of nations and diverse civilizations, but which is likewise the hearth of the greatest of religious inspirations.

Krishna, followed by a band of disciples, went from place to place, spreading his teaching.

> "The body, he taught[5], envelope of the soul that dwells in it, is a finite thing; but the soul that is within is invisible imponderable, eternal.

---
5 *Baghavadgita*

"The fate of the soul after death contains the mystery of rebirth. As the farthest depths of heaven are open to the radiance of the stars, so are the depths of life crystallized by the light of this truth.

"When the body is dissolved, when wisdom is in the ascendant, then does the soul depart for the regions of the pure beings; those that have knowledge of the Highest. When the passions predominate, then the soul again returns to dwell amongst those who are absorbed by earthly matters. In like manner, the soul that is darkened by ignorance of matter is drawn once more by the attraction of unreasonable beings.

"Every rebirth, happy or unhappy, is the consequence of deeds performed in anterior existences.

"But there is a still greater mystery. To attain perfection, one must acquire the science of Unity, which is above wisdom; one must elevate oneself to the divine Being who transcends both the soul and the mind. This divine being is also in each one of us.

"You bear within yourself a sublime friend whom you do not know, for God resides in the interior of every individual, but few know how to find Him. The person who sacrifices his desires and his works to the Being from whom all things proceed and by whom the Universe was made, by this sacrifice attains to perfection: for he who finds within him happiness and contentment, and within him also, light, is one with God. Then, know it well, the soul that has found God is delivered from rebirth and from death, from old age and from sorrow, and drinks of the waters of immortality."

Krishna spoke of his own nature and of his mission in words upon which it is well to meditate. Addressing himself to his disciples:

> "You and I, said he, have several rebirths. Mine are known to myself alone, but you do not even know your own. Although I am no longer, by my nature, subject to birth or to death, every time that in this world virtue fails and vice and iniquity prevail, then do I make myself visible; thus do I show myself, from age to age, to save the just, to punish the wicked and to rehabilitate virtue.
>
> "To you have I revealed the great secrets. Tell them only to those who are able to comprehend them. You are my chosen ones, you see the goal where others discern but a stretch of the road."[6]

Upon these words was the secret doctrine founded. Despite the successive alterations it underwent, it still remained the source to which, in darkness and in secrecy, the great thinkers of antiquity resorted for inspiration.

The morals that Krishna preached were not less pure:

> "The evils with which we afflict our neighbors likewise follow us, as our shadow follows our body. The deeds we do for love of our fellow being are those that will weigh most in the heavenly scales. – If you frequent the good, your examples will be useless: fear not to live amongst the wicked, to return them to good. – The virtuous person is like a great tree whose beneficent shade imparts freshness and life to the plants that surround it."

---

6 Baghavadgita

His language attained sublimity when he spoke of abnegation and of self-sacrifice:

> "The honest person should fall beneath the blows of the wicked, like the sandalwood tree which perfumes the axe that struck it."

When the sophists asked him to explain God's nature to them, he answered:

> "Infinity and space alone can comprehend the infinite: God only can understand God."

He also said:

> "Nothing that Is can perish, for all that Is is contained in God. The wise person mourns neither for the living nor for the dead. For never have I ceased to be, nor you, nor any man, and never shall we cease to be, any of us, beyond this present life."[7]

On the subject of communication with spirits:

> "Long before they shed their mortal figment, souls that have done nothing but good, acquire the faculty of conversing with those souls that have preceded them in the spiritual life (Swarga)."[8]

---

7 Mahabharata.
8 Baghavadgita.

This the Brahmins still teach today, in the doctrine of the Pitris. At all times, the evocation of the dead has been one of the forms of their liturgy.

Such are the principal points of the doctrine of Krishna, and one may still find them in the zealously preserved sacred books of the sanctuaries of Southern Hindustan.

The Brahmins mainly borrowed the social organization of India from their religious conceptions. According to the ternary system, they divided society into three classes; but this organization degenerated after a while into a system of sacerdotal and aristocratic privileges. Heredity imposed its harsh rules upon all natural aspirations. Woman, so free and honored in Vedic times, became a slave. Society became frozen into a rigid mold, and India's decadence was the inevitable consequence thereof. Petrified in her castes and dogmas, India has slept the lethargic sleep that resembles death, and which even the tumult of foreign invasions has been unable to disturb. Will she ever awake: this God only can tell.

The Brahmins, after establishing social order, killed India by an excess of repression. They likewise divested the doctrines of Krishna of all moral authority, burying them under an overlying mass of gross and material formula. If one considers only the external and vulgar side of Brahmanism, its puerile rules, pompous ceremonial, and complicated rites, as also the fables and legends of which it is so prodigal, it appears to be nothing more than an accumulated heap of superstition. It would, however, be a mistake to judge of it by its external semblances, for Brahmanism, like all the other ancient beliefs, must be divided into two separate parts. The first is its gross faith and teaching, filled with fictions that are calculated to captivate the common people and induce them into the ways of servitude. To this order belongs the dogma of metempsychosis, or the reincarnation of guilty spirits in the shape of animals, insects of plants, manifestly a scarecrow designed to terrorize the weak; a shrewd system imitated by Christianity in its conception of the myths of Satan, of hell and of eternal torment.

Quite another matter is the secret teaching, the grand esoteric tradition. This attains to the highest and purest flights of speculation concerning the soul and its destiny, and the great Universal cause. But to find these one must venture into the mystery of the pagodas' dark recesses, search their hidden manuscripts, and consult their learned Brahmins.

Something like six hundred years before the Christian era, one who was the son of a king, Sakya Mouni, the Buddha, fell a prey to an absorbing sadness, an immense pity for the sufferings of people. India was then undermined by corruption following upon the decadence of religious traditions, and the abuses of a domineering theocracy. Renouncing both greatness and luxury, the Buddha turned his back upon his palace and went out into the silent woods. After long years of meditation he reappeared, bringing to the Asiatic world that which, if not a new faith, was at least a new rendering of the Law.

According to Buddhism[9] desire is the cause of sin, suffering, death and reincarnation. It is desire and passion that rivet us to the material body and awaken in us a hundred never satisfied and ever recurrent cravings, which become so many tyrants. Life's loftiest aim is to rescue the soul from the lusts of the flesh: this may be achieved by reflection, by austerity, by the sacrifice of the ego, by enfranchisement from the despotism of personality and self. Ignorance is the sovereign ill from which misery and suffering

---

9 See Léon de Rosny, « *Le Boudhisme;* » Burnouf, « *La Science des Religions.* »

arise, and the first step towards the betterment of one's condition, be it present or future, is the acquirement of knowledge.

Knowledge includes the science of nature, both visible and invisible; likewise the study of the human being and of the principles that govern all things; these are absolute and eternal. The world having, by its own activity, emerged from a state of uniformity, is in perpetual evolution. Beings, descended from the Great Unity, to solve the problem of perfection, which is inseparable from freedom, are on their return to perfect righteousness. They re-enter the world of matter to labor for the fulfillment of their task of improvement and elevation. This may be accomplished through science, according to an *Upanishad*; or through love, according to a *Purana*.

Science and love are the two essential factors of the universe. So long as the being has not acquired love, it is condemned to follow the chain of terrestrial reincarnations.

Under the influence of such a doctrine the instinct of selfishness sees its circle of action become more and more circumscribed. The being learns to include all that lives and breathes in the same love. And this is but one stage in the evolution which must finally lead it to love nothing but the eternal principle from which all love emanates and to which all love must necessarily return. This is the state of Nirvana.

Nirvana is a word which, diversely commented upon, has been the cause of much misunderstanding. According to the secret doctrine of Buddhism[10] Nirvana is not, as the Southern Church and the high priest of Ceylon inculcate, a loss of individuality or the absorption of the being into nothingness: it is the conquest of perfection by the soul, and the latter's definite enfranchisement from ulterior transmigrations and rebirths in this world.

---

10 Sinnett, « *Esoteric Buddhism.* »

Each soul works out its own destiny. The present life with its sorrows and joys is but the consequence of the good or bad actions that were freely performed by the same individual in his anterior existences. The present is explained by the past, not only for the world taken as a whole, but for each individual that forms part of it. That which is known as Karma is the sum total of merits or demerits acquired by an individual being. This karma represents to him, at any stage of his evolution, the starting-point for the future, and the cause of all distributive justice:

> "I, the Buddha,[11] who have wept with the tears of all my brothers, whose heart has been broken by the grief of a whole world, I smile and am content, for freedom is. Oh, listen, you who suffer. Behold! I show you the truth. All that we are is the resultant of what we have thought. That is founded upon our thoughts; that is made of our thoughts. If a man speaks and acts from out of a pure though, happiness will follow him like a shadow. Hatred has never been appeased by hatred. Hatred can be vanquished only by love. As the rain passes through an ill-roofed house, so passes passion through a thoughtless spirit. By reflection, by moderation, by self-dominion, the human being makes of himself an island that no storm can devastate. The human being returns, to reap that which he has sowed. Such is the doctrine of Karma."

Most religions counsel righteousness for the sake of a future reward: a selfish and mercenary motive, from which Buddhism is greatly free. "Do good," says Léon de Rosny[12] "because righteousness is

---
11 *Dhammapada.*
12 « *La Morale du Boudisme.*»

nature's supreme object." It is certain that by obeying this law, one experiences the only unalloyed satisfaction; the highest that can be experienced by a being liberated from the trammels of flesh and desire, those perpetual causes of suffering and disappointment.

The Buddhist's compassion, like his charity, is extended to all beings. All beings, to his way of thinking, are destined to experience Nirvana. In "beings," he includes animals, vegetables, even inorganic forms. All forms of life are linked together according to the great law of evolution and transformation. Nowhere, in the universe, is life non-existent. Death is but an illusion, it is one of the agents of that life which incessantly seeks renewal and transformation. Hell – to the esoteric initiates – is none other than remorse and a lack of love. Purgatory is omnipresent: you will find it wherever body is to be found and wherever matter evolves. It exists upon this globe as well as in the depths of the starry firmament.

The Buddha and his disciples practiced the Dhyâna or contemplation, ecstasy. The spirit, in this state of exaltation, communicates with the souls that have departed from earth.[13]

Exoteric or vulgar Buddhism, which towards the sixth century, after bloody fights caused by the Brahmins, was driven back to the two extremities of India, has undergone diverse vicissitudes and numerous transformations. One of its branches or churches, the southern one, seems, in some of its interpretations, to incline towards atheism and materialism. That of Tibet has remained deistic and spiritualistic. Buddhism has also become the religion of Chine, the world's largest empire; today, its faithful number a third of the world's population. But everywhere and wherever it has spread, from the Ural to Japan, its primitive traditions have been clouded and altered. There, as elsewhere, the material forms of worship have stifled thought's high aspirations: the rites, the superstitious

---

13 Eug. Bonnemère, *L'Âme et ses manifestations à travers l'Histoire*.

ceremonies, the vain formula, the offerings and devices, the barrels, and the prayer mills, have taken the place of ethical teaching and of the practice of virtue.[14]

The principal doctrines of the Buddha have, however, been happily preserved in the Sutras.[15] Some wise men, heirs to the science and powers of the ancient ascetics, also possess, it is claimed,[16] the secret doctrine in all its fullness. They seem to have chosen their residence far from the human tribe, upon those high plateaus whence the plains of India appear distant and dim as in a dream. It is in that pure atmosphere and in the stillness of solitude that the *Mahatmas* elected to dwell. Masters of secrets that defy both pain and death, they are said to pass their days in meditation, awaiting that uncertain hour when humanity's moral condition will make its possible for them to divulge their arcane. Unfortunately no well authenticated fact has yet been submitted to substantiate these sayings; and it remains to be proved that the Mahatmas really exist.

In the last twenty years great efforts have been made to spread the Buddhist doctrine through the western hemisphere; but our race, avid of activity, life and liberty seems but little inclined to adopt this religion of renunciation, of which Orientals have made a doctrine of voluntary extermination and intellectual effacement. In Europe, the conquests of Buddhism have been limited to a few men of letters, who likewise favor Tibetan esotericism. This latter belief opens some strange vistas to the mind. The theory of the days and nights of Brahma, Manvantara and Pralaya, extracted

---

14 G. Bousquet, *"Revue de Deux Mondes,"* March 15,1876.
15 G *Le Lalila Vistara,"* translation of Foucaux; *"Le Lotus de la Bonne Loi."* Translation of Eug. Burnouf..
16 Sinnet, *le Bouddhisme ésotérique.*

from the ancient religions of India, seems to conflict a little with the conception of Nirvana.

In any case, the mere thought of these stupendous periods of diffusion and concentration, at the end of which the Great First Cause absorbs all beings and remains quiescent and lethargic, brooding over worlds dissolved makes the brain reel. The theory of the seven constitutive principles of the human being: that of the seven planets[17], on which the wheel of life in its ascension movement proceeds, also constitutes the original view and is subject to examination.

In this faith, one fact stands forth. The law of charity, as proclaimed by the Buddha, is one of the most powerful appeals to righteousness that this world has ever heard; but, to borrow a sentence from Léon de Rosny:[18] "This calm law, this empty law – empty because it rests upon nothing – has remained unintelligible for the majority, whose aspirations it slights, and to whom it fails to extend the reward they crave."

Buddhism, despite its blemishes and its shadows, remains nevertheless one of the greatest religious conceptions that the world has yet received; a doctrine all of love and equality, a powerful reaction from the caste distinctions instituted by the Brahmins. In some points it offers striking analogies with the Gospel preached by Jesus of Nazareth.

---

17 Instead of seven, the only ones known in ancient times, today one counts eight principals in our solar system. The existence of a ninth and others is still suspected beyond Neptune, because of the disturbances undergone by this planet.

18 « La Morale du Bouddhisme, » Léon de Rosny.

3

Egypt

At the gates of the desert rise the temples, the pylons, the pyramids: a forest of stone beneath a fiery sky. Couchant and unfathomable sphinxes overlook the plains, and rock-quarried cities of the dead open their profaned portals upon the banks of the silent river. This is Egypt, strange land and venerable book in which modern man is scarcely beginning to spell the mystery of the ages, with their manifold races and religions.[19]

India, as most Eastern cultures tell us, has given to Egypt its civilization and its faith; while other authorities contend that at a very early day the land of Isis had already its own traditions. These were the heritage of an extinct race, that of the red people who came from out of the west,[20] whom terrible struggles with the white men, combined with geological cataclysms, have almost exterminated. The sphinx of Giza, which predates the great pyramid by several thousand years, [21] was erected by the red people near

---

19 See Lenormant's and Maspéro's works.
20 See Ed. Schuré, "*Les Grands Initiés*" (p. 116), the discoveries of Leplongeon and H. Saville in Central-America, and the work of Roisel and d'Arbois de Jubainville about the Atlantis.
21 A papyrus of the fourth dynasty (4000 B.C.E.) relates that the sphinx had been accidentally found beneath the sand which had covered it for centuries (Lenormant, "*Historie d'Orient*").

to where the Nile flowed into the sea;[22] it is one of the rare remaining monuments of those distant times.

The deciphering of the hieroglyphs, and that of the papyri found in the tombs, enables us to reconstruct the history of Egypt, and with it that ancient doctrine of the Verb-Light, the threefold divinity, at once intellect, force and matter: spirit, soul and body, which offers a perfect analogy with the philosophy of India. Here as there, we discover beneath a coarse overgrowth of ritual the same hidden thought. The soul of Egypt, the secret or her vitality and of the part that she played in history lies hidden in the occult doctrine of her priests, carefully masked by the mysteries of Isis and Osiris, to be pondered over in the depths of the temples, by the initiates of all ranks and all countries.

The sacred books of Hermes expounded, in austere guise, the principles of this doctrine. They composed a vast encyclopedia, compounded of all human knowledge. All of these books have not reached us. The religious science of Egypt has been principally retraced for us by the hieroglyphic readings; the temples, in themselves, are huge volumes, and one may say that in the land of the Pharaohs the very stones have voices.

Of modern scientific individuals, Champollion was the first to identify three species of writing in the manuscripts and on the Egyptian monuments.[23] This confirms the opinion of the ancients, that the priests of Isis employed three different species of characters: the first, *demotic*, were clear and simple; the second, *hieratic*, had a symbolical or figurative sense; the others were *hieroglyphs*. This is what Heraclites conveyed by the words, "speaking, signifying and hiding."

---

22 The present delta was formed by successive deposits of the Nile.
23 Champollion, « *L'Egypte sous les Pharaons.* »

The hieroglyphs were of threefold signification and undecipherable without a key. Into these signs entered the law of analogy that governs the three worlds, natural, human and divine, which allowed of the expression of the threefold aspects of all things, with a combination of numbers and figures by which the harmonious symmetry and unity of the universe were reproduced. Thus could a single hieroglyph convey principles, causes and effects, and to the adept this language was intensely forceful.

The priest, who might belong to any social rank, even the lowest, was the true ruler of Egypt; the king, chosen and initiated by the priest, was but a mandatory governor. Lofty aspiration united with deep wisdom watched over the destiny of the land. In the midst of a barbarous world, situated between ferocious and passionate Assyria and wild Africa, the land of the Pharaohs was like an island against which the billows vainly strove, and in which were preserved the pure doctrine and all the hidden lore of antiquity. Sages, philosophers and chiefs, Greeks, Hebrews, Phoenicians and Etruscans, all came hither to seek inspiration.

Through them, religious thought, gathered at the shrine of Isis, spread along the Mediterranean coasts, giving birth to other civilizations, diverse and often dissimilar, according to the nature of the race that received them: monotheistic with Moses in Judea, polytheistic in Greece with Orpheus, but uniform as regards their hidden principle and mysterious essence.

The popular worship of Isis and Osiris was a brilliant mirage displayed to the crowd. Beneath the pomp of public show and ceremonial, the vital teaching lay hidden, only revealing itself in the little and the great mysteries. Initiation itself was attended by serious difficulties and genuine danger. The physical and moral tests were many and lengthy. An oath of secrecy was exacted and the slightest indiscretion was visited with death. This redoubtable discipline imparted remarkable force and authority both to the initiation and to the secret doctrine. As the adept progressed, the veils parted before him, the light shone brighter and the symbols took on life and speech.

The sphinx, with woman's head on bull's body, with lion's claws and eagle's wings, was the symbol of a human being merging from the depths of animality to attain to a new condition. The human being was the great enigma, bearing within him the visible traces of his origin, epitomizing all the elements and forces of lower nature.

The bizarre gods, with heads of birds, mammals and serpents were so many other symbols of life in its innumerable guises. Osiris, the solar god, and Isis, the great nature, were everywhere honored, but above them there was an unnamed god, of whom one spoke but low and fearfully.

The neophyte was obliged before all else to attain self-knowledge. The hierophant thus instructed him:

> "O soul that is blind, arm yourself with the torch of mystery, and in the terrestrial night you will find your luminous double, your celestial soul. Follow this divine guide, take him for your genius, for he holds the key of your past and future existences."[24]

At the end of his trials, shaken by the emotion of many hairbreadth escapes, the initiate would perceive a woman's figure, bearing a roll of papyrus, who advanced towards him:

> "I am your invisible sister, she said, I am your divine soul, and this is the scroll of your life. It contains the full pages

---
24 Admonition to the initiate, from "*The Book of the Dead.*"

of your past lives and the blank pages of your life to come. Some day I will unroll them before you. Now that you know me, call, and I will come!"

Finally, roofed by the starry night, on the terrace of a temple overhanging sleeping Memphis, or Thebes, perchance, the high priest would recite to the adept the vision of Hermes; a vision which was orally transmitted from pontiff to pontiff and engraved in hieroglyphs upon the walls of subterranean crypts.

One day Hermes saw the heavens and the worlds, and the life that universally flourished in all places. The voice of the light that flowed through the infinite revealed to him the divine mystery:

> "The light that you have seen is the divine intellect that contains all things in their might, and the image of every created being as well. The darkness is that material world in which the people of this earth abide. But the fire that flames from the depths is the divine Word: God is the Father, the Word is the Son. Their union is Life.
>
> "As to the spirit of the human being, its destiny has two sides: captivity in matter; elevation in the light. The souls are the daughters of heaven, and their journey is a trial. During their incarnation they lose all recollection of their celestial origin. Captives of matter, enamored of life they fall like a rain of fire through the regions of Sorrow, of Love and of Death, until they attain that terrestrial prison in which you groan thyself and where the divine life appears like a vain dream.
>
> "Base and wicked souls remain enslaved to the earth by multiple rebirths, but virtuous spirits ascend with strong wings to the superior spheres, where they regain sight of

the divine things, through which they become imbued with the lucidity of a conscience enlightened by sorrow, and with the will which is acquired by battling with life. They become luminous, for within them they find the divine, through which their deeds are made radiant. Strengthen then your heart, O Hermes, and comfort your darkened spirit by the contemplation of yon flights of souls ascending the ladder of spheres which leads to the Father; and there all ends and all eternally begins. And the seven spheres cried together; 'Wisdom! Love! Justice! Beauty! Splendor! Science! Immortality!"[25]

To which the pontiff added:

"Ponder this vision; in it lies the secret of all things. The more you learn to know it, the more you will see its limits, for the same organic law governs all worlds.

"But the veil of mystery conceals the great truth. The total knowledge can only be revealed to those who have undergone the same trials as we have. Truth must be proportioned to the intellect; it must be veiled from the weak, whom it would craze, and it must be hidden from the wicked who would find in it a weapon with which to destroy. Enclose it in your heart that it may speak through your works. Science will be your strength, the law your sword, and silence your shield."

The science of those priests of Egypt in many ways surpassed modern science. They controlled magnetism and somnambulism,

---

[25] Extract from *"Pimander,"* the most authentic of the Hermes Trismegistus writings.

cured by means of artificial sleep and practiced suggestion; all of which they designated "magic."[26]

The highest ambition of the initiate was to acquire these powers, whose emblem was the crown of the Magi.

> Learn, it was said, what this crown signifies. Every will that unites with God to manifest the truth and to accomplish justice participates, even in this life, in the divine power over human beings and things: this is the eternal recompense of emancipated spirits.

The genius of Egypt was submerged by a flood of invasions. The school of Alexandria saved some remnants of it which were transmitted to dawning Christianity; before the advent of this latter, the Greek initiates had, however, introduced some of the hermetic doctrines into Hellas. That's where we will find them.

---

26 Diodorus of Sicily and Strabo both relate that the priests of ancient Egypt were capable of provoking clairvoyance, which they applied therapeutically. Galen mentions a temple near Memphis, which was renowned for its hypnotic cures.

4

Greece

Of all initiative people there are none whose mission has been made more brilliantly manifested than the Hellenes. Greece has initiated Europe into beauty's entire regal splendor; from her outstretched hand civilization has poured, and after a lapse of twenty centuries her genius still radiates a warm glow over the world. Hence, in spite of reactions, backslidings, internal struggles and final downfall, will Greece ever remain a subject worthy of admiration.

Greece has rendered in a clear tongue the obscure beauties of Oriental wisdom. She first expressed them with the aid of those twin celestial harmonies that she humanized – music and poetry. Orpheus and Homer sounded their first notes to the hearkening world.

Later, Pythagoras, an initiate of the Egyptian mysteries, after listening to the harmonious rhythm introduced by the nascent genius of Greece into speech and song, discerned it in all things: in the onward march of the spheres, those future abodes of the human being, as they majestically roll through space; in the accord of the three worlds, natural, human and divine, which sustain, complete and balance one another for the production of life in its ascending stream and infinite spiral. Born of this tremendous vision, there came to him the conception of a triple initiation, through which many possessed of the eternal principles, might learn, by purification, to free themselves from earthly ills and attain perfection. From this arose the great system of education and reformation which produced so many sages and heroes, and to which Pythagoras gave his name.

Finally, Socrates and Plato, by popularizing the same principles and by enlarging their scope, inaugurated the reign of open science instead of that of the secret lore.

Such was the role of Greece in the history of the development of thought. Initiation exercised, at all times, a preponderating influence over the destinies of that country. It is not in the political fluctuations that agitated this mobile and impressionable race that one must look for the highest manifestations of Hellenic genius. At its best it was to be found, neither in somber and brutal Sparta, nor yet in Athens, the brilliant and frivolous; but rather at Delphi, at Olympus, at Eleusis, those sacred strongholds of the pure doctrine. There it appeared in its full strength at the celebration of the mysteries. There philosophers, poets and artists gathered together to receive the hidden instruction which, clothed in brilliant metaphors and burning verse, they afterwards rendered to the people. Above the turbulent cities, ever ready to rend one another; above the shifting forms of politics that passed from aristocracy to democracy and into the rule of tyrants, a supreme power dominated Greece; that of the Amphictyons council, whose seat was at Delphi, and which was composed of initiates of a superior degree. This council alone saved Hellas in the days of her peril, by imposing peace on the rivalries of Sparta and Athens.

In the days of Orpheus the temples already possessed the secret science.

> "Listen, said the master to the neophyte,[27] listen to these truths, not to be spoken to the crowd, but which are the main stay of the sanctuaries. GOD is one, and ever like unto Himself; but the Gods are innumerable and diverse, and that because Divinity is infinite and eternal. The greatest are the souls of the stars...
>
> "You have entered with a pure heart into the realm of mystery. The solemn hour is at hand when I shall conduct you to the very fount of life and light. Those who have not lifted the heavy veil which hides the unseen marvels from the eyes of people are not yet sons of the Gods...."

To the mystics and adepts:

> "Come and rejoice, you that have suffered; come and rest you that have struggled. By your past sufferings, by the effort that has brought you here, you will vanquish, and if you believe in the divine words, you have already won. For after the long circuit of troubled existences, you will meet as one spirit in the light of Dionysus.[28]
>
> Love, because all must love. But love the light and not the darkness: and during the journey bear the goal in mind. When the spirits return to the light, they bear, like hideous stains upon their ethereal bodies, all the sins of their life. To efface that expiation is necessary, and they

---

27 Orphic hymns
28 According to Pythagoras, Apollo and Dionysus are two revelations of the Spirit of God, which is eternally manifested in the world.

must return to the earth.... But the pure, the strong, go on to the sun of Dionysus..."

⁓

An imposing figure towers over the group of Greek philosophers. It is Pythagoras, who of Ionia's sons was the first to coordinate and reveal the secret doctrines of the East, and to bind them in one great synthesis that embraced moral, science and religion. His academy at Croton was an admirable school of lay initiation. His life work was a prelude to that great wave of thought which extended from Plato to Jesus and was to raise the deep-lying strata of ancient society: the very ripples of which were destined to lap upon the far ends of the Continent.

Pythagoras had spent thirty years of study in Egypt. To a vast knowledge he united a marvelous intuition, lacking which, reason and observation often fail to discover the truth. By the light of these gifts he raised a stately monument to esoteric science, the principal lines of which we feel compelled to indicate:

"Essence itself eludes the human being, the Pythagorean doctrine tells us,[29] The human being knows but the things of this world, wherein the finite combines with the infinite. And how can he know them? Because, between him and these things there is a harmony, an affinity, a common principle, and this principle was given them by the One, who likewise bestowed upon them, together with their essence, measure and intelligibility.

"Your own being, your soul, is a tiny universe. But it is stormy and full of discord. Therein, you must strive to

---
29 See Shuré's "Les Grands Initiés;" also his "Pythagore," p. 329.

establish unity in harmony. Then only will God descend into your conscience, then only will you participate in His power and make of your will a hearth-stone, an altar to Hestia, a throne of Jupiter.

The Pythagoreans named spirit or intellect the active and immortal part of the human being. To them the soul was the spirit, enwrapped in its fluidic and ethereal body. The fate of Psyche, the human soul: her descent into and captivity by the flesh, her struggles and sufferings, her gradual re-ascension, her triumph over human passions and her final return to the light, all of which symbolized the drama of life, was represented in the mysteries of Eleusis as being the all-important knowledge.

According to Pythagoras,[30] the material evolution of the worlds and the spiritual evolution of the souls are parallel, coincidental and explicable the one by the other. The great soul, diffused throughout nature, animates matter which vibrates under its impulse and produces all forms and all beings. Conscious beings, after long efforts, extricate themselves from matter, which in their turn they dominate and govern in the course of their innumerable existences. Thus the invisible explains the visible, and the development of material creation is a manifestation of the divine Spirit.

If one searches the physical treatises of the ancients for their conception of the structure of the universe, one encounters gross and childish notions. But these are but allegorical. The secret teaching conveys very different notions of the universal laws. Aristotle tells us that the Pythagoreans were aware of the Earth's motion around the sun. The conception of terrestrial rotation occurred to Copernicus when he learnt from a passage in Cicero that

---

30 Consult the *"Vers dorés de Pythagore,"* in the French of Fabre d'Ollivet; also *"Pythagore et la Philosophie pythagoricienne,"* by Chaignet.

Hycetas, a disciple of Pythagoras, had imputed a diurnal motion to the globe. In the third degree of initiation, the dual motion of the earth was taught.

Like the priests of Egypt, his masters, Pythagoras was aware that the planets are outcasts of the sun, around which they revolve: that each star is a sun lighting other worlds; and that each with its train of satellites constitutes another system, another universe, governed by the same laws as obtain in our own. But these notions were never committed to writing; they formed a part of the oral teaching which was imparted under bond of secrecy. The vulgar would not have understood, but would have deemed them contrary to their mythology and therefore sacrilegious. [31]

The secret science likewise taught that an imponderable fluid everywhere prevails, impregnating all things. A subtle agent, it can be modified by volition, refined and condensed according to the power and elevation of the souls that utilize it, and weave their astral garment out of its substance. It is a link between matter and spirit; all things, whether thoughts or deeds, are recorded in it and reflected by it as pictures by a mirror. Thanks to the properties of this fluid and to the action exercised upon it by the will, the phenomena of suggestion and of thought-transmission become explicable. The ancients metaphorically termed it "the veil of Isis" or "the mantle of Cybele," which enfolds all that lives. This same fluid serves as a means of communication between the visible and the unseen, between human beings and discarnate spirits.

The science of the occult formed one of the most important branches of the reserve teaching. It had succeeded in deducing from the bulk of phenomena the law of analogy that unites the material to the spiritual world. It methodically developed the transcendental faculties of the soul, thus making thought reading

---

[31] See Schuré's « *Les Grands Initiés.* »

and second sight[32] possible. The deeds of clairvoyance and divination performed by the oracles of Grecian temples, by the sibyls and Pythoness, are vouched for by history, but many strong minds deem them apocryphal. One must assuredly allow for exaggeration and for legend, but recent discoveries of experimental psychology show us that therein there was something more than superstition. These experiments bid us more carefully to examine a cohesive conglomeration of facts, which in former days was based upon certain fixed principles, and which formed the objective of a science as profound as it was comprehensive.

Those faculties are to be found, as a rule, only in persons of extraordinary purity and elevation of character, and they moreover require a long and patient cultivation. Delphi has known some such subjects. The oracles reported by Herodotus, concerning Croesus and the battle of Salamis, prove it. Later, abuses intermingled with these practices. The scarcity of subjects induced the priests to be less scrupulous in their choice; divinatory science became corrupt and fell into disuse. Its final disappearance was universally considered, according to Plutarch, as a great misfortune.

All Greeks believed in spirit intervention in human affairs. Socrates possessed a daemon or familiar genius. When at Marathon and at Salamis, the Greek legions triumphed over the overwhelming Persian invasion, their strength was multiplied by the conviction that they were being seconded by invisible legions. At Marathon, the Athenians were convinced of the presence of two shining warriors who were fighting in their ranks. Ten years later, an inspired Pythoness, from the eminence of her tripod, indicated to Themistocles the means by which Greece might be saved.

---

32 Also known as remote viewing. Editor's note.

Indeed, were Xerxes victorious, a barbaric Asia would overflow Hellas, stifling her genius and retarding by twenty centuries the fruition of thought to its ideal perfection. The Greeks, who were but a handful, defeated the huge Asiatic army, and, conscious of the unseen power that had come to their aid, they rendered homage to Pallas-Athena, a titular divinity, symbolical of spiritual power. This solemn event took place upon the headland of the Acropolis, which is silhouetted between the blue and dazzling sea and the majestic outlines of Pentelicus and Hymettus.

Such a popular participation in the mysteries would naturally contribute to the dissemination of occultism. It developed among the initiated a consciousness of the invisible forces, which spread, in a modified degree, to the people. Universally, in Greece, in Egypt and in India, the mysteries hinged upon the same important fact: the knowledge of the secret of death, the revelation of successive lives, and communication with the unseen world. The effect of these examples and exhortations was such as to strongly influence the people, imparting to them an incomparable peace, serenity and moral force.

Sophocles alluded to the mysteries as "the hopes of death," while Aristophanes relates that all who participated in them led pure and holy lives; for thereunto were admitted no conspirators, perjurers or debauchees.

Prophyrus warns us that:

"At the hour of death our spirits should be as during the mysteries; that is, exempt from desire, choler, envy or hatred."

In the following terms Plutarch asserts that interchange with the spirits of the departed does exist:

"Righteous spirits generally intervened in the mysteries: although the perverse sometimes attempted to enter therein."

Proclus informs us:[33]

"In these mysteries, the gods (the word here signifying all manner of spirits) show many forms of themselves, appearing in a great variety of shapes, amongst which is the human form."

The esoteric doctrine formed a link between philosopher and priest, which accounts for their good understanding and the inconspicuous role of the priesthood in Hellenic civilization. This doctrine taught people to curb their passions, and to cultivate will and intuition. Through a gradual process of training, the adepts of superior rank succeeded in discovering and controlling some of the hidden secrets of nature: by the exercise of will-power they compelled some of the world's active forces to produce phenomena, apparently supernatural phenomena, which really were but the manifestation of laws unknown to ignorant minds.

Socrates, and after him Plato, in Attica pursued the task undertaken by Pythagoras. Socrates, who wished to remain free to teach the truths that his reason discovered, would never consent to be initiated. After the death of Socrates, Plato departed for Egypt and was there admitted to participate in the mysteries. He returned to Greece, entered into some understanding with the Pythagoreans, and founded his academy; but being an initiate he could not speak freely. In his works the doctrine appears somewhat

---

33 In Plato's Dialogues, "The Republic."

obscure; nevertheless the theme of the soul's migrations and reincarnations is set forth in Phaedrus, Phaedo and Timaeus.

> "Certain it is that the livings are born of the dead and that the souls of the dead are born again (Phaedrus)."

One will also recall the allegorical scene that Plato introduces at the end of his *Republic*. A genius having gathered from the Fates the destiny and diverse conditions of humanity, exclaims:

> "Divine souls, return you into human bodies and therein undertake a fresh career. Here are all the destinies that life offers. Choose freely, but remember that the choice is irrevocable, wherefore, if it is bad, do not accuse God."

These beliefs had reached the ear of Rome. Ovid speaks of them in his *Metamorphosis* (chap. XV); and Cicero in *The Dreams of Scipio*, (chap. III). In Virgil's sixth book of *The Aeneid*, Aeneas encounters Anchise, his father, in the Elysian Fields, and from him learns the law of reincarnation. All the great Latin authors assure us that all men of talent are assisted and inspired by their familiar genii.[34] Lucanius, Tacitus, Apuleius, as well as the Greek Philostratus, frequently refer in their writings to dreams, apparitions and evocations of the dead.

To recapitulate, we cannot too often repeat that the secret doctrine, mother of all religions and philosophies, assumes different aspects with the different ages, but that its foundation is ever the same. Born of India and of Egypt, it has thence journeyed westward, following the flood of migration. We shall find it

---

34 Consult, Cicero's « *De Univers;* » Ammianus Marcellinus, Hist., I., 20, c. 6, p. 267.

in all lands which the Celts have occupied. In Greece, concealed within the mysteries, it stands revealed in the teaching of such masters as Pythagoras and Plato, clothed in poetic and pleasing guises. The pagan myths are like golden gauze that drapes in shimmering folds the pure lines of Delphic wisdom. The school of Alexandria condensed the principles thereof and infused them into Christianity's young and ardent blood.

The scriptures were already illuminated by the esoteric science of another branch of initiates, the Essenes – as a dark vault is lighted by a dazzling gleam of sunshine. Into this source Christ dipped, as into a live and inexhaustible spring, borrowing of its vivid imagery and lofty flights. Thus, through the lapse of centuries and the upheaval of nations, do we ever find the undying traces of a secret teaching, which is at the base of all great religious and philosophical conceptions, and is universally identical. The sages, philosophers and prophets of all times and all lands have drawn from it the energy and inspiration which makes all things possible, which transforms both individuals and social organizations by forwarding them upon the path of progressive evolution.

There would seem to be some mighty spiritual current which mysteriously flows through the deep places of history. It appears to issue from that unseen realm that governs and surrounds us, where dwell and act those transcendental spirits who have ever guided this human race, with which they still commune.

5

Gaul

To ancient Gaul a great doctrine was given. There it lived and thrived in a powerful and hitherto inexperienced form, and from it consequences were deduced such as were elsewhere unknown. "There are three primitive unities," the Druids proclaimed, "God, Light and Liberty." When India had already settled into castes of rigid limitations, the Gaelic organization was founded upon universal equality, community of belongings and electoral rights. No other people of Europe possessed to the same degree the conviction of immortality, justice and liberty.

It is with reverence that we should study the Gaelic philosophical tendencies, for Gaul is our great ancestor, and we find in her, strongly accused, all the qualities and all the defects of our race. There is nothing more worthy of our respect and inquiry than the doctrine of the Druids, who distinctly were not the barbarians as has been wrongly believed for centuries.

For a long while all that we knew of the Celts was what the Catholic and Latin writers chose to tell: of these we have some right to be suspicious, for was it not to their interest to belittle our ancestors and misconstrue their beliefs? Caesar's *Commentaries* were written with an evident eye to posterity. Philo and Suetonius both testify to the fact that this work is manifestly full of misrepresentations and voluntary errors. Certain fathers of the Church, however, such as Cyril, Clement of Alexandria and Origen, are careful to distinguish the Druids from the idolatrous herds, and assign to them the distinction of "philosophers." Among the ancient authors, Lucan, Horace and Florus considered the Gaels as custodians of the mysteries of birth and death.

The progress of Celtic research,[35] the publication of the *Triades* and of the *Songs of the Bards*,[36] allow us to gather from a clearer source a truer appreciation of the beliefs of our forefathers. Druidical philosophy, as we must now broadly view it, conforms alike with the secret doctrines of the Orient and with modern spiritualistic thought in agreement with which it asserts the progressive lives of the spirit in its progress up the ladder of worlds. This virile doctrine imbued the Celts with such indomitable courage and self-assurance that they went forth to death as to a feast. Where the soldiers of Rome covered themselves in steel and iron, the hardy Celts stripped off their clothes and fought bare chest. They prided in their wounds and deemed the artifices of warfare to be no better than cowardice, hence their many defeats and final downfall.

Their belief in a future existence[37] was so great that they often made loans redeemable in a future life. They confided messages to the dying, to be delivered to the dead. They called the remains of dead warriors "torn envelopes", and these they abandoned on

---

35 See Gatien Arnoult's « *Philosophie Gauloise*; » H. Martin's « H*istoire de France*; a. Pictet's « *Bibliothèque de Genève*; » Dumesnil's « *Imortalité*; » Reynaud's « *L'Esprit de la Gaule*. »

36 "*Cyfrinach Beirdd Inys Prydain*," Ed. Wllliams, "British Bards."

37 See César, "Commentaires," I. VI, chap. XIV: "The druids initially wanted to persuade us that the souls do not die, but rather, that after death, they pass into other human bodies" (*non interire animas, sed ab aliis post mortem transire ad alios*).

the field of battle, to the amazement of their foes, as unworthy of further consideration.

The Celts had no notion of hell. For this in *Pharsale* (Song 1st) Lucan thus praises them:

> "To your minds, the shades bury themselves not in Erebus' somber regions; but the spirit flies straight away to animate other bodies in other worlds. Death is but the midway of a long life. They are happy, these men that know not the supreme fear of the grave. Hence their heroism in bloody battle and their scorn of death."

These ancient people were chaste, hospitable and true to their pledge. In Druidical institutions, we find the highest expression of Celtic genius. They were not a sacerdotal body: the title "Druid" was equivalent to "sage" or "scientist", leaving those who bore it free to choose their own field of action. Some, designated by the title of "eubage," president at the religious ceremonies; but the majority devoted themselves to the education of youth, to the practice of justice and to the cultivation of science and poetry. Great was the political influence of the Druids, whose chief ambitions lay in the unification of Gaul. In the land of the Carnutes they instituted an annual assembly at which the deputies of the Gaelic republics would meet to discuss the important interests of the country. The Druids were chosen by election; twenty years of study were required as a preliminary to initiation.

Their worship was held under the green canopy of the woods, and its symbols were all borrowed from nature. A primeval forest was the temple: with columns innumerable, with emerald vault illumined by the sun's golden shafts that reached down to the mossy floor, flecking it with a thousand intricate designs. The moaning wind and shivering leaves filled this great green temple with a volume of mysterious sound that inclined the subdued soul to reverie. The oak, the most sacred of trees, was the emblem of divine might; the evergreen mistletoe represented immortality. A heap of boulders formed the altar, for "a carved stone is a dirty stone," these austere men would say! No object wrought by hand of man was allowed to deface their sanctuaries, for the Celts had a horror of idols, and of the puerile forms of the Roman worship.

That their principles should not be tainted nor materialized by symbolism the Druids went as far as to forbid all plastic art, even to written precepts. They solely entrusted the tenets of their doctrine to their bards and initiates, which accounts for the scarcity of documents relating to this epoch.

The human sacrifices, for which the Celts have been so harshly condemned, were, in the main, but legal executions. The Druids, who were both magistrates and chief executioners, made, of condemned criminals, a holocaust to the Supreme Power. An interval of five years elapsed between sentence and execution. Eager to rejoin their dear departed in happier spheres, eager to ascend the circle of felicity, the Celts gaily mounted the sacrificial stone, and death come to them in the midst of a song of joy. But in Caesar's time, these immolations had already fallen into disuse.

Teutates, Esus and Gwyon were only in the Celtic Pantheon the personification of force, light and mind. Above these reigned the infinite Power, whom they worshipped by the consecrated stones, in the majestic silence of the forests. The Druids taught the Oneness of God.

According to the *Triads*, the soul is formed in the depths of the unfathomable abyss, "anoufn." There it assumes the rudimentary forms of life; it only acquires conscience and freedom after having been for a long while captive to the lower instincts. The bard Taliesin, famous throughout Gaul, thus sings:

> *"Having existed since all time in the bosom of the great waters, I was born neither of Father nor yet of Mother, but from Nature's crude forms; from the twigs of the birch, from the fruits of the forest, from the flowers of the mountain. I have frolicked in the night, I have slept in the dawn. I have been a viper in the lake, an eagle upon the mountain tops, a wolf in the woods. Then did Gwyon (the sacred spirit), the sage of sages, stamp me with his seal and I acquired immortality. A long, long time ago I was a shepherd. Long did I wander over the Earth, before I became learned in science. At last I shone amongst the high chiefs. Robed in sacred robes, I have held the sacrificial bowl. I have dwelt in a hundred worlds; I have moved through a hundred circles."*[38]

The Druids held that the soul, in its tremendous flight, passes through three successive circles corresponding to three successive conditions. In "anoufn" it endures the tyranny of matter; this is the animal period. Then it enters into "abred," the circle of the migrations that people the worlds of trials and atonements, of which the Earth is one.

Often, in each circle, is the soul incarnated. Finally, at the cost of an incessant struggle, it casts off all corporeal influences and passes out of the circle of incarnation to attain "Gwinfyd," the circle of the happy worlds of felicity. To it are spirituality's enchanting horizons then unfolded. Higher still are revealed the profound depths of "ceugant," the circle of the Infinite which, encompassing

---
38 Barddas, cad. Goddeu.

all others, belongs to God alone. Far from bordering upon pantheism, like most of the Eastern faiths, Druidism was quite oppositely inclined, as well because of its exalted ideal of the Divinity as by its high conception of life.

The *Triads* hold that the human being is neither the plaything of fate nor yet the slave of a capricious will. He himself molds and shapes his own destiny. His objective does not lie in the pursuit of temporary gratification, but in that elevation which is attained through self-sacrifice and duty accomplished. Life is a battlefield where the brave conquers his ranks. Such a doctrine exalted heroic qualities and purified morals. It was as remote from puerile mysticism as from the deceitful platitudes of the theory of nothingness; it seems, however, to have erroneously maintained that[39] the culpable soul which persists in wrong-doing may lose the fruit of its labors and retrograde to the lower degrees; that it may even be reduced to that germ level whence it will be necessary to begin again his tedious and painful ascent.

Still, as the *Triads* add, loss of memory will at least enable it to take up the struggle without the clogging fetters of past remorse or hatred. Finally, in "Gwynfid," with memory it regains its vision of the entirety of its existence and can piece together the fragments of lives scattered throughout a succession of ages.

The cosmologic knowledge of the Druids was extensive. They were aware of the fact that our planet whirls through space, describing a wide circle around the sun. This appears in the song of Taliesin, called the song of the world:[40]

> *"I will ask the bards, and why the bards would not answer?*
> *I will ask them what it is that upholds the Earth in such*

---

39 Triad 26, "Triades Bardiques," published. by Celtic School of Glamorgan
40 Barddas, cad. Goddeu.

manner that, the prop removed, still the Earth falls not. But, what could thus uphold it? A mighty traveler is the Earth! While ever ceaselessly advancing, still she is constant to her course; how admirably contrived this course must be that the Earth should not leave it!"

Caesar, himself so little versed in such matters, tells us in his "*Commentaries*" that the Druids taught many things concerning the size and shape of the Earth, the motion of the stars, the mountains and precipices of the moon. They taught that the universe, although eternal and immutable as a whole, undergoes a constant transformation in its parts: that life, thanks to an endless circulation, fills and animates it in every region. Lacking the means of observation that modern science possesses, one wonders how the ancient Celts could formulate such theories.

There is ample testimony that the Druids communicated with the unseen world. From within stone enclosures, they evoked the dead. Druidesses and female bards rendered oracles. Several authors relate how Vercingétorix was conversing, beneath the canopy of the dark woods, with the souls of departed heroes, who had died for their country. Before raising Gaul against Caesar he went to the Isle of Sein, the ancient dwelling of the Druidesses. There, in clash of thunder and a blaze of lightning,[41] a spirit appeared that predicted his defeat and martyrdom.

The commemoration of the dead is of Gaelic origin. On the first of November the feast of the spirits was celebrated: not in cemeteries – for the Celts did not honor dead bodies – but in every house the bards and the seers evoked the spirits of the dead. Our forefathers peopled the moors and the woods of wandering

---

41 Bosc and Bonnemère, « *Histoire nationale des Gaulois.* »

spirits: the Duz and the Korrigan were but so many souls in search of reincarnation.

The teaching of the Druids was molded, politically and socially speaking, into institutions befitting their standards of justice. Confessing one ruling principle and conscious subjects of one universal destiny, the Celts possessed both liberty and equality.

In all Gaelic republics the chiefs were elected by the assembled people. The over ambitious and the would be usurpers were punished, according to Celtic law, by fire. The women were seers and prophetesses; they were admitted to the councils and held sacerdotal offices. They were subservient to themselves alone, and chose their husbands. Property was collective, all the land belonging to the republic; with them hereditary rights did not exist. Elections decided everything.

The long Roman occupation, followed by the Frankish invasion and by the introduction of feudalism, caused the loss of our true national traditions. But one memorable day of the old Gaelic blood surged in the veins of the people, and the Revolution swept away in its turmoil those two foreign importations: the theocracy that Rome had given and the monarchy engrafted by the Franks! Ancient Gaul lived anew in the France of 1789.

One important thing, however, was lacking: the notion of solidarity. Druidism certainly inculcated the conceptions of right and liberty, but if the people of Gaul were aware of their equality, they lacked the sentiment of fraternity: hence the want of unity that determined its downfall. After being bowed beneath the weight of twenty centuries of oppression, purified by misfortune, enlightened by fresh knowledge, the nation has at last become unified and undivided.

The law of love and charity, Christ's great gift to humanity, has come to complete the Druidical teaching and to construct a noble philosophical and moral synthesis.

From out of the womb of the dark ages, like a resurrection of the very spirit of ancient Gaul, there arises a radiant figure. Already, in the first centuries of our era, the bard Myrdwin, or Merlin had prophesied the coming of Joan of Arc. It was in the shade of the mystic oak, next to the table of stone, that she so often heard "her voices." She was a pious believer, but above the earthly church she placed the Church eternal: the only one she would obey in all things. [42]

No other testimony of spiritual intervention in the history of any nation is at all comparable to this touching story of the virgin of Domrémy. At the beginning of the fifteenth century, France was being slowly strangled by England's iron grip. With the assistance of a young girl, a child of eighteen, the unseen powers reanimated a demoralized people, rekindled an extinct patriotism, quickened a petrified nation into active resistance and saved France from dissolution.

Joan never presumed to act until she had consulted "her voices;" whether on the field of battle or when confronted with her judges, these ever inspired her actions and her words. For one moment only, when in her dungeon at Rouen, did these voices seem to desert her. Then it was that, exhausted by suffering, she consented to recant. As soon as the spirits left her she became a mere woman, weakened and submissive. Then the voices spoke

---

42 Consult the "*Procés de Rehabilitation de la Pucelle,*" contained in the documents of the college of Charts.

again; immediately she regained courage and replied to her judges:

> The voices told me that it was treason to recant. The truth is this: God has sent me and what I have done was well done.

Sanctified by her dolorous passion, Joan has given humanity a sublime example of self-sacrifice, a subject for deep meditation, and universal admiration.

6

Christianity

The belief in one only God, the mother conceptions from which Christianity was to emerge, was born in the desert. Across Sinai's stony solitudes, towards the Promised Land, Moses, an Egyptian initiate, led the chosen people: that people through whom the monotheistic conception, until now confined within the mysteries, was to create a religious wave which would eventually flood the world.

Considerable was the part played by the people of Israel, whose history was like a hyphen placed between the East and the West, between the secret science of the temple and democratized religion. Despite its general confusion and many blemishes, despite the somber exclusionism which is one of its characteristic traits, Judaism's great merit lies in the adoption and complete assimilation of the all-important conception of the Unity of the Creator: a conception, vaster than it could dream, a conception which will prepare the way for the fusion of all nations into one universal family, ruled by one Father, and under one Law.

The prophets only, before Christ's coming, could dimly foresee or imagine such a glorious and distant prospect. Such was the ideal, unseen of the multitude, which the Son of Mary was to touch and transform into a vision of ineffable splendor. His disciples disseminated it amongst the pagans, and the dispersion of the Jews contributed to its diffusion. Ever serenely progressing amid crumbling civilizations and the havoc wrought by the time, it will remain indelibly engraved in the hearts of people.

A little while before the dawn of our era, when the power of Rome was most prevalent and predominant, the secret doctrine began to retrograde and its authority to pale. True initiates had grown scarce, thought was becoming materialized, and high ideals corrupted. Lethargic India fell fast asleep and dreamed dreams; extinguished was the lamp of Egypt's temples; Greece, given over to the rhetoricians and sophists, reviled its wise men, banished its philosophers, profaned its sacred mysteries. The oracles became dumb, superstition and idolatry invaded the temples, Roman debauchery took the world, a giant tidal wave of saturnalia, bestial lust and intoxication! From the apex of the Capitol the sated she-wolf rules both rulers and nations: in a bloody apotheosis Caesar, Emperor and God, holds sway.

Still, upon the distant shores of the Dead Sea, there are some who yet hold to the tradition of the prophets and to the secrets of the pure doctrine.

These, a handful, are the Essenes, a group of initiates whose colonies extend to the banks of the Nile. They openly professed the practice of healing, but their secret object was other and higher: in pursuance with this, to a select few, they revealed the higher laws governing life and the universe. Their doctrine was almost identical with that of Pythagoras. They admitted pre-existence and the soul's successive incarnations, and rendered to God the worship of the spirit.

Their initiation, like that of the priests of Memphis, was gradual and required several years of preparation. Their morals were beyond complain, their lives were spent in contemplation, far from political strife and from the plotting of a grasping and envious priesthood.[43]

It is most certainly amongst these Essenes that Jesus spent the years preceding His apostleship; years concerning which the Scriptures are sealed. All tends, however, to substantiate this surmise: the identity of His views with those of the Essenes, the aid they lent Him at several times, the free hospitality extended to Him as an adept, and the final fusion of their order with the first Christians, a fusion from which esoteric Christianity emerged.

If Christ had not the superior initiation, His soul, which overflowed with light and love, was great enough to supply all the elements that His mission required. Never did greater spirit pass through the world. A divine serenity radiated from His countenance; in Him all the perfections blended to form and ideal beauty and an ineffable loveliness. His heart throbbed with a boundless pity for the poor and lowly; in it reverberated the sorrows, woes and sufferings of all humanity. To alleviate these sufferings, to staunch these tears, to comfort, to heal, to save, He unhesitatingly surrendered His own life and offered Himself as a willing sacrifice to the elevation of humanity. When He appeared on Calvary, livid with the pallor of death, nailed to the infamous cross, He still found strength in His agony to pray for those that were torturing Him: "Father, forgive them, for they know not what they do."

Of all the great missionaries, Christ, the foremost, confined to the people those truths which, before Him, belonged to the privileged class alone. Through Him, was the hidden teaching rendered accessible to all, even to the humblest; when the mind was incapable of receiving it, its appeal was sent straight to the heart. This teaching He presented to them in a way that the world knew

---

43 See Josephus's "*Wars of the Jews,*" II; and Philo *On the Contemplative Life.*

not as yet, with a passionate love, a winning sweetness, a communicative faith that thawed the frosts of skepticism, and, conquering his Hearers, made of them His devoted followers.

What He called "preaching the kingdom of heaven to the humble" simply consisted in making known to all people the facts of immortality and the existence of their common Father. Intellectual treasures which the too frugal adepts had meted out but with prudence, Christ spread them over the great human family; millions of beings bowed down to earth, who knew nothing of destiny and waited, in uncertainty and suffering, for the new word which was to console and warm them. His words and teachings He gave forth ungrudgingly; they were moreover consecrated by His passion and death. The cross, that ancient emblem of the initiates which was to be found in the crumbling temples of Egypt and of India, became, through Jesus' Passion, the symbol of the elevation of a humanity rescued from the depths of darkness and from the ditch of inferior passion, to attain finally eternal life, the life of the regenerated spirit.

The Sermon on the Mount condenses and contains the whole teaching of Jesus. In it, the moral law is revealed with all its consequences; human beings are told that brilliant qualities contribute neither to their improvement, nor to their happiness, but that in their stead they must cultivate the humble hidden virtues of humility, charity and righteousness:

> *"Blessed are the poor in spirit:*[44] *for theirs is the kingdom of heaven. Blessed are those who mourn, for they will be comforted. Blessed are the meek, for they will inherit the earth. Blessed are those who hunger and thirst for righteousness, for they will be filled. Blessed are the*

---
44 Simple" and "honest" minds was undoubtedly implied

merciful, for they will be shown mercy. Blessed are the pure in heart, for they will see God."[45]

So spoke Jesus, and His words open unknown perspectives to the human being. In the depths of His heart wells the spring of future happiness: "The kingdom of God is within you!" This every one may realize who practices self-command, the forgiveness of injury and the love of his neighbor.

Love, in Jesus' estimation, comprised all religion and all philosophy:

> "But I tell you who hear me: Love your enemies, do good to those who hate you, bless those who curse you, pray for those who mistreat you. If someone strikes you on one cheek, turn to him the other also. If someone takes your cloak, do not stop him from taking your tunic. Give to everyone who asks you, and if anyone takes what belongs to you, do not demand it back. Do to others as you would have them do to you. If you love those who love you, what credit is that to you? Even 'sinners' love those who love them. And if you do good to those who are good to you, what credit is that to you? Even 'sinners' do that."[46]

Of such love, God Himself sets us the example, for are not His arms ever open to him who repents? This is set forth in the parables of the Prodigal Son and the Lost Lamb.

> "Your Father that is in heaven does not want one of these little ones to perish."

---

45 Mathew V: 3-8
46 Luke VI. 27-34 Mathew V: 44 -48

Is not this a denial of eternal damnation, the conception of which has been falsely attributed to Jesus?

If Christ be sometimes severe and speaks wrathfully, it is to those Pharisees that are assiduous at their devotions but neglect the moral law. To Him a schismatic Samaritan is more deserving than the Levite who scorned the wounded. He disapproved of superficial manifestations of piety and exclaimed against such priests:

> "Woe unto you, scribes and Pharisees, hypocrites! For you devour widows' houses, and for a pretense make long prayer: therefore you shall receive greater damnation".

To the devout who seek atonement in fasting and in prayer, he says:

> "It is not that which goes into the mouth that defile a man: but that which come out of the mouth, this defile a man."

He admonishes those who are partial to lengthy prayers:

> "Your Father knows what things you have need of, before you ask Him."

Jesus condemned the hierarchical priesthood when he cautioned His disciples to choose neither leader nor master. His faith was the inner faith, the only one worthy of a lofty spirit. This He expresses in the following admonition:

> "But the hour comes, and now is, when the true worshippers shall worship the Father in spirit and in truth, for the

> Father seeks such to worship Him. God is a spirit: and they that worship Him must worship Him in spirit and in truth."

He demands only fraternal love and righteous living:

> "Love your neighbor as yourself and be perfect as your Father which is in heaven is perfect, for this is the law and the prophets."

This precepts states, with simple eloquence, the highest aim of initiation, the striving after perfection, of which the attainment likewise comprises power and felicity. In addition to these teachings, intended by Jesus for the lowly, there are others in which the hidden doctrine of the Essenes is sketched in flashes of light.[47] Such elevation is beyond the reach of the multitude, hence it came to pass that in the course of centuries, and Evangelical translators and interpreters have altered the original form and corrupted the sense. In spite of these alterations it is easy to reconstruct the original if one but discards a superstitions clinging to the letter, setting mind and reason in its place. This is especially evident in the Gospel according to John.

> "In My Father's house are many mansions. I go to prepare a place for you. I will come back and take you to be with me that you also may be where I am." [48]

---

[47] In Mark IV, 10-13 will be found: "Unto you it is given to know the mystery of the kingdom of God: but unto them that are without, all these things are done in parables." The same thought is expressed by Matthew, XIII, 11 and 13. For other details about the secret doctrine of the Christ, see "*Christianity and Spiritism,*" Léon Denis, chap. IV, notes 4, 5, 6, etc.

[48] John XIV, 2, 3.

The house of the Father is the infinite heaven with the worlds that populate it and the life that animates these worlds. These are the innumerable stations of our road, stations in which we shall rest if we follow the precepts of Jesus. Jesus Himself will come to teach us through His example and courage, in order that we can reach these worlds so far transcend than our own.

In the following words will read the assertion of the souls' successive lives:

> "I tell you the truth, no one can enter the kingdom of God[49] unless he is born of water and the Spirit. Flesh gives birth to flesh, but the Spirit gives birth to spirit. You should not be surprised at my saying, 'You must be born again.' The wind blows wherever it pleases. You hear its sound, but you cannot tell where it comes from or where it is going. So it is with everyone born of the Spirit."

When his disciples sought him, asking: "Why then do the teachers of the law say that Elijah must come first?" Jesus replied "But I tell you, Elijah has already come, and they did not recognize him." And then the disciples understood that he was talking to them about John the Baptist:[50]

> "Truly I tell you, among those born of women there has not risen anyone greater than John the Baptist; yet whoever is least in the kingdom of heaven is greater than he (...) And if you are willing to accept it, he is the Elijah who was to come. Whoever has ears, let them hear."[51]

---

49 John III, 5-8.
50 Matthew XVII, 11-13
51 Matthew XI, 11, 14 and15.

The goal for which each and all of us must strive is plainly pointed out. It is the reign of the "Son of Man:" of the Christ social: in other words, the reign of truth, justice and love. The gaze of Christ was ever directed towards the future, towards those days that have been promised us:

> "But very truly I tell you, it is for your good that I am going away. Unless I go away, the Advocate will not come to you; but if I go, I will send him to you. (…) I have much more to say to you, more than you can now bear. But when he, the Spirit of truth, comes, he will guide you into all truth. (…) [52]

At time he would depict the eternal truths, with dazzling colors and flame-like words. His apostles could not always follow Him, but he relied upon time and events to germinate these principles in the consciousness of humanity, as rain and sun sprout the grain entrusted to the earth. Such was the intent of the ringing words which he spoke to his disciples:

> "Heaven and Earth shall pass away, but My words shall not pass away."

Jesus' appeals were addressed both to heart and mind. Those who could have understood neither Pythagoras nor Plato were stirred to the soul by Nazarene's eloquent apostrophes; and therein is the secret of the superiority of his religion. In order to receive the wisdom of the temples of Egypt and Greece, it was necessary

---

52 John XVI, 7, 12 and 13. These words are interpreted by the Church as predicting the coming of the Holy Spirit, some months later, to the apostles; but if mankind (to whom this prophecy was made) was not able to apprehend the truth, why should it be better fitted to receive it only fifty days later?

to undergo the degrees of a long and painful initiation; whereas through charity all could become good Christians and brothers in Jesus.

Gradually, the transcendent truths became veiled. Those who possessed them were supplanted by those who only thought they did and thus material dogma dethroned the pure doctrine. Christianity, in expanding, lost in value what it gained in extent.

To the profound science of Jesus was added the fluidic power of the superior initiate, of the soul free from the yoke of passions, whose will dominates matter and commands the subtle forces of nature. Christ was gifted with the second sight: his gaze went to the bottom of minds and conscious; he healed with a word, with a gesture, with the laying on of hands, and even by His mere presence. Beneficent effluvia arose from his person, and evil spirits fled at his command. He communicated at will with the spiritual powers from whom in his hours of trial he derived the moral strength that sustained him on his painful way. At Tabor his frightened disciples saw him conversing with Moses and Elias. Thus, later, after the crucifixion, they will see him appear in the radiance of his ethereal fluidic body, of which Paul spoke in these terms: "If there is a natural body, there is also a spiritual body," [53] and whose reality has likewise been attested by modern psychology.

The apparitions of Jesus after His death may not be doubted, for they alone account for the persistence of the Christians faith. After the martyrdom of the Master and the dispersal of His disciples, Christianity was morally dead. The apparitions

---

53 1 Corinthians XV, 44: In this same epistle (XV. 5-8) St. Paul enumerates the apparitions of Jesus, after His death. He reckons these to be six, amongst which was the one to the five hundred, "of whom several are still living." The last was that upon the road to Damascus, which converted Paul from a relentless enemy to the Christians into a most ardent apostle.

and discourses of Jesus could alone restore faith and energy to His apostles.

Some writers have denied the very existence of Christ, attributing all that has been written about Him to anterior traditions or to the Oriental imagination. Thus has a faint wave of opinion been started, the tendency of which is to reduce the origins of Christianity to the status of legend.

The New Testament undoubtedly contains many errors. Several events which it chronicles are to be found in the history of other ancient peoples: some of the acts attributed to the Christ likewise figure in the lives of Krishna and Horus. On the other hand there are many historical proofs of the existence of Jesus of Nazareth, which proofs are all the more peremptory because they originate from the very adversaries of Christianity. All Jewish Rabbis recognize the fact of His existence. Thus the Talmud bears witness:

> "On Easter Eve, Jesus was crucified, for having given Himself over to magic and sorcery."

Tacitus and Suetonius likewise mention the martyrdom of Jesus and the rapid progress of Christianity.[54] Fifty years later, Pliny the Younger, Governor of Bithynia, officially reported this movement to Trajan, and his report has been preserved.

Moreover, how would it be possible to admit that the belief in a mere myth could have inspired the early Christians with such enthusiasm, courage and steadfastness in the face of martyrdom? How indeed could this have enabled them to overthrow paganism,

---

54 Tacite, *Annales*, XV, 44 ; Suétone, *Vitæ* ; Claud., 25; Neron 16.

to conquer the Roman Empire and, gradually, the entire civilized world? A religion that lasts twenty centuries and revolutionizes the half of a world can certainly not be founded upon a fiction. If we trace the cause that has produced a mighty result, we shall invariably find an eminent personality at the root of every great idea.

As to the theories that makes of Jesus one of the three Persons of the Trinity, or else a purely fluidic being, these seem to be equally baseless. In uttering these words: "Let this cup pass from Me…" Jesus revealed himself a human being, subjected both to fear and to weakness. Jesus often spoke of Himself as "the Son of Man." This expression can be counted twenty five times in Matthew. Like ourselves, Jesus has suffered and has sorrowed, and this human suffering brings Him closer to us; and in becoming more akin to us His virtue and His supreme example are rendered still more admirable.

The coming of Christianity has brought about admirable results. It has brought to the world the idea of humanity which antiquity has not known in its extended sense. This ideal, vitalized in the person of Jesus, has gradually expanded, and today is manifest throughout the West, with the social consequences that follows from it. To this conception we must add those others of moral law and eternal life which until then had been the exclusive property of sages and scholars. Henceforth, the human being's highest duty is manifestly to prepare the world, by every effort of his individual and social life, for the reign of God, which is that of Truth and Justice: *"Let Thy kingdom be on Earth, as it is in Heaven."*

This reign can be realized but by the perfection of all people, by the constant progress of their souls and society. These notions therefore contain in them an unlimited power of development. It is not surprising that after twenty centuries of incubation, of obscure labor, they have scarcely begun to produce their effects in the social order. Christianity contains, in latent state, all the elements of true progress, but since the first centuries it has deviated, and its true principles ignored even by its official representatives, have passed on into the spirit of the people, even into those who, no longer claiming nor believing themselves to be Christians, nevertheless unconsciously carrying in them the ideal dreamed by Jesus.

Neither to the churches nor to the so-called institutions of divine right – which is none other than the reign of the Force – shall we find the heritage of Christ transmitted; for these are but pagan, or barbarous, institutions. The spirit of Christ dwells in the soul of the people. In its strivings after a higher life, in its constant reaching towards some social condition more consonant with the notions of justice and solidarity, this great humanitarian stream reveals itself; a stream whose source is upon the heights of Calvary and whose current is sweeping us towards a future in which the infamy of pauperism, ignorance and war, whether internal or foreign, will be unknown.

Catholicism has vitiated the pure and beautiful doctrines of the Gospel by its conceptions of redemption through grace, of original sin, of hell, of atonement. In each century numerous councils have promulgated new dogmas, each of these being further removed from the teachings of Christ. Luxury and simony have overrun the pure faith. Through fear has the Church ruled the world, in contradistinction to Jesus' reign of love and charity. It has armed the nations, one against another; it has systematized persecution and caused oceans of blood to flow.

Vainly has science, in its onward march, pointed out the contradictions extant between Catholic teaching and the real nature of things; the Church has replied by anathematizing science as an invention of Satan. A great gulf divides the Roman doctrines from the ancient wisdom of the initiates, who was the mother of Christianity. In this chaos materialism alone has prospered, everywhere spreading its insidious roots.

Religious sentiment, on the contrary, has perceptibly weakened. Dogma no longer exercises the slightest influence upon society. The human mind, grown weary of the restrictions to which it had been subjected, hastened towards the light; it has broken these weak bonds, so as to unite with the great minds who belong to no one race or sect, but whose thought enlightens and console all humanity. Enfranchised from sacerdotal tutelage it asserts its right henceforth to think, act and live, by itself.

We only want to speak of Catholicism impartially. We cannot forget that it was the faith of our forefathers, that it has cradled innumerable consideration. Moderation, however, must not exclude criticism. When we look closely into it, we are forced to the following conclusions: The infallible Church has erred both in its physical conception of the universe and in its moral conception of human life. The Earth is no more the most important center of the universe than this life is the only stage of our progress and struggles. Work is not a punishment, but rather a means of regeneration whereby the human being may be strengthened and elevated. The distorted view, which Catholicism takes of life, has reduced it to a hatred of all progress and civilization, as the last article of the Syllabus unreservedly states:

> "Anathema to him who says: The pontiff of Rome could and should be reconciled to and harmonize with modern progress, liberality and civilization"

Catholicism attributes all of our own weaknesses to the Supreme Being; it represents Him as a kind of spiritual executioner who consigns to everlasting torment to those feeble creatures that He Himself has made. Human beings, who were born to happiness, succumb, as a crowd, to the temptations of the evil one, and go forthwith to hell. Thus God's helplessness would equal His lack of foresight, and Satan would be cleverer than He!

And is this the Father of whom Jesus spoke when He bade us forget, in His name, the wrongs that we have suffered, when He tells us to render good for evil, and to practice mercy, love and forgiveness? Thus would a good and compassionate individual be superior to God!

We forget, it is true, that in order to save the world, God has sacrificed His own Son, one of the Trinity, part and parcel of Himself. But here again we stumble upon a monstrous blunder, which Diderot thus epitomizes: "God, to appease God, has killed God!"

Catholicism has obscured the conscience by its dark and terrible conceptions of a vengeful God. He has disheartened the man of thought; He taught him to stifle his doubts, to annihilate his reason and his most beautiful faculties, to depart from all those who sincerely and truthfully sought the truth, to esteem those who bear the same yoke as himself.

Besides its erroneous teaching, there are innumerable abuses: paid prayers and ceremonies, taxes levied upon sin, confession, relics, Purgatory, the repurchase of the soul, finally the dogmas of the Immaculate Conception, of papal infallibility and temporal power; which latter stands in flagrant violation of the precepts of Deuteronomy (XVIII: 1 and 2), which prohibit priests from possessing the goods of the world or from sharing in any inheritance, "the Lord Himself being their heritage" – all of which goes to show how far Catholicism has drifted from the true sense of the Holy Books.

Still, it remains true that the Church has done good work. It has had its days of greatness; it has raised dams before the advancing flood of barbarism; it has endowed the world with many charitable institutions. But now, as though petrified within its shell of dogma, it alone remains stationary, while all else moves and progresses. From day to day science is expanding and human reason takes its rise.

Nothing escapes the law of progress, not even religious beliefs. These may have satisfied the requirements of a backward epoch, but the time is at hand when these beliefs, imprisoned in their formulas as in iron belt, must expand or perish. Thus is it with Catholicism. Having given to history all that it had to give, and being now powerless to fecundate the human mind, that mind deserts it, pursuing its tireless advance towards greater and nobler conceptions. The Christian idea will not die out, however; it will be transformed to appear again in a newer and purer form. The day will come when Catholicism, with its dogmas and rituals, will be but a vague recollection, as indistinct as the Roman and Scandinavian paganism are to us; but the great figure of the Crucified One will forever tower over the centuries. Of His teachings three things will subsist, because these three are the expression of the everlasting truth; the unity of God, the immortality of the soul, and human brotherhood.

In spite of religious persecutions, the secret doctrine has withstood the havoc of the centuries. One can follow its traces throughout the Middle Ages. At a very remote time, some Jewish initiates had already consecrated two celebrated works to it – the Zohar and the Sepher-Jeshirah – the combination of which forms the Kabbalah, one of the chief works of esoteric science. [55]

Primitive Christianity carries the strong imprint. The early Christians believed in the pre-existence of the soul and in its survival in other bodies; as we witness in those words of Jesus relating to John the Baptist and Elijah, as well as in the questions the apostles asked concerning the man who was born blind and who seemed "to have incurred this punishment because of sins committed before he was born." [56] The belief in reincarnation was so universal amongst the Jews that the historian Josephus reproached the Pharisees of his day for only conceding the transmigration of the soul to the worthy. [57] This they called Gilgul, or the rotation of souls.

The Christians likewise evoked the souls of the departed, with whom they were in communication. Numerous indications of this appear in the Acts of the Apostles.[58] Saint Paul, in his First Epistle to the Corinthians, describes, under the name of "spiritual gifts" all types of mediumship.[59] He claimed to be directly instructed in evangelical truth by the spirit of Jesus.

The inspirations were sometimes attributed to evil spirits, which were also referred to as the "Spirit of Python."

---

55 Consult Ad. Franck's fine work, "*La Cabbale.*"
56 John IX: 2.
57 Josephus' "*Wars of the Jews,*" vol. VIII, chap. VII.
58 Acts of the Apostles VIII: 26; XI: 27, 28; XVI: 6, 7; XXI: 4.
59 XIV: 26-29; XV: 44. Mediums were then denominated "prophets." In the Greek text, "spirit" almost invariably appears without other qualification. St. Jerome was the first to affix the "holy"; it remained for the French translators of the vulgate to crystalize the form into "Saint-Esprit," or "Holy-Spirit", or "Holy-Ghost."

> "Dearly beloved, said John the Evangelist, believe not in every spirit, but first prove if it be of God."[60]

The spiritist practices were current during several centuries. Almost all the Alexandrian philosophers, Philo, Ammonius Saccas, Plotinus, Porphyry, Arnobius, professed to be inspired by superior genii. Saint Gregory thaumaturge received from St. John the symbols of the faith of the Spirit.

The school of Alexandria then shone brightly; all the great currents of human thought there seemed to meet and to blend in. From this celebrated school sprang a galaxy of brilliant minds, whose endeavor it was to combine the philosophy of Pythagoras and of Plato with the traditions of the Jewish Kabbalah and with the tenets of Christianity. They thus hoped to form a final doctrine of broad and far-reaching tendencies, a religion both universal and imperishable. This was Philo's dream. Like Socrates, this great thinker was counseled and inspired by a familiar spirit, through the intermediacy of whom he even wrote when sleeping. [61]

So it was with Ammonius and Plotinus, of whom Porphyry relates that he was inspired by a "genius," "not of those termed demons, but of those which are called gods" [62] Plotinus has written a book upon "familiar spirits."

Iamblichus, like others, was versed in theurgy and communicated with the unseen.

Of all the champions of esoteric Christianity, Origen is the best known. This man of genius, saint as well as great philosopher, establishes in his writings [63] that the inequality of people is caused

---

60 Ep., I, IV, 1.
61 Philon, « *De Migrat. Abraham,* » p. 393.
62 Bayle, *Diction. phil. And hist.*, art. Plotin.
63 « *De Principiis.* »

by their unequal merits. What he terms "medicinal" punishment is, he maintains, the only punishment compatible with divine mercy and justice, the effect of which is progressively to purify the soul in a series of existences before it can be admitted into heaven. Amongst the Fathers of the Church, many shared his views,[64] resting upon the revelations of the spirits to prophets and mediums.[65]

Saint Augustine, the great Bishop of Hippo, in his treatise *De cura pro mortuis*, speaks of occult manifestations, adding:

> *"Why not attribute these occurrences to the spirits of the departed, and why not believe that Divine Providence makes good use of all that may instruct, comfort or intimidate man?"*

In his *City of God*,[66] speaking of the lucid and ethereal body, which is the envelope of the soul and which preserves the image of the carnal body, this Father of the Church alludes to theurgical preparation, of the kind called Teletes, which enabled him to communicate with spirits and angels, and to receive wonderful visions.

On the subject of the plurality of lives asserted by Origen, Augustine expresses himself thus in his Confessions:

> *"Has not my childhood succeeded another dead age before it?"*
>
> *"Even before that time, have I been anywhere? Was I someone?"*

This other passage of his works seems even more significant to us:

---

64 See the « *Histoire du Manichéisme,* » Beausobre, II. 595.
65 Origen, « *Contra Celsum,* » pp. 199, 562.
66 « *De Civit. Dei,* » livre X, chap. IX et XI.

"I am sure that amongst the Platonists I shall find many things not incompatible with our dogmas. ... This voice of Plato which, of all philosophers, was the clearest and the most vibrant, rings again out of the mouth of Plotinus, who so resembles him that they seem to be contemporaries; although they are so separated by time that the first of the two appears to be resuscitated in the other. [67]

Saint Clement of Alexandria[68] and Saint Gregory of Nyssa, express themselves in the same way. The latter states[69] that "the immortal soul must be healed and purified, and if this has not been accomplished during its terrestrial life, the healing takes place in future and subsequent lives."

In many circles, the spirits fought against the nascent dogmatism of the Church and supported the heresiarchs. They lamented that the simple teachings of the Gospel should be so obscured by fabricated dogmas, which were imposed upon human credulity despite the protest of reason. They indignantly rose against the already scandalous luxury of the bishops.[70]

These revelations were so many hindrances to the official Church. From them the heretics derived their arguments and their strength, and sacerdotal authority was thereby shaken. With reincarnation and the succession of lives, with the redemption of the faults committed through trial and labor, death had ceased to be a fearful thing, and every person was free to liberate himself from the earthly purgatory by his own individual efforts and progress; all of which went to make the priest dispensable. The Church, finding

---

67 *"Augustini opera,"* I, p. 294.
68 *Stromat,* book VIII, Oxford, 1715.
69 « *Grand discours catéchétique,* » vol. III, chap. VIII, ed. Morel.
70 Abbey de longueval, « *Histoire de l'Eglise Gallicane,* » I, 84.

it unable to open at will the gates of heaven or hell, foresaw that its power and prestige alike would vanish.

It, therefore, thought it wise to impose silence upon all partisans of the secret doctrine; to renounce spiritualistic communications and to denounce their teachings as inspired by the devil. It is from this time that Satan acquired an ever-growing importance in the Christian religion. All that embarrassed the latter was attributed to him. The Church announced herself to be the only living and permanent prophet, and God's sole interpreter. Origen and the Gnostics were condemned by the council of Constantinople (553); the secret doctrine disappeared with the prophets, and the Church was left free to accomplish at leisure her task of absolutism and immobilization.

It was then that the priests of Rome became blind to the light that Jesus had shown the world, and relapsed into darkness. The night they had coveted for others settled upon themselves. The temple ceased to be, as in former days, the sanctuary of truth, and Truth forsook the altar to seek some hidden refuge. It fled to the poor; it inspired those humble missionaries and obscure apostles who sought, taking as their textbook the Gospel of St. John, to establish in distant parts of Europe the simple and pure religion of Jesus, the religion of love and equality. Their doctrines were smothered by the smoke of the pyres or drowned in the streams of blood.

The entire history of the Middle Ages is full of these tentative advances of thought, of glorious awakenings promptly followed by despotic religious and monarchical reaction, which led to periods of gloomy silence.

Yet, under diverse semblances, sacred science was preserved by the secrets orders. The Alchemists, the Templars, the Rosicrucians and others, still reassured its principles. The

Templars were mercilessly persecuted by the official Church, which of all things feared the secrets schools and their influence upon the mind. Under the pretext of sorcery and diabolical pacts, most of them were destroyed by fire and steel.

The Reformation succeeded in rescuing half of Europe from the tyranny of Rome. The Protestant religion is superior to Catholicism, in that it rests upon the principle of free examination. Its morality is more precise, and it retains more of the Evangelical simplicity. Because of its excessive devotion to the letter of the law and to the dogmatic baggage to which it has still partially clung, Protestant orthodoxy cannot be considered as the last word in religious renovation.

In spite of the efforts of theocracy, the secret doctrine has not been lost. Long it lay quiescent, by all unseen. The councils of the Inquisition and the henchmen of the Holy Office flattered themselves that they had exterminated it; but beneath the stone that sealed its sepulcher it still lived, like the sacred flame that burns in solitude throughout the night.

Even within the clergy there were always hidden supporters of these ideas of pre-existence and communication with the invisible. Some of them dared to raise their voices.

Already in 1843, in one of his commendations, M. de Montal, Bishop of Chartres, spoke in these terms:

> *Since it is not forbidden to believe in the soul's pre-existence, who can tell what may not have passed from mind to mind, in the dim bygone ages?*

Cardinal Bona, the Fénelon of Italy, in his treatise *On Spiritual Discernment*, thus expresses himself:

One may well wonder that there have been people of sound judgment who could altogether deny the reality of apparitions and the communication between spirits and the living; or attribute these either to a deceived imagination or to demoniacal artifice!

Lastly, very recently, Mr. Calderone, director of "*Filosofia della Scienza,*" of Palermo, published some letters addressed by Mgr Louis Passavalli, archbishop, vicar of the basilica of Saint-Pierre of Rome, to Mr. Tancredi Canonico, Senator and Minister of Justice, regarding reincarnation. Here is one of the principal passages. [71]

"It seems to me that if one could propagate the idea of the plurality of the existences of the human being, as well in this world as in others, as an admirable means to carry out the merciful designs of God, in the expiation or purification of the human being, with the aim of finally returning it, worthy of Him and the immortal life of the Heavens, one would have already taken a tremendous step, because that would be enough to resolve the most confused and most difficult problems, which currently agitate the human intelligences. The more I think about this truth, the more it appears grand and fertile to me, in practical consequences, for the religion and the society."

Louis Archbishop

---

[71] Voir « *Annales des Sciences Psychiques,* » Septembre 1912, p. 284.

7

Materialism and Positivism

Thought, like the ocean, has its ebb and flow. When the human mind allows itself to overstep the borderland of exaggeration, then, sooner or later, a vigorous reaction is sure to set in. Excesses provoke counter excesses. After centuries of submission and blind faith, the world, grown weary of the somber idealism of Rome, has swung back to the tenets of nothingness. Hasty assertions have challenged furious denials; the battle once begun, the pickaxe of materialism has wrought woeful breaches in the stronghold of Catholicism.

Materialism is gaining ground. Rejecting the dogmas of the Church as unacceptable, a great many cultured minds were moved by the same impulse to desert the spiritualistic cause and their belief in God as well. Thrusting all metaphysical conceptions aside they sought for the truth by the direct observation of phenomena, using what is known as the experimental method.

Materialism may be summarized as follows: there is nothing but matter. Each molecule is endowed with inherent properties, by virtue of which the universe and all it contains were made. The idea of a spiritual principle governing the world is purely hypothetical: the world governs itself by inevitable and mechanical laws. Matter, and matter only, is eternal. Made out of dust, to dust we must return. That which we call soul, the entirety of our intellectual faculties and conscience, is nothing more than an organic function which disappears with death. "Thought is a brain secretion," Carl Vogt tells us, and he further says:

> "The laws of nature are invisible forces that regard neither morality nor good-will."

If matter is everything what then is matter? The materialists themselves could not satisfy us as to this; for matter, as soon as one seeks to analyze its hidden essence, melts away, vanishing like a deceitful vision.

Solid change into liquids and liquids into gas; after the gaseous state comes the radiant state, then, by innumerable and even more subtle phases of refinement, matter becomes imponderable. It becomes that ethereal substance which fills space, so rarefied as to resemble utter void, if the light did not make it vibrate through it. The worlds bathe in its waves as in those of a fluid sea.

So, from degree to degree, matter disappears in an invisible dust: and everything is summed up in into force and motion.

All bodies, organic and inorganic, be they mineral, vegetable, animal, human beings, worlds or stars, are, according to science, but an aggregation of molecules: and these molecules themselves are composed of atoms, separated from one another and in a state of continuous motion and perpetual renewal.

The individual atom is invisible, even by the aid of the most powerful microscope; it is so tiny that thought can scarcely conceive of it.[72] These molecules, these atoms, are active; moreover, they move, circulate and revolve in ceaseless vortices, throughout which the shape of the body is only maintained by virtue of the law of attraction.

It may then be said that the world is formed of invisible atoms which are governed by immaterial forces. Matter, as soon as one examines it, vanishes like smoke. Its reality is but apparent and can furnish us with no basis for certainty. In the spirit alone do we find some certainty, some permanent reality; to the spirit alone is the world revealed in its living unity and eternal splendor; the spirit alone is privileged to look upon it and to grasp its harmony. In the spirit the universe knows, reflects and possesses itself.

And the spirit is yet more; it is the hidden force, the will, which governs and directs matter – *mens agitat molem* – and gives it life. All molecules and all atoms, we have said, are in a state of incessant activity and renewal. The human body is like a vital torrent of which the waters are incessantly replenished. Each particle is replaced by other particles. The brain itself is subject to these changes, and our entire body is renewed every few years.

One cannot say that the brain produces thought: the brain is but the instrument of thought. Throughout the perpetual manifestations of the flesh our personality never ceases to exist, and with it our memory and will. There is in the human being an intelligent

---

72 The theory of an indivisible and indestructible atom, which during 2000 years served as a basis for physics and chemistry, has just been relinquished by science in consequence of the discoveries made by Curie, Becquerel, G. Le Bon, etc. Berthelot, in his "*Synthèse Chimique,*" in 1876, called this theory a subtle and ingenious fiction. "Which shows us," Le Bon declared (in the *Revue Scientifique*, October 31, 1903), "that some of the dogmas of science have no more body to them than had the ancient divinities." Sir W. Crooks had already declared matter to be but a mode of motion. (*Proc. Roy. Soc., No. 205, p. 472).* Thus fell the principle prop that sustained the whole materialist fabric.

and conscious force that regulates, according to life's necessities, the harmonious movements of the atoms: a principle which transcends and survives matter.

It is the same with all things. The material world is but the outward aspect, the changeable appearance, the manifestation of a substantial and spiritual reality which dwells within. As the human self does not proceed from variable matter but from spirit, so is the self of the universe not to be found in the stars and other heavenly bodies which are its component parts, but in the unseen Will, in the invisible and immaterial Power which directs the hidden springs and regulates all evolution.

Materialist science sees only one side of things. In its inability to determine the laws of the universe and of life, after having proscribed the hypothesis, it is obliged to return to it and to leave the experiment to give an explanation of the natural laws.

Such was the case when the atom, which is beyond the ken of the senses, was designated as the basis of the spiritual world.

Mr. J. Roury, a materialist of repute, frankly acknowledges this contradiction in his analysis of Haeckel:

"We can know nothing," he says, "of the composition of matter."

Were the world but a composite of matter governed by blind force, or in other words by chance, we should not have this regular and continuous succession of the same phenomena recurring in accordance with established order; nor should we witness that intelligent adaptation of the means to the end, that harmony of laws, forces and proportion, which is manifest throughout nature. Life would be the accident, the exception, rather than the rule. One would be at a loss to account for this tendency, this impelling power which at all stages of the world, from the advent of the most elementary forms of life, steadily directs the vital current in successive progression towards ever more perfect forms. Aimless, blind and inconsequent, how of itself could matter multiply and develop according to that grand plan whose outlines are apparent to any attentive observer? How could it coordinate its countless molecules and elements in such manner as to fashion all of nature's marvels; from the stars that revolve in space to the organs of the human system, the brain, the eye, the hearing, down to the insect, the bird, the flower?

The progress realized by geology and prehistoric anthropology has cast a high light upon the remote history of the primitive world; but the materialists were mistaken in thinking that their theories had found a new point of support in the law of evolution. One essential truth is evolved from these researches: it is the certainty that nowhere does brute force obtains absolute mastery. On the contrary, we see that intelligence, will and reason triumph and reign. Brute force does not in itself suffice to assure the preservation and development of the species. Of all beings, the one which has conquered the Earth and dominated nature is not physically the strongest, the most invulnerable – but it is intellectually the best equipped.

Since its beginning the world tends to an ever higher order of things. The law of progress manifests itself in the Earth's transformation during the progression of cycles and in the progressive stages of humanity. Throughout the slow march of the universe a purpose is discernible: a purpose towards which all tends: this purpose is the Good and the Better. The history of the earth bear eloquent witness.

It will no doubt be objected that struggle, suffering and death are at the bottom of everything. To which we reply that effort and struggle are an ineradicable condition of progress. As to death, far from signifying oblivion, as we shall show by and by, it marks the entrance of the being into a new phase of evolution. One capital fact stands forth from the study of nature and from the annals of history: everything that exists has a cause. In order to comprehend this cause we must rise above matter until we attain the level of the intellectual principle, even of the living and conscious Law which will expound to us the order of the universe: just as the experiences of modern psychology have elucidate the problem of life.

A philosophical doctrine is appraised according to its ethical consequences and by the effect it produces upon social life. Considered from this standpoint, the theories of materialism, based upon fatalism, are as poor an incentive to spirituality as they are unfit to direct the conscience. Their purely mechanical conception of the world, of the laws of life, is contrary to the notion of liberty and consequently to that of responsibility.[73] Of the battle of life they make an inexorable law in which the weak are bound to succumb to the strong: a law that would forever destroy the human being's faith in a coming reign of peace, love and brotherhood, branding it an impracticable dream. By penetrating into the minds, they can only bring about indifference and selfishness among the happy, violence and despair among the disinherited, and the demoralization in all.

There are, unquestionably, both honest materialists and virtuous atheists; but their virtue and honesty do not arise from the doctrines they profess, but if they are such, it is in spite of their opinions and not because of them, it is by a secret impulse of their nature, and because their conscience has been able to resist all sophisms. It is undeniably a fact that when materialism denies

---

73 Buchner and his followers did not hesitate to declare that "Man is not free, he follows where his mind directs (*Force and Matter*)

free will, when it attributes all mental and moral qualities to mere chemical combinations or to the secretion of the gray matter of the brain, when it considers genius a form of neurology, it shoulders a weighty responsibility in attacking human dignity and depriving human life of all nobler incentive.

Once convinced that nothing awaits us beyond the grave and that human justice is final, we might ask ourselves: "What is the use of struggling and suffering? Of what use is pity, courage, and righteous living? Why constrain or curb our appetites and desires?" Leave humanity to itself, deprive it of the just and discerning power that sustains it, to where then would it drift, to whom would it look in its dark hours of need?

Were there in the universe neither reason nor justice nor love, if it contained nothing more than a blind force crushing people and things beneath the dead weight of a remorseless and soulless fatality, then indeed are idealism, righteousness and morality but so many lying illusions. It is not in them but in brutish realism: not in duty, but in pleasure that the human being must seek the purpose o life; and in order to realize it, he must eschew all vain sentimentality.

If we come from nothingness merely to relapse into nothingness; if a like fate of oblivion awaits both the criminal and the righteous individual, the egotist and the devoted person; if, as the whim of chance may elect, some are doomed to perpetual toil and some fore-ordained to pleasure and luxury: then, and why not proclaim it, hope is a chimera, for there can be no consolation for the afflicted, and no redress for the victims of an unkind fate. Meanwhile, the human being is whirled around in unison with the revolving globe: purposeless, senseless, denuded of all guidance, perpetually renewed by birth and death, between which two events he passes away, leaving behind him no more trail than does a spark ejected into the vault of night.

Under the influence of such doctrines, silence becomes the lot of conscience, which must efface itself before brute force: a calculating spirit takes the place of enthusiasm, and the soul's high aspirations give way to the love of pleasure. Then everyone will think only of himself.

The weariness of life and the temptation to suicide will haunt unfortunate humanity. The waifs of fortune, the world's dispossessed, will experience nothing but hatred for those who possess, and in their fury they will arise and rend this crude and material civilization to pieces.

But not! Thought and reason rise in vehement protest against such dreary doctrines. The individual, they urge, has not struggled, suffered and worked merely to end in nothingness. No, matter is not the final goal. There are laws that transcend it: laws of order and harmony, and the universe is something more than an unconscious machine. How indeed could blind matter govern itself by clever and wise laws? How, could it deprived of reason and sentiment, produce reasoning and thinking beings, capable of discerning good from evil and just from unjust? What! We have a human soul that is capable of carrying love to the point of self-sacrifice, a soul in which the senses of good and evil are deep-rooted, and we would make of it the product of an element which bears no trace of such qualities! We are sentient, we love, we suffer, and yet we would be the offspring of a deaf, mute and inexorable cause. If so, we should be better and more perfect than it!

Such reasoning is an outrage upon logic. One cannot admit that the part is superior to the whole, that intelligence can proceed from an unintelligent cause, or that a purposeless nature can procreate beings capable of pursuing a settled plan.

Common sense tells us, on the contrary, that if intelligence, the love of good and beauty are in us, they must come from a cause which possesses them to a superior degree. If in all things a certain order is manifested, if in the world's fashioning we can trace a plan, then it is because a thought has elaborated them and a reason has conceived them.

We will not now swell further upon these questions, to which we will return later, but will pass on to another doctrine that has much in common with materialism; that is called positivism.

This philosophy is either more subtle or less frank than materialism: it will neither affirm nor deny. Setting aside all metaphysical study, all research as to the initial cause; it asserts that as the human being can know nothing of the principle of things, consequently, the study of the causes of the world and of life would be superfluous. All his method relates to the observation of the facts ascertained by the senses and the laws which connect them. It admits only experience and calculation.

However, the rigor of this method had to bend before the demands of science, and positivism, like materialism, despite its horror of the hypothesis, was forced to admit theories not verifiable by the senses. Thus it speculates upon matter and force, whose inner essence it cannot ascertain: it acquiesces in the principles set forth by the laws of attraction, of the correlation of forces, of the astronomical system, as established by Laplace, all of which lie beyond the province of experimental demonstration.

Moreover, we have we not seen Auguste Comte, the founder of Positivism, after rejecting all religious and metaphysical considerations, hark back to the occult and mysterious attributes of things[74], and finally end by advocating a worship humanity: one, moreover, provided with ceremonials and salaried priests? The positivists, to be sure, have disowned such vagaries. We shall not

---

74 As to this, consult Durand de Gros' "*Ontologie*," published in 1871; a remarkable work that refutes the positivist doctrines.

therefore dwell upon this point any more than upon that peculiarity which appears in the life of Littre – that eminent, erudite and venerated chief of modern atheism – when he allowed himself to be baptized on his deathbed after receiving the frequent visits of a Catholic priest. Such startling recantations of the principles of a lifetime are, however, worth putting on record.

These two examples set by the masters of positivism demonstrate the helplessness of those doctrines which deny the carvings of religion and morality. They go to prove that nothing can be founded upon negation and indifference; that in spite of all sophisms there comes an hour when the Hereafter overwhelms the most hardened skeptics.

Still we will not deny that Positivism has had its *raison d'être*, not that it has rendered undoubted service to the mind by forcing it to a closer reasoning and a nicer preciseness, and to a greater liberality where demonstration is concerned. Weary of metaphysical abstractions and of philosophy's footless discussions, the founders of positivism strove to place science upon a solid ground. Unfortunately the basis they chose happened to be so restricted that their edifice lacked both capacity and solidity. In their endeavor to limit the scope of thought they stifled the best faculties of the soul: in discarding the conceptions of space, of the infinite and the absolute, they deprived mathematics, geometry and astronomy of all possible avenues of development and progress. Significantly enough, it is precisely in this stellar astronomy, rejected by Comte as one of the unknowable, that many of the world's most brilliant discoveries have been made.

Positivism could not possibly supply that moral basis which conscience demands. The human being here below has not only rights to exact, but also duties to fulfill, which is an essential condition of social order. But a person must know where his duty lies before he can go expected to perform it, which seem difficult when he lacks even the knowledge of the object of his own existence, of his being's antecedents and purpose? How can we conform to the general rule, to use Littre's words, if we refuse to explore the moral kingdom or to analyze the phenomena of conscience?

It was a praiseworthy intention that prompted a few positivist and materialist thinkers to found what they termed "Independent Morality," by which they meant a morality stripped of all theological conceptions and faith or creed influences. Thus they thought to provide a neutral field where all well-meaning minds might meet. They forgot, however, that in suppressing liberty, morality is rendered vain and powerless. The human being, deprived of freedom, is but a machine, and morality and machinery have little in common. Besides, that a conception of duty should be workable, all must accept it: and what kind of a notion of duty can you build from a mechanical theory of the universe?

Morality is not a basis, a starting-point: it is a consequence following from certain principles, the apex of a philosophical conception. Hence is independent morality doomed to remain a sterile theory, a generous illusion that can exert no influence on morals.

The positivists have contributed by a close study of matter to the enrichment of some branches of human knowledge, but they have lost sight of the unity of the universe, with its higher laws. Confined within narrow walls they resemble the miner, who by delving ever more deeply into the bowels of the earth brings some of its treasure to light, but thereby forfeits the privilege of green fields and sunny skies.

The positivist schools have not even adhered to their own program: after declaring that the experimental method was alone conducive to truth, we have seen them deny themselves to themselves, denying *à priori* an entire order of phenomena of psychic nature, into which we will later examine. It is noteworthy to observe that positivism has displayed such disdainful incredulity towards these phenomena, as have the most bias intolerant churchmen.

Positivism cannot then be considered as the topmost rung of the ladder of science, which indeed rises endlessly, adding to itself as it mounts. Positivism is no more than a temporary form of philosophical evolution. Centuries upon centuries have not rolled by, the thoughts of sages and philosophers have not been amassed, but to end ingloriously in a theory of the unknowable. Thought is ever changing, ever progressing, and reaches each day a little further. Yesterday's unknown will be tomorrow's knowledge. The onward march of the human mind has no limits: to circumscribe it is to ignore the law of progress, to disregard truth.

8

The Moral Crisis

It is manifest, as we have endeavored to show, that the great world of thought is divided between two opposing and contradictory schools. Viewed in this light, our epoch is one of trouble and transition. Religious faith has grown lukewarm and the outline of the philosophy of the future appears only to a minority of researchers.

The present age is certainly a great one as reckoned by the sum of progress accomplished. With its powerful appliances modern civilization has transformed the Earth's surface: by lessening distances it has brought the nations nearer together. Education has been generalized and institutions have been improved. Right has replaced privilege and liberty triumphs over the spirit of routine and authority. A great battle is fought between a past that strives against death, and a future that struggles to be born. Stimulated by this struggle the world is restive and pushes onward: an irresistible impulse urges it on, and the road traversed and the results accomplished lead us to expect even more wonderful achievements.

If, however, the physical and intellectual progress which have been realized are truly remarkable, on the other hand, moral progress is null. As regard this, the world seems rather to be retrograding: Human societies are so feverishly absorbed by politics, by industrial and financial enterprises, that they sacrifice spiritual welfare to material ease.

If civilization dazzles us by the display of some magnificent achievements, like everything human, it has its dark side. Certainly it has, in a measure, improved the conditions of life, but in satisfying, it has increased the requirements of the individual: in sharpening his desires and appetites, it has stimulated his sensuality and depravity. The craving for pleasure, luxury and wealth is growing ever more imperious. The individual feels that he must acquire and possess, regardless of the cost.

This is the cause that has brought about those shameless speculations, which are being constantly transacted in broad daylight. This is the cause of that deterioration of character and conscience which we behold: of that fervent worship rendered to wealth, a true idol whose altar has been replaced where fallen divinities used to reign.

Science and industry have multiplied the wealth of humanity, but this wealth has been of direct benefit only to a small portion of its members. The livelihood of the poor is still precarious, and fraternity fills more space in oratory than in the heart. One can still starve in the streets of a wealthy capital. Factories and manufacturing centers have become hotbeds of physical and moral corruption: veritable infernos of labor.

Drunkenness, prostitution and debauchery everywhere spread their poison, checking life at its outset and impoverishing the generations to come: while the public leaves sow defamation and falsehood, and an unhealthy literature excites brains and debilitates souls.

Each day despair makes further ravages. In 1820, France recorded fifteen hundred suicides: today they number more than eight thousand. For lack of energy and moral sense, eight thousand beings each year are driven to abandon life's fruitful struggle and to seek relief in what they deem to be oblivion. The number of crimes and punishable offences has increased three times these last fifty years. In the ranks of condemned criminals the proportion of adolescents is considerable. Must we not attribute this state of things to environment, to the bad example set to children, to the weakness of parents and to the lack of family training? All this is true and there is more besides.

The evils we endure arise from the fact that notwithstanding the strides of science and the broadening of education, the human being is still ignorant of himself. He knows little of the laws of the universe; he knows nothing of the forces that are within him. The "know thyself" of the Greek philosopher has remained for the vast majority of humans a sterile appeal. The individual of today knows no more than twenty centuries ago, from where does he come, to where he is going, or what the real purpose of his existence is. No teaching has revealed to him an accurate idea of his function in this world, of his duties or of his destiny.

The human mind undecidedly vacillates between the inducements proffered by two powers.

On the one hand come the religions, followed by their cortege of errors and superstitions, their spirit of domination and intolerance, but attended likewise by the consolations of which they are the source and such faint gleams of primordial truth as they still retain.

On the other hand stands science: materialistic in essence as in tendency, with its cold negations and its penchant for individualism; but followed also by a goodly retinue of substantial results and discoveries.

Such are the two giants – a religion without evidence, and a soulless science – which confront, defy and contend with one another; an endless struggle, since each responds to an imperious craving of man, one speaking to his Heart, the other addressing his mind and reason. And around these accumulate the ruins of wrecked hopes and shattered aspirations. Gracious feelings are dying out, discord and hatred are taking the place of peace and good-will.

In the perplexity of this confusion, conscience has lost its way. Falteringly and haltingly it feels its way, often unable amidst the general uncertainty to distinguish the good from the bad. The moral dilemma of those unfortunate beings who are already bowed down by the burden of life, is made well-nigh intolerable by the limited choice offered as a reward for their sufferings. On the one hand, annihilation; on the other, an inaccessible paradise, or an eternity of torture.

The consequences of this conflict are everywhere visible: in the family, in the schools, in society. Virile education is a thing of the past, for neither science nor religion are any longer capable of producing strong souls properly equipped against the perils of life. Philosophy, by solely addressing itself to a few abstract minds, is abdicating its rights, hence its influence upon society.

How will humanity come out of this state of crisis? There is but one way: to find a common ground where sentiment and reason, those two sturdy forces, may unite for the good and the salvation of all, for every individual; has within him these twin forces by whose dictation he, turn by turn, thinks and acts. Their accord imparts balance and harmony to his faculties, multiplies his powers of action and brings some rectitude and unity of effort into his life; while their discord leads to inevitable confusion. That which takes place in each of us is likewise manifest in society as a whole and causes the moral disorder which afflicts it.

To put an end to it, it is necessary that the eyes of all, great or small, rich or poor, men, women or children, should be open to the truth; that a new and universal teaching should come to enlighten all souls as to their origin, duty and destiny.

These are the all important truths which alone can serve as the foundation for the virile education that will render humanity truly strong and free. Their importance is paramount, as well for the individual whom they direct in his daily round of work, as for the social body whose institutions and relations they regulate. The human being's conception of the universe and of its laws, of the part which he will be expected to enact upon this vast stage, affects his entire life and influences his every determination. According to the dictates of this conception, the individual plans his career and elects the goal for which he must strive. It is useless to endeavor to elude these problems: they impose themselves upon our minds, they dominate us, overcoming our reluctance by their greatness, in short they are the pivot on which hinges all civilization.

Every time that some fresh conception of life and the world penetrates into the human mind, it gradually passes from brain to brain, until all law, order and morality become impregnated with it.

The conceptions of Catholicism created the civilization of the Middle Ages, and molded its feudal, monarchical and authoritative system. Then the reign of favoritism and privilege obtained on Earth, as in heaven. These ideas still survive, although the modern world has no room for them. Unfortunately, although we have discarded the ancient beliefs, we have found nothing to substitute them. Materialistic and atheistic positivism discerns nothing in life beyond a transient combination of matter and force: in the laws of the universe, a brutal mechanism, in which they can trace no token of justice, solidarity or responsibility. Such a point of view could not fail to cause a general relaxation of all social bonds, a pessimistic skepticism, contempt of law and order, which could lead us to the abyss.

To some, the materialistic doctrines have brought discouragement: to others, increased covetousness, and to all the worship of flesh and profit. Under their tutelage a generation has risen: a generation deprived of ideal, devoid of faith in the future, of conviction while pursuing the wholesome struggle of life, doubting itself and doubting everything else.

Dogmatic religion was leading us to arbitrariness and despotism, but anarchy and nihilism are the inevitable outcome of materialism. Hence must we fear it as a pitfall, a cause of decline and decadence.

Perhaps we may find these assessments excessive, and we may be accused of exaggeration. In this case, it would suffice for us to refer to the works of the eminent materialists and to cite their own conclusions.

To take one example amongst many, M. Jules Soury[75] tells us:

"Of all things in the world the most vain and useless is the birth, life and death of those innumerable parasites, fauna and flora that move and vegetate like a living mold upon the surface of this tiny planet. A chief condition of their being, indifferent in itself, albeit necessary since it exists, is the merciless struggle of each against all, of violence versus cunning, in which love will appear, at least to every thinking being, as a sinister dream, a hallucination so painful, that beside it, oblivion would be a blessing."

---

75 In his *"Philosophie Naturelle,"* p. 210.

"But if we are truly the children of nature, if it has created us and given us being; we, in our turn, have endowed it with all those ideal qualities in which, to our eyes, it stands arrayed; we ourselves have spun the luminous veil in which she shows itself to us. The eternal illusion which enchants or torments the heart of the human being is therefore his own undoubted handiwork.

"In this universe where all is silence and darkness, man alone on this planet is watching and suffering, for he only, together with his lower brothers perhaps, meditates and thinks. Hardly yet does he begin to comprehend the vanity of that in which he had believed and loved; the mockery of beauty, the deceit of goodness, the irony of all human science. After having naively worshipped himself in his gods and his heroes, now that neither faith nor hope are his, he suddenly discovers that nature itself is slipping away from him; that, like all the rest, it was but an illusion and a deception."

Madame Ackermann, another materialist and a poetess of real talent, does not hesitate to exclaim:

"I will not say to humanity, progress! Rather will I bid it die! For no progress can ever rescue thee, poor humanity, from the misery of thy earthly condition!"

And these are not merely the views of a few writers. By means of novels and short stories, through the medium of a literature that dishonors the beautiful name of naturalism, they have penetrated even into the humblest circles.

Having concluded that nothingness is preferable to life, one need not wonder that the individual should find labor disgusting, nor is it hard to understand why discouragement and demoralization have grown so prevalent! Such beliefs are ill-fitted to inspire high aspirations, let alone the courage needed to face hardships, or the resolution to encounter adversity.

A society that has no hope or belief in a future state is as a man lost in the desert, as a leaf whirled by the wind. It is good that ignorance and superstition should be combated, provided a rational belief is supplied in their place. To walk through life with a firm step, secure from weakness and faltering, one must possess a robust conviction, a faith that transcends the world of matter: one must absolutely keep the goal in sight and unswervingly strive to attain it. A sound and enlightened conscience is the surest defense in the battle of life.

But if we are persuaded of our ultimate oblivion, if we believe that life is to have no tomorrow and that death is the eternal extinguisher; then logically, personal interest and material satisfaction should have precedence over every other consideration. What do we care for a future that we are never to know? In what capacity will we speak of progress, reforms, and sacrifices? If our life is only an ephemeral existence, then by all means let us make the most of the passing hour, culling its pleasures and turning away from its pain and its duties. Such is the inevitable conclusion of materialism as daily uttered and daily enacted about us.

What ravages can we expect from these doctrines in the midst of a rich civilization, already well developed in the sense of luxury and physical gratification?

Nevertheless idealism is not quite dead. The human soul is, at times, aware of its own wretchedness; it experiences the inadequacy of this life and the necessity of a hereafter. Some kind of intuition still throbs in the soul of the people. For centuries deceived, they have become incredulous regarding all dogmas: incredulous but not skeptical. Vaguely, confusedly, the people still believe in justice, and still aspire. The Creed of Remembrance is exemplified by the touching manifestations of the second of November, which carry crowds to the tombs of their beloved dead; it also denotes a certain confused instinct of immortality.

No! The people are not atheists, since they have faith in an immanent justice, and in liberty: for both of these subsist by the sanction of the eternal and divine laws. This sentiment, the greatest and noblest that pertains to the soul, will prove our salvation: there it would suffice that all should learn that this conviction, inherent in us, is likewise a very law of the universe; that it rules all beings and all worlds; that through it right must finally triumph over wrong, and life must emerge from death.

While aspiring to justice, the people are striving for its realization. This they seek in politics, in economics, in the principle of association. The power of the people has started a vast ramification of worker's associations which embraces all nations: a socialist group which embraces all nations, and, marching under one single banner, makes the same appeals and the same demands everywhere it is heard. Therein lies, and let us not be mistaken as to its importance, not only a most edifying spectacle for the thinker, but likewise a matter of weighty future consequence.

If it seeks its inspiration from the materialistic and atheistic doctrines, it will become an instrument of destruction, for its action will take the form of violent outbursts and dire revolutions. Restrained by wisdom and moderation, it may affect the happiness of humanity. Let a beam of heavenly light descend upon these myriad workers: let some divine ideal animate these crowds that hunger for progress; then at last, shall we see the old social forms dissolve and melt into a new world based upon universal right, justice and solidarity.

⁓

The present hour is a time of crisis and renewal. The world is in fermentation, corruption is in the ascendant: the mighty shadow spreads and the peril is great, but behind the shadow we perceive the light, and behind the peril, salvation. Society cannot perish: if it bears within it the germs of decomposition, there likewise are those of transformation and redemption. Decomposition confirms death, but it also heralds the new birth; it is the prelude to another life.

And from where will proceed this light, this salvation, this redemption?

Surely not from the Church, which is incapable of regenerating the human mind.

Not from science, which cares neither for conscience nor for character but only for that which concerns the senses: devotion, virtue, justice, love, all that enters into the making of noble characters and wholesome societies – none of these appertain to the domain of the senses.

That the moral level should be raised, that the two streams of superstition and skepticism, which terminate in a sea of sterility, may be checked, a new conception of life and of the universe is indispensable; one which, based upon the study of nature and conscience, upon the observation of facts and the principles of reason, may at last determine the aim of our life and regulate our onward progression. What we require is a belief which affords an incentive for improvement, a moral sanction and a strong conviction as to our ultimate fate.

But this conception and this teaching we already have: and daily they are becoming better known. In the midst of the disputes, above the divergences of philosophical schools, a voice has made itself heard – the voice of the dead. The dead have revealed themselves from beyond the grave, more alive than when they stood among us in the flesh; in the light of their revelations the veil has fallen, which hid from us the future life. Their precepts will conciliate all conflicting creeds, and will cause a new flame to arise from the ashes of the past. In the philosophy of the spirits, we find again that secret doctrine which ran like a golden vein through the quartz of the ages, but renovated and now cleansed of its dross. Its shattered remnants have been gathered and bound together by a powerful cement, and even now frame an edifice vast enough to accommodate all nations and all civilizations. To ensure its duration, it sits it on the rock of direct experience, constantly renewed. Thanks to it, the certainty of immortality becomes clearer in the eyes of all, together with the innumerable existences and the unceasing progress that await us in the successive cycles of times.

Such a doctrine is bound to transform all the nations and classes of the world: conveying light where all is dark: melting, with its heat, the icy selfishness that lies at the heart of the human being: revealing to all people the laws that unite them with the bonds of a close solidarity. t will reconcile with peace and harmony. Through it we shall learn to act with one heart and with one mind. Humanity, conscious of its strength, will advance with a firmer step towards its magnificent destinies.

In the second part of this work, we shall proceed to detail the essential principles of this doctrine, after which we shall cite the experimental proofs and recorded facts upon which it rests.

Second Part
The Great Problems

9

The Universe and God

Transcending the problems of life and destiny we are brought face to face with the greater conception of God.

If we ponder nature's law, if we follow up that ideal beauty which is the inspiration of all art, we shall universally find, everywhere and always, above and beyond all else, the conception of a Superior Being: necessary and perfect, eternal source of righteousness, beauty and truth, in whom law, justice and supreme reason are met.

The world, physical and moral, is governed by laws, and these laws, formulated after a predetermined plan, denote a profound understanding of that which they govern. They do not proceed from a blind cause, for chance and chaos could not produce order and harmony; they do not emanate from the human being: so ephemeral a being, limited as to time and space, could hardly be credited with creating permanent and universal laws. To explain them logically, one must ascend to the generating cause of all things. One could scarcely conceive of intelligence unless associated with some being; but this being is not linked with the chain of beings; rather it is the Father of all, the very well spring of life.

Personality must not here be understood in the sense of some definite being in a definite shape, but rather as implying all the faculties that go to make a conscious whole. Personality, in the highest acceptation of the word, is the conscience: it is in this sense that God may be conceived of as a person, or rather as the absolute personality, and not as a being possessing form and limitations. God is infinite and cannot be individualized – that is to say, separated from the world.

As to the idea of relinquishing all study relating to the First Cause, as useless and unknowable, to quote the Positivists, we wonder if it is really possible for an earnest mind to rest content in total ignorance of the laws that regulate its existence. The search for God is necessary. It is nothing more nor less than the study of the great Spirit, of the principle of life that animates the universe, and is reflected in each of us. Everything becomes secondary when it comes to the principle of things. The notion of God is inseparable from that of law, and especially from that moral law, without which no society can prosper. The belief in a transcendent ideal fortifies the conscience and sustains the being in its hour of trial. It is the consolation and reliance of those who despair: the supreme refuge of the afflicted and the oppressed. Its soft beams, like those of the dawning day, bring a ray of hope to the downcast spirit.

The existence of God can certainly not be demonstrated by direct and tangible proofs; for God does not enter into the domain of the senses. The Divinity has hidden behind a mysterious veil: possibly to compel us to seek it – the highest and most fruitful task that can be given to the mind – and also to leave us the merit of the discovery. But there is within us a power, a sure instinct which brings us to it, asserting its reality with a more positive authority than all demonstrations and analyzes.

In all times, in all climates – and this is the actuating idea in all religions – the human spirit has experienced the necessity of looking beyond those fluctuating and perishable things that make up the material life and which are unable to afford him any complete satisfaction: it looks beyond, to that which, in the universe alone is fixed, permanent and immutable, perfect and absolute, with which all intellectual and moral power are identified. This he finds in God, without whom there can be no certainty, no confidence or security, and deprived of whom we are at the mercy of every lurking suggestion of doubt or passion.

We may be objected to the fatal use which religions have made of the idea of God. But what matter the varied forms which human beings have portrayed the divinity? To us, they are so many fabled deities pictured by the feeble intellect of humanity in its infancy, it shapes grotesque, poetic, or alarming, according to the intelligences that have conceived them. Human thought, grown somewhat more mature, has discarded these old conceptions, has forgotten these phantoms and the evils that were perpetrated in their name, to elevate itself, impelled by an overpowering need, towards Eternal reason, towards God. God! Soul of the world, Universal Center of light and love, in whom we live as the bird lives in the air or the fish in the sea, through whom we are united to all that is, has been and ever will be!

All religious conceptions of God were based upon a so-called supernatural revelation. Today we still admit of a revelation of the higher laws, only this revelation is now both rational and progressive: it has been conveyed to us by the logic of events and by the contemplation of the world. It is contained in two volumes that ever lie open before us: the book of nature, in which the divine works appear in majestic characters, and the book of conscience, wherein the precepts of morality are engraved. The instructions imparted by the spirits, which have been gleaned and gathered from every quarter of the world by simple and logical processes, all tend to confirm these assertions. It is in virtue of this two time teaching that the human mind is enabled to communicate with divine reason in the realm of universal nature; by the aid of which it may dimly surmise somewhat of the beauty and harmony that lie therein.

⁓

When the silence of the night enfolds the Earth, when all is still in the human dwellings, if we lift our eyes to heaven's infinite vault we shall find it all aglow with countless scintillations. Radiant stars and dazzling suns, attended by their planet train, revolve through space in myriad force. Even in the most remote regions, stellar groups unfold like luminous scarves. Vainly does the telescope search the heavens, nowhere can it assign a limit to the universe: perpetually worlds follow upon worlds, and suns upon suns: everywhere are the countless stars multiplied until they appear like a brilliant dust floating in the bottomless void of space. What human word could depict you, O marvelous diamond of the casket of heaven! Sirius, greater twenty times than our sun, which in itself is equal to more than a united million of Earths like ours. Aldebaram, Vega, Procyon: pink, blue, crimson: stars of opal and sapphire, that ceaselessly lavish their multi-colored beams through space, whose beams, in spite of their velocity of seventy thousand leagues per second[76], only reach us after a journey requiring hundreds and thousands of years. And you, far distant nebulae, procreators of suns, universes in formation, trembling, barely discernible stars, gigantic radiators of heat, light, electricity and life, shining suns and colossal spheres; and you, innumerable peoples, races and sidereal humanities who dwell therein! Our feeble voice

---

76 N.T.: 70000 leagues per second = $8.69989e{+}8$ miles per hour

vainly endeavors to proclaim your splendor: impotent, faltering, it is hushed, while still our dazzled gaze contemplates the endless procession of the stars.

And when the eyes, weary of the vertiginous depths, return to more neighboring worlds and rest upon the planets, own daughters of our sun, who like us gravitate around the common center, what do they observe on these surfaces? Continents and seas, mountains and plains, heavy wind-blown clouds, snows, and ice fields gathered around the poles! We find that these worlds possess air, water, light, heat, seasons, climates, days and nights; in a word, all the conditions of terrestrial life, which may entitle us to consider them as the residences of other human families, and to believe, with science, that they are, were, or some day will be, inhabited. These all, flaming stars, secondary planets, satellites, wandering comets: these all, suspended in space, move, grow distant, come nearer, and travel over their determined orbits, impelled at a terrific speed through the limitless regions of space. Everywhere are motion, activity and life manifest, throughout the stupendous panorama of the universe, peopled by worlds innumerable, forever restlessly in the depths of the heavens.

A law regulates this formidable circulation: the universal law of gravitation. It alone sustains and directs the celestial bodies, guiding the obedient planets in their course around the luminous suns. This law governs everything throughout the entire nature: from atom to star. The same force which, under the name of attraction, restrains the worlds in their orbits, is that which, known as cohesion, groups molecules and presides over the formation of chemical bodies.

If after this rapid glance cast towards heaven, we compare the Earth on which we dwell to those powerful suns that are poised in the ether, we perceive that alongside of them the earth would hardly seem as great as a grain of sand, as an atom floating through infinitude. The Earth is one of the least of the stars of heaven. Still how much harmony there is in its contour, how variegated is it raiment! Consider the outline of its continents and the sharp peninsulas with their island wreaths; see its imposing seas, the lakes, and the forests, the vegetation, from the cedar that grows upon its heights to the tiniest flower that nestles beneath the leaves; enumerate the living things that inhabit it – the birds, insects and plants – and you will recognize that each of these, admirable in itself, is a masterpiece of art and precision.

Consider the human body; is it not a living laboratory, an instrument whose mechanism touches perfection? Note the circulation of the blood and the wonderful system of valves: does it not remind you, by its intricacy, of a steam engine? Examine the structure of the eye, a more complex contrivance than any that the human being has attempted; the ear, so admirably adapted to receive the sound waves; the brain, whose convolutions are like those of an opening flower. Let us consider all this, then, leaving the visible world, let us descend lower upon the ladder of life and seek those kingdoms that the microscope discovers to our view: let us observe the swarms of species and families, the multiplicity of which stupefies the intellect. Each drop of water, each grain of sand is a world, and the infinitely small beings which inhabit these are governed by laws as precise as those that rule the giants of space. Everywhere we find life, embryos, and germs. Millions of infusoria are moving in the cells of organic beings, in each drop of our blood, in the cells of the organized bodies. A fly's wing, the least atom of matter, is populated by legions of parasites. And all these animalcules are supplied with means of locomotion, with a nervous system, with sensitive organs, all of which go to make of them complete beings, armed for the struggle and necessities of life. In the very depths of the ocean, eight thousand meters deep, dwell frail and phosphorescent creatures that make their own light and that are endowed with eyes to see it.

Thus a boundless fecundity chairs the formation of the beings. Nature is in perpetual childbirth. As the ear of wheat is embryonically contained in the grain, the oak in the acorn, the rose in the bud, so is the genesis of future worlds being elaborated in the depths of starry skies. Life everywhere engenders life. From grade to grade, from species to species, it rises in an endless chain from the simplest and the most rudimentary organism, to the thinking and conscious being, the human being.

A grand unity governs in the world. One single substance, ether or the universal fluid constitutes in its infinite transformations the innumerable variety of bodies. This element vibrates to the action of the cosmic forces. According to the velocity and number of its vibrations, it produces heat, light and electricity, otherwise known as the magnetic fluid. Let these vibrations condense, and at once the bodies appear.

All these forms are linked together, all these forces are held in balance, and by a perpetual interchange are united in close solidarity. From mineral to vegetable, from vegetable to animal and to the human being; from the human being to superior beings, the refinement of matter, the ascension of force and thought are rhythmically and harmoniously accomplished. A sovereign law regulates the manifestations of life according to a uniform plan, while an invisible bond unites all worlds and all souls.

Out of the work of beings and things there arises an aspiration for eternity, for perfection. All effects, no matter how divergent they may appear, in reality converge towards one Center: all tendencies coordinate to form one whole, to evolve towards one end, God, the center of all activity and final objective of all love and all thought.

The observation of nature shows us in all places the action of a hidden will. Matter universally obeys some force which organizes and directs it. All cosmic forces finally resolve themselves into motion, and motion signifies Life and Being! Materialism accounts for the world's formation by a blind dance and the fortuitous bringing together of the atoms. But have we ever seen the random toss of the letters of the alphabet produce a poem? And what a poem is that universal life! Has anyone ever seen a conglomeration of elements of itself produce an imposing building or a mechanism of complex and complicated structure? Of itself, matter can achieve nothing: blind and unconscious atoms would be powerless to unite to any purposeful end. The harmony of the world is only explicable by the intervention of a will. It is through the action of force upon matter, by the existence of wise and profound laws that this will makes itself manifest in the order of the universe.

Often has it been objected that all is not harmony in nature. If nature produces marvels, it likewise procreates monsters. Evil everywhere is found side by side with good. If slow evolution seems to be fitting the world to become the stage of life, one must not overlook the waste of life nor the fierce struggle it engenders. One must not forget that earthquakes and volcanic eruptions sometimes rend our planet and destroy, in the space of a few minutes, the work of generations.

Yes, accidents doubtless occur during the travail of nature, but they do not exclude the notion of order and finality; on the contrary, they strengthen our contention, for we might wonder why all is not accidental?

The conformability of cause to effect, of the means to the end, of the body's organic parts to one another and to their environment and conditions, is manifest. Nature's industry, which in many ways resembles human's, being sometimes superior to his, is in itself an evidence of the existence of a plan: the working of the elements that contribute to the realization denotes an occult cause, infinitely wise, and infinitely powerful.

As to the argument derived from the existence of monsters, this arises from a faulty deduction. Monsters are but misdirected germs. If a man stumbles and breaks his leg, should we therefore hold nature or God responsible? In the same way, owing to disorders or accidents during gestation, the germ may be misplaced in the womb of the mother. We are in the habit of dating life from birth, from the time of the being's first entrance into the world, but life's real starting-point is far more remote.

The argument drawn from the existence of scourges originates from a wrong understanding of the purpose of life. Life was not designed merely for our satisfaction: it is useful and necessary that in it we should encounter hardships. We were born to die, and we are surprised that some people die by accident! Temporary beings in this world, from which we shall take nothing with us into the hereafter, we lament the loss of possessions that would in any case have been lost to us in the course of nature. These cataclysms, catastrophes and scourges inculcate a teaching of their own. They remind us that we do not need to expect from nature pleasure only, but above all such things are propitious to our education and advancement: that we were not placed here below to enjoy and to slumber but to struggle, work and suffer. They remind us that the human being was not designed merely for this earth, but that he must look higher and attach himself in a limited measure to earthly things, and that his being is not destroyed by death.

The doctrine of evolution does not exclude that of the primary and of the final causes. The highest ideal one could form of a creator is of one who could create a world capable of developing itself by its own strength, without requiring incessant intervention and continual miracles.

Science, as it advances in the knowledge of nature, has been able to bring back God, but God has grown in retreat. The Eternal Being, as measured by the theoretical standpoint of evolution, towers majestically over the fantastic God of the Bible. That which science has forever destroyed is the notion of an anthropomorphic God, framed in man's image, and exterior to the physical world. A higher standpoint has taken its place: that of an immanent God ever present in the matrix of the universe. The idea of God no longer expresses that of any concrete personage, but rather a Being in whom all beings are. Nor is the universe that creation[77] evolved from nothingness of which religion tells.

The universe is a stupendous organism animated by an everlasting life. As our own body is governed by a central will which directs its actions and ordains its motions; as we, each of us, through the modifications of our flesh, feel ourselves alive in the permanent unity that we name soul, conscience or self: so in like manner does the universe, in its varied and multiple aspects, know, reflect and possess itself in a living unity, in a conscious reason, which is God.

The Supreme Being does not exist outside of the world, of which He is the essential and integral part. He is the central unity, in which all affiliations meet and harmonize; He is the principle of love and solidarity, by which all individuals are brothers and sisters. He is the center from which all spirit forces such as wisdom, justice and righteousness proceed and radiate throughout eternity.

---

[77] According to Eug. Nus (« *A la Recherches des Destinées,* » chap. XI.), the Hebrew verb which we interpret as signifying *created*, really means, *to pass from principle to essence.*

There is, therefore, no such thing as a spontaneous or miraculous creation: creation is continuous, without beginning or end. The universe has always been, containing within itself its principles of force and motion, likewise its own purpose. The world, in its parts, is constantly renewed; as a whole it is immutable. Everything changes and evolves by the continual play of life and death, but nothing perishes. While, in the heavens, suns are obscured and extinguished, and worlds, grown aged, disintegrate and disappear, so, elsewhere, new systems are elaborated, new stars radiate and new worlds are born to light: alongside of death and decrepitude, fresh humanities burst forth in eternal rejuvenation.

Thus the grandiose work continues, throughout boundless time and boundless space, by the work of all beings, in solidarity with one another, and for the benefit of each one. The universe unfolds to us the spectacle of an unceasing evolution in which all participate. One immutable principle presides over this work: it is that of a universal unity, a divine oneness, which embraces, connects and directs all individualities, all personal activities, causing them to converge towards one common ideal, which is perfection in the fullness of life. [78]

While the laws of the physical world all testify to a sublime creator, the moral laws, through reason and conscience, has eloquently spoken of a principle of justice, a universal providence.

---

78 There is *One*, self-procreated, and from this *One* all things have proceeded, and He is in them, He enfolds them, and no mortal has beheld Him, but He beholds them all (Orphic hymns).

The panorama of nature – the heavens, the mountains, the sea – suggests the conception of a God, somewhere hidden in the universe.

Conscience shows Him, or at least something of Him, to be within us: and this something is the sentiment of duty and righteousness, a moral ideal, to attain which the thoughts of our brains and the impulses of our hearts alike are striving. Duty sternly demands: it is imperious, and its voice coerces the powers of the soul. It possesses that authority which compels the human being to sacrifice oneself. It alone imparts some dignity and some nobility to life. The voice of conscience is the inner manifestation of a power superior to matter, of a live and active reality.

Reason, likewise, also speaks of God. Our senses acquaint us with the outside world, the world of effect: reason, which is superior to experience, reveals to us the world of causes. The one collects facts which the other classifies and from them deduces laws. It alone demonstrates to our satisfaction that at the origin of motion and life there must be intelligence: that the lesser cannot contain the greater, any more than the unconscious can produce the conscious, which would, however, be the case if we admit of a universe that ignores itself. Reason before experience has discovered the universal laws; experience has but tested the discoveries of reason and proved them correct. But there are degrees in reason, which is a faculty not equally shared by all men: hence the difference and inequality of their opinions.

If the individual knew how to meditate and how to concentrate; if he could clear his soul of every passion wrought shadow, if he could tear the thick veil which prejudice, ignorance and sophistry have spun; if he could see to the bottom of his conscience and reason, there would he find the principles of an inner life, in diametrical contradiction with those he had previously held. In this inner principle he would discover affiliations which would put him in contact with all nature, with the universe and with God: a glimpse which would contain a foretaste of the life that awaits him in the higher worlds beyond the grave. Therein, likewise, he would find the mysterious book in which all the doings of his life are set forth in indelible characters, to transpire with dazzling brightness at the hour of death.

Sometimes a powerful voice rises from the depths of our being, a strong voice is uplifted, intoning a chant both deep and sad: it resounds above the frivolous cares and pursuits of our worldly life, reminding us of our duty. Woe to him who refuses to hear it! A day will come when remorse will teach him not to reject in vain the warnings of conscience.

It is there, in this intimate sanctuary, that we must seek God. God is in us, or at least there is a reflection of Him in us. However, what is cannot be reflected. The soul reflects God as the dewdrops mirror the sunbeams, each according to its clearness and purity.

It was through this inner perception, and not through the experience of the senses, that men of genius, great missionaries, and prophets knew God and his laws, and revealed them to the peoples of the earth.

Further than this is it possible to define God? For to define is to limit! Confronted with this great problem, human incapacity manifests itself. God imposes himself upon our minds, but He surpasses all analysis. The Being that fills time and space is not to be measured by those that are limited by space and time. To define God would be to circumscribe, almost to deny Him.

The secondary causes of universal life are explicable; but the First Cause, in its immensity, remains inscrutable. We shall be able to understand it only after passing through death many times.

We can only repeat that God is life, reason and conscience in their plenitude. He is the ever active cause of all that is: the great communion to which every being must come to draw the life that will enable him to contribute, proportionately to his growing faculties and elevation, to the universal harmony.

And here we pause, finding ourselves far indeed from the God of religions: that "mighty and jealous" One, who surrounds Himself with lightning, whose worship demands bloody victims and whose condemnation is eternal. The anthropomorphic gods have served their time. We still hear of a God to whom human passions and weaknesses are attributed, but His jurisdiction is each day growing less.

The human being, thus far, has only looked upon God through own being: and his conception has accordingly varied with the faculty that he has used as a ground glass. Viewed through the prism of his senses, God is multiple: all of nature's forces are gods, thus polytheism was born. Considered by the intellect, God is manifold, spirit and matter: hence arises duality. To pure reason He appears triple: soul, mind and body. This conception has given birth to the Trinitarian religions of India and to Christianity. Perceived by the will and rendered more precise by the inner perception, which is a slowly assimilated property, like all the acquired faculties of genius, God is Unique and Absolute. In Him the three fundamental principles of the universe combine to compose one living unity.

Thus is explained the diversity of systems and religions, the purity of which is measured by the purity and enlightenment of those who conceived them. Viewed from a high standpoint, the clash of ideas, of religions and of historical events, become quite comprehensible and reconcilable in a higher synthesis.

The conception of God, in the diverse forms that it has assumed, has oscillated between two reefs upon which many systems have been wrecked. The first of these is pantheism, which concludes in the final absorption of all beings in the great whole. The other is the notion of infinitude, which removes God to such a remote distance from the human being, as to make all interchange between them seem impossible.

Certain philosophers have disputed the conception of infinitude. Incomprehensible as it seems, one cannot, however, quite discard it, since it reappears in all things. What, for example, is better established than the exact sciences? They are based upon numbers, without which there can be no mathematics, but it would be impossible, did one consecrate hundreds of years to the task, to find the numeral that would express the infinite numbers that thought conceives. This is true of time and space. Beyond the limits of the visible world, thought seeks other realms that constantly evade it.

A single philosophy seems to have successfully evaded these two difficulties and reconciled their conflicting principles: it is that of the Gaulish Druids. In Triad 48[79] we find the following:

"Three necessities of God: to be infinite in Himself, to be finite by analogy with the finite, and to be in harmony with each state of existence in the circle of the worlds."

Thus, according to this teaching, which is at once simple and rational, the infinite and absolute being by itself becomes relative and

---

[79] *"Bardic Triads,"* Cyfrinach Beirdd Inys Pryddain.

finite with its creatures, unfolding unceasingly under new aspects, in proportion to the advancement and the elevation of souls.

His revelation, or rather the education that He gives to humanity, through the embassy of His great spirits, is gradual and progressive. A providential intervention is manifest in history, by the presence, at critical times in the midst of humanity of those chosen spirits whose mission is to introduce the innovations and discoveries necessary to their progress, or to teach the spiritual principles needful for their regeneration.

As to the question of the being's final absorption in God, Druidism found a way out of that by imagining the *Ceugant*, a superior circle enclosing all other circles, the exclusive abode of the Divine Being. In this way, evolution and the soul's progression, following the circle of the infinite, could have no end.

Let us revert to the problem of evil, which has preoccupied so many minds, and to which we have but incidentally referred.

Why does God, skepticism objects, the first cause of all that is, allow evil to exist in the universe?

We have seen that physical evil, or what is so termed, appertains in reality to the order of natural phenomena, whose noxious character is explained as soon as one has grasped the true reason of things. The eruption of a volcano is not more extraordinary than the ebullition of a jar of water. The thunderbolt which destroys trees and houses is akin to the electric spark, the vehicle of thought; and it is thus with all violent phenomena. Physical pain remains! But this we know to be the outcome of sensitivity which in itself represents a magnificent conquest that the being has only achieved after long stages in the inferior forms of life. Pain is a necessary warning, a stimulus applied to human's activity. It compels us to return within ourselves and to think: it aids us to curb our passions. Pain is a vehicle to perfection.

But moral evil, we are asked – vice, crime, ignorance, the triumph of the wicked and the downfall of the just – how can you explain them?

To begin with, from what standpoint does one judge of such things? If the human being can perceive but the narrow strip of ground where he dwells, if of life all he knows is contained in his short stay upon Earth, how then can he know the eternal and universal order?

To weigh good and evil, truth and untruth, justice and injustice, we must rise above the narrow limits that enclose this life and consider the totality of our destiny. Evil then appears but as a transitory state, inherent to out globe – as one of the lower phases of the creature's evolution towards righteousness. It is neither in our world, nor in our time that ideal perfection can be looked for, but rather in the immensity of worlds and in the eternity of time.

If, however, we observe the slow evolution of species and races through the ages; if we consider prehistoric man, the anthropoid of the caverns whose instincts are savage and whose life is wretched, if we take this as a starting-point and compare it with the results achieved by present civilization, we shall clearly perceive the constant tendency of men and things towards an ideal perfection. Evidence itself proves this much to us: life is ever being improved, transformed, enriched, the sum total of good is ever increasing and that of evil is diminishing.

If one notices occasional pauses, and even retrogression, in this progression towards a better state, one must recollect that the human being is free, and that he can choose for himself the direction in which he would proceed. His improvement is only possible when his will is in accordance with the law.

Evil, which is in opposition to divine law, cannot be the work of God; it is that of the human being and the outcome of his freedom. But evil is like a shadow and has no real existence; it is rather the effect of contrast. As darkness is dispersed by light, so does evil disappear at the coming of righteousness. Evil is, in a word, but the absence of goodness.

It is sometimes said that God could have made the soul perfect, and thus have spared it the vicissitudes of earthly life. Without questioning God's power to create beings similar to Himself, we will reply that, were this be the case, life and its universal activity, variety, work and progress would be purposeless: the world would be frozen into a state of rigid perfection. Is not the magnificent evolution of the being through the fields of time preferable to a dreary and eternal repose? Would an unmerited and underserved welfare be good; and were it obtainable without effort, would its value be appreciated?

Before the vast progression of our existences, each of which is a struggle towards light – before this sublime ascension of the being, as it rises from circle to circle towards perfection, the problem of evil disappears.

To leave the lower regions of matter and to ascend all the rungs of the hierarchy of the spirits, to shake off the yoke of passion and to conquer all virtue and all science, such is the purpose for which Providence has created our souls and designed the worlds, those predestined stages of our struggles and labors.

Let us believe in and let us bless it; let us place our trust in that generous Providence which has fashioned us all for our good; let us recollect, if we seem to detect flaws in its handwork that they proceed from our ignorance and faulty reason. Let us believe in

God, the Great Spirit of nature, who presides over the final triumph of justice throughout His universe. Let us rest our trust in His wisdom, in which we shall find compensation for all suffering, joy for all our pain; and let us proceed with a resolute heart towards the destiny that he has chosen for us.

It is good, it is comforting and sweet to be able to follow the path of life with a serenely uplifted head, feeling assured that even when exposed to the stress of storm, or when enduring the most bitter trials, in the darkness of a dungeon or in the depths of a mountain abyss, a Providence – some divine law – is watching over us and guiding our actions; and that our struggles, sufferings and tears are themselves the foundation of our future glory and happiness. In this thought lies the whole strength of the righteous individual.

10

The Immortal Spirit

The study of the universe has led us to the study of the soul, to the research of that principle by which we are animated and our actions are directed.

Physiology teaches us that the different parts of the body are renewed every few years. Through the action of the two great vital currents a perpetual molecular exchange is at work within us: those that have been eliminate from the organism being replaced by others which alimentation produces. Our entire physical being is subjected to perpetual change, from the soft matter of the brain to the toughest parts of the bony structure. Our body dissolves and forms again many times during life. Notwithstanding these constant transformations and throughout all the modifications of the material body, we still remain the same individuals. The substance of our brain may be renewed, but our thought survives and with it our memory, the recollection of a past in which our actual body has not taken part. In us, there is a principle distinct from matter, an indivisible force that persists and subsists in the midst of these perpetual changes.

We know that matter cannot of itself organize and produce life. Devoid of unity, it disintegrates and endlessly crumbles away. In us, on the contrary, all the faculties, all the intellectual and moral forces meet in a central unit that groups, enlightens and binds them together: and this unit is the conscience, the personality, the self – in a word, the soul.

The soul is the principle of life, the cause of all sensation: it is the invisible, the indissoluble force which governs our organism and harmonizes the different parts of our being.[80] The faculties of the soul have nothing in common with matter. Intellect, reason, judgment, and will, are quite another thing from the flesh that clothes our muscles. It is the same with consciousness, with the privilege we have of weighing our actions, of discerning good from evil. This intimate language which is ever whispering to all beings, to the humblest as to the highest; that voice whose murmuring accents may discredit the brightest glory, is free from all material suggestion.

Conflicting currents contend within us; appetites and passionate desires clash with our reason and with the voice of duty. Were we but matter, we should not experience these struggles, this indecision: we should merely drift, without regret or remorse, to our natural tendencies. As it is, our will frequently in conflict with our instincts. Thanks to the will we can escape from the influence of matter; we can subjugate it and make it our obedient tool.

Do we not see people, born under the most difficult conditions, overcome all obstacles, poverty, sickness, infirmity, and attain to the highest rank by dint of energetic and unremitting effort? And is not the soul's superiority to the body still more strikingly proclaimed by the great examples of self-sacrifice and abnegation which history sometimes record? Nobody knows how the

---

80 This by means of a vital fluid that transmits its orders to the body. We shall presently speak more at length of this third element which constitutes the subtle body or perispirit, which endures beyond death, and, inseparable from the soul, accompanies the latter through all its peregrinations.

martyrs to duty, how the victims of some truth that anticipated its appointed time of revelation: how all of those who, for humanity's sake, were persecuted, maltreated, tortured, while undergoing the direst suffering, even to the threshold of death, inspired by a great belief, were still able to dominate matter and to silence the outcry of their mortified flesh.

If there was only matter in us, we would not see, when our body is plunged into sleep, the mind continue to live and act without the help of any of the five senses, proving thereby that activity is an essential condition of the spirit. Magnetic lucidity, the faculty of distant vision without visual aid, the foretelling of future events, and thought penetration, are so many evident proofs of the existence of the soul.

Thus, be it weak or strong, ignorant or enlightened, a spirit lives in us, which governs the body, which is under its direction, only a servant, a simple instrument. This spirit is both free and perfectible, hence responsible. Subject to its own free will, it is open to transformation and amelioration. In some perplexed, in others luminous, an ideal ever lights its way. The higher the ideal, the nobler and the more useful are its works. Happy the soul that a noble enthusiasm sustains: be it love of truth, of justice, or country, or humanity! Its ascent will be rapid, its passage here below will leave deep traces, a furrow from which will rise a blessed harvest.

The existence of the soul once established, the problem of immortality forthwith arises. This is a question of the deepest importance: for immortality is the sole sanction of morality; it is the only conception that satisfies our notion of justice that can fulfill the highest hopes of humanity.

If our spiritual entity remains intact and persists, in spite of the molecular renewal and the continuous transformation of our material body, its dissociation and final disappearance would be equally powerless to disturb its existence.

We have seen that in the universe nothing perishes. When chemistry and physics both demonstrate that not an atom can be lost, that no force can disappear, how is it then possible to believe that the very unit which summarizes all the powers of the intellect how can we then conceive that this unit, this self, could be dissolved? How can we believe that this conscious self, in whom life emerges from the chains of fatality, can be annihilated?

Not only logic and morality, but as we shall later demonstrate, the facts themselves – facts of a sensible order, both physiological and psychological – all go to prove, by establishing the persistence of the human soul, that this soul will be found beyond the grave to be identical with that which, by thought and action, it made itself in this present life.

Were death to end all, were our destinies to be cramped within the narrow limits of this fugitive life, should we then be haunted by these aspirations for a better and more perfect state, of which there is nothing in this world to suggest the possibility? Should we be pursued by that unquenchable desire to experience and to know? If all is to be obliterated by the grave: then why these yearnings, these dreams, these inexplicable desires, this powerful human cry which echoes down the chambers of the centuries, these infinite longings, these irrepressible surging towards light and progress? Are they then but the attributes of a passing shadow, of an aggregation of molecules which vanishes as soon as it is formed? If so, what is this earthly life: so short, that even at its lengthiest it does not allow us to attain to the confines of science: so powerless, so bitter, so full of disillusion, that in nothing can it utterly satisfy us: even to that extent, that when thinking to have grasped the object of our desire, unsatisfied, we still reach forth for something else – something ever beyond, ever unattainable! The persistence we display in pursuing, in spite of all disappointments, an ideal that is not of this world and a happiness which ever eludes us, sufficiently indicates that there is something beyond the present life. Nature would not bestow upon the human being, hopes and aspirations that are never to be realized. The unlimited cravings of the soul necessarily imply life unlimited.

11

The Plurality of Lives

In what form does immortal life unfold, and what is in reality the life of the soul? To answer these questions we must revert to the problem of life, start at its beginning and follow it through.

We know that upon this Earth life first reveals itself in the simplest and most elementary aspects, to rise gradually, by a constant progression, from form to form, from species to species, to the level of the human type which is the apex of terrestrial creation. Gradually, as the being is developed and refined, sensitivity increases. Slowly, blind instinct makes way for intellect and reason.

Does this imply that each soul has traveled this scale of progressive evolution, whose low degrees plunge into a dark abyss? Before it has been allowed a conscience and freedom, before it has attained to the fullness of its free will, has it necessarily been constrained to sojourn in rudimentary organisms, to assume life's inferior semblances? The study of human nature, which still bears the impress of bestiality, would lead us to believe that such is the case. The question, however, remains pending. [81]

It is repugnant to the requirements of justice that animals, like humans, must not live and suffer merely to end in nothingness. A continuous, ascending chain seems to unite all kingdoms: the

---
81 See « Life and Destiny,», chap. IX, *Evolution and Purpose of the Soul.*

mineral to the vegetable, the vegetable to the animal and the latter to humans. It can connect them doubly, to the material as to the spiritual. These two forms of evolution are parallel and interdependent, life being but a manifestation of the mind.

Be that as it may, the soul, having reached the human state, and having acquired consciousness, can no longer retrograde. In every degree, the forms it assumes are the expression of its own value. God should not be accused of having produced hideous and malignant forms. The being can bear no other semblance than that which is the outcome of the habits and tendencies that it has contracted. It sometimes happens that human souls choose weak and sickly bodies to repress their passions and acquire the qualities necessary for their advancement, but in a lower state of nature no choice can be exercised, the creature coming perforce under the dominion of such attractions as it has cultivated in itself.

This gradual development may be marked by any attentive observer. Among domestic animals differences of character are appreciable. In some species certain animals seem to be far more advanced than others, some being susceptible to affection and devotion, and moreover possessing qualities which bring them decidedly nearer to humans. One must credit them with the existence of a soul in embryonic form, since matter is incapable of love or sentiment.

It would be difficult to conceive of anything grander, more just or more conformable to the law of progress, than this ascension of the soul, occurring by successive stages, during which they form themselves, ridding themselves, little by little, of gross instincts, shattering their shell of selfishness, to be replaced by reason, love and liberty. It is sovereignly just that all should undergo the same apprenticeship and that no being should attain to a superior state until he has acquired the necessary aptitudes for it.

When the soul, having attained to the human state, has achieved its autonomy and moral responsibility and acquired the sense of duty, it has not therefore attained its final end, nor finished its evolution. Its real task, far from being achieved, is now beginning. The struggles of the past are but a prelude to those the future holds in reserve. Its rebirths on Earth in carnal bodies will follow in constant succession. Each time, it will take up again with rejuvenated organs the work of self-perfection that death had interrupted, to carry it on, and progress still a little further. The soul, an eternal traveler, must thus gravitate from sphere to sphere towards righteousness and infinite reason, ever acquiring higher rank, ever growing in science, wisdom, virtue and love.

Each of our terrestrial existences is but an episode of our immortal life. No soul in this short space of time could rid itself of all its vices and errors, of all the coarse desires that are so many vestiges of its past lives, so many proofs of its origin.

By estimating the time that humanity has required from its first appearance upon Earth to arrive at its present degree of civilization, we can understand that for it to fulfill its destinies and ascend from light to the absolute, towards the divine, the soul will require an unlimited stretch of time and of recurrent lives. [82]

---

[82] The law of reincarnation is not only approved by reason, it is also sustained by facts. De Rochas' experiments concerning the regression of memory, and those earlier ones of Spanish experimenters – Colavida and Marata, recorded by the Spiritualistic Congress of 1900 – demonstrate that where subjects are in a state of complete magnetic sleep the deep strata of the memory which appear dumb and dark when the subject is in a waking state – can be caused intensely to vibrate. The subject then recalls the least episodes of his childhood, as well as events appertaining to his anterior existences. Through such researches, a web of proof is gradually evolved, establishing the reality of being and pre-existence; and human individuality is revealed under entirely new aspects. (See, for the whole of these experiments, our book *"Life and Destiny,"* chap. XIV.)

(Read the records of the Spiritist and Spiritualistic Congress of Paris, in 1900, p. 349-350; and concerning the experiments of Col. de Rochas, Dr. Sollier and Dr. Comar, consult the *Revue Scientifique et Morale du Spiritisme*, July and August Nos., 1904)

The plurality of existences can alone explain the diversity of character, the variety of aptitudes, the disproportion of moral endowments – in a word, all the disparities that we notice about us.

Were it not for this law, one might vainly wonder why some possess talent, nobility and fine minds, while to others folly, vice, passions, and vulgar instincts are allotted.

What could one think of a God, who while granting us but one corporeal life, should have bestowed upon us such unequal gifts, and should have allotted to humanity, whether civilized or uncivilized, possessions of such different value and so divergent a spiritual level?

Were it not for the law of reincarnation, iniquity would rule the world. While the influence of environment, heredity and educational differences have their importance, yet they do not suffice to explain these anomalies. We notice that members of the same family, of the same flesh and blood, brought up with the same ideas, differ in many ways. Frequently have good men fathered monsters – did not Marcus Aurelius beget a Commodus? – and, again, are not many celebrated and admirable men descendants of parents who were not only obscure but morally worthless?

If all took its rise in this present life how could we account for so great an intellectual discrepancy, for so many degrees of vice and virtue, for so many social ranks? An impenetrable mystery would surround precocious genius and those powerful minds whose youth assimilates science without effort, while others grow pallid with plodding, to remain mediocre all their days despite their efforts.

This enigma is resolved by the doctrine of multiple lives. Those who excel by their intellect or virtue are those that have lived more, labored more, and acquired thereby greater experience and skills.

The soul's progress and ennoblement depend wholly upon the amount of work and energy which it expends in the battle of life. Some souls courageously encounter and rapidly surmount the barriers that separate them from the higher life, while the effortless and sterile existences led by others keep them stationary for centuries. But these inequalities, the cause of which lies in the past, may be redeemed and leveled by our future lives.

The human being, we repeat, is his own artisan; he makes himself by gradually developing the forces that are in him. Vacillating at the start, his life gradually becomes more intelligent and purposeful as he attains manhood and enters into complete possession of himself. His freedom, however, still remains subject to the natural laws that ensure his preservation. Thus do fate and free-will balance and correct one another. Freedom and, consequently, responsibility, are ever proportionate to the soul's progress.

Such is the only rational solution of the problem. Through the succession of times, on the surface of thousands of worlds, our existences unfold, pass and renew. In each passing, a little of the evil which is within us is eliminated, and our strengthened and purified souls are able to advance yet a little along the sacred path, until the time, when liberated at least from the necessity of painful reincarnations, they have conquered by their merits the access to the higher circles – where beauty, wisdom, power, and love, everlastingly shine.

12

The Purpose of Life

This being understood, clarity is made in us and around us. Our road becomes clearer: we know what we are, and where we go.

Henceforth material pleasure will cease to be our object, and an ardent endeavor towards self-improvement will take its place. The supreme aim is perfection: the road that leads to it is the road of self-improvement. The road is long, and is traversed step by step. The distant end appears to recede as one approaches it, but, at each stage passed, the being collects the fruit of its sorrows; He enriches his experience and develops his faculties.

Our destinies are all identical. There are no privileged or cursed beings. All must trudge the same tremendous road and, through a thousand obstacles, are called to fulfill the same ends. We are free, it is true, to accelerate or slow down our progress, to plunge ourselves into vulgar enjoyment; free to squander away entire existences in vice and idleness; but sooner or later the sense of duty will awaken, then will pain quicken our apathy, and we shall find ourselves obliged to take up our burdens and move on.

Between one soul and another, there is but the difference of a degree – a difference that the future will find opportunity to erase. In making use of our free-will, we have not all traveled the same road, thence arises the intellectual and moral disparity among human beings. But we, all of us, children of the same Father, must perforce gather closer to Him in the succession of our lives; and so finally form only one family: the great family of spirits, which inhabits the whole universe.

The world has no longer room for such conceptions as an eternal Paradise or an endless Hell. We see in immensity only beings pursuing their own education and rising by their efforts within the universal harmony. By these deeds each prepare his own place, and the consequences of these deeds revert to him, binding and enthralling him. When his life has been the plaything of passion and sterile of good results, the being is lowered and his good standing accordingly sinks. To wash these stains away he must seek reincarnation in worlds of trial, that suffering may purify him. This purification accomplished, his evolution will begin again. There are no eternal trials; but the trials must be in just proportion to the sins committed.

We have no other judge and no other executioner than our conscience; but when this conscience is liberated from the bonds of matter, it becomes imperious and persistent. In the moral as in the physical order there is nothing beyond cause and effect, a sovereign, immutable and unerring law ordains these. That which we may ignorantly deem an injustice of fate is but the reparation exacted for past transgressions. Human fate is the settlement of the debt contracted by us unto the law.

Our actual life is therefore the direct and inevitable outcome of our anterior lives, just as our future life will be the resultant of our present actions. When the soul comes to animate a new body it brings with it, at each rebirth, the accumulation of its qualities and defects, all the good and evil harvests that we sown in the past. So, in the succession of our lives, we construct our moral edifice with our own hands, we build up our future, we prepare the environment in which we are to be reborn, the site that we are to occupy.

With the law of reincarnation, sovereign justice shines upon the worlds. Each being in possession of reason and conscience becomes the contriver of his fate. He forges or shatters at will the chains that rivet him to matter. The pitiful condition of some people is thus explicable, for each guilty life must be redeemed. The hour comes when the proud soul must be born again in humble or servile condition, when the idle spirit must submit to painful labors. He, who has caused another to suffer, will in his turn likewise suffer.

But the soul is not bound for ever to this lowly planet; when it has acquired the necessary qualities it departs for more enlightened worlds. It traverses the fields of space strewn with stars and suns. Among the multitudes that people infinity, a place for it will be found. Still progressing in this new environment, the soul will endlessly add to its store of moral wealth and knowledge. After an incalculable number of deaths and rebirths, of falls and ascents, finally delivered from reincarnation, it will enter into the enjoyment of the heavenly life, where it will share in the direction of beings and worlds, contributing by its own deeds to the universal harmony and to the fulfillment of the divine plans.

Such is the mystery of Psyche, the human soul. Engraved upon it, the soul bears the law of its own destiny, to learn to decipher the precepts and to unravel the mystery of which constitutes the true science of life. Each spark gathered from the divine fire, each conquest over self, with its desires and egotism, fill it with ineffable joy, greater in proportion to the greatness of the difficulty overcome. Such is our promised heaven, and this heaven is not remote, for we have it within us. Happiness or remorse, power or degradation – these all, consequences of his deeds, has the individual ever with him, imbedded in his deepest self. These voices, harsh or melodious, that stir within him, are the faithful interpreters of the eternal laws; their volume grows greater as he rises higher on the road of perfection.

The soul is a world: a world in which light and shade are still intermingled; the more closely we study it the more we walk from surprise to surprise.. In its folds lie the germs of all power, waiting the fecundating hour to spring forth in sheaves of light. As the soul becomes purer, its perceptions increase. All that which delights us in its present condition, gifts of talent or flashes of genius, are insignificant indeed compared to what it will some day acquire, when it attains to the higher planes. Vast already are its hidden resources: its inner essence, subtle and varied, source of keen impressions, the exercise of which is ever hindered by the clumsy body, its envelope. Some transcendental souls alone, detached by anticipation from earthly things and purified by self-sacrifice, have felt the first fruits of this world. But they have found no words to describe their rapture, and men in their blind ignorance of the soul's true nature and of the treasures it conceals, have laughed at that which they name illusion and chimeras.

13

Trial and Death

The object of existence being fixed, higher than fortune, higher than happiness, a whole revolution takes place in our views. The Universe becomes an arena through which the souls goes forth fighting for its elevation, which may be obtained, but at the price of much effort, self-sacrifice and suffering. Suffering, be it physical or moral, is one of the essential requisites of evolution, potent instrument of development and progress. It teaches us to know ourselves, to govern our passions, and to love our neighbors. The soul's most necessary acquisitions are love and science. The more one knows, the more one loves, and the greater is our elevation. Suffering obliges us to inquire into the causes that produced it, so as to oppose and overcome them, and the knowledge of these causes awakens in us a quicker sympathy for those who suffer.

Pain is the supreme purifier, the instiller of patience, resignation and austere duty. It is the furnace in which selfishness is melted and pride dissolved. Sometimes, in the darkest hours, the much tried soul rebels, denying God and His justice; but when the storm is spent and the soul can calmly face its grief – it discovers that suffering has made it better, more pitiful and more helpful.

All the vicissitudes of life contribute to our improvement. Through suffering, humiliation, infirmity and adversity, the better one emerges from the worst. Thus does it come to pass that suffering predominates over happiness, here below. Hardship tempers the character, quickens sentiment and subdues the proud and hasty spirit.

Physical suffering also has its object, it chemically loosens the bonds that unite the spirit to the flesh; it liberates the spirit from the coarse fluids which even after death envelop it, holding it down to the lower regions.[83]

Let us not rail against suffering, for it alone may rescue us from indifference and voluptuousness. It carves the spirit, imparting to it the purest outlines, the most gracious beauty.

Our trials are the infallible corrective of our inexperience. Providence acts towards us, like a vigilant mother towards an unruly child. When we remain deaf to its appeals and stubborn to its admonition, it leads us to encounter disappointment and failure, well knowing that adversity is the best teacher of wisdom.

Such is the fate of most of us here below. Under a sky that often lowers, still must we follow the arid path, our feet lacerated by its stones and thorns. A black-robed spirit, the spirit of grief, is our guide. Grief, blessed and holy, since it alone by shaking our being, releases it from the petty vanities to which it so obstinately clings, making it apt to feel what Is truly noble and beautiful..

---

83 This attribute of suffering explains in some cases, the brief term of those children who die at a tender age. These souls had already acquired upon Earth sufficient knowledge and virtue to ascend to higher regions, but were withheld by some remnant of materialism which stopped their flight, and so returned to complete their purification by suffering.

In the light of these revelations death loses its terrifying aspect, it now appears nothing more than a necessary transformation, a renewal. In reality, nothing dies. Death is but an appearance. The outer shape alone is affected: the principle of life, the soul, remains in its permanent, indestructible unity. It finds itself beyond the grave, in its fluidic body, in full possession of its faculties and such attainments, aspirations, virtues and powers as it had acquired during its earthly life. For these are the imperishable of which the Gospel speaks, when it says: *"Do not store up for yourselves treasures on Earth, where moth and rust destroy, and where thieves break in and steal."* They are the only treasures we can take with us to use in the life to come.

Death, and the reincarnation which follows after a certain interval, are the two essential forms of progress. By interrupting the narrow habits that we have contacted, they bring us into a different environment, they give our thoughts a new impulse; they compel us to adapt our minds to the thousand faces of the social and universal order.

When the evening of life is at hand, when our life is about to be turned, like the page of a book, to make room for a fresh page, then does the wise person review his past and take stock of his deeds. Happy then, the person who can say: *"My days have been well fulfilled"*! Happy is the one who has received his trials with resignation and endured them with courage! What though they rent his spirit asunder – was it not that the bitterness and gall thereof might find an outlet? The sage, as he muses over the trials of an arduous life, will bless the sufferings he has endured: With a tranquil spirit he will quietly await the signal for his departure.

Let us then bid good-bye to the theories that picture death as an outlet into nothingness, or as the prelude to endless torment! Farewell then, you dark phantoms of theology; you relentless creeds, pitiless condemnations and excruciating torments, farewell! Make way for hope and for life eternal! Behold, from out of the tomb, there rises not a dark mist, but a shining light.

Have you ever watched the diaphanous winged butterfly, as it sheds the shapeless chrysalis, into which a repulsive caterpillar is enclosed? Have you marveled at the insect which began by crawling over the ground, and now flits so freely and gladly away through the warm sunshine, fragrant with the sweetness of roses? The phenomenon of death has no truer symbol than this, for man also is a chrysalis which death decomposes. The human body, a garment of flesh, goes back into nature's laboratory; but the spirit, having accomplished its work, rushes toward a higher life – to that spiritual life which follows the corporeal, as day follows night, and which separates our incarnations one from another.

Assured of these truths we shall no longer fear death, but shall steadfastly look it in the face, like our fathers, the Gauls. No more will there be fear, nor tears, nor mournful preparations, nor mourning chants. Our funerals will be celebrated by a feast at which we shall render thanks for the release of a soul from bondage and its happy return to its true fatherland.

Death is the great revealer. In the hours of trial when all that surrounds us seems immersed in darkness, do we not sometimes wonder?

"Why was I born, why was I not allowed to remain without, in the dark and quiet night, where one feels not and suffers not, but where one merely sleeps the eternal sleep?" And in these anguished moments a far-off voice is lifted, and reaching us replies: "Suffer that you may grow and be purified! Learn that your destiny is a great one. This cold Earth is not to be your grave, those worlds that shine in the remotest heavens are your future abodes: they are God's heritage to you. You are forever a citizen of the universe;

You belong to future centuries as to past centuries, and at the present time you are preparing your elevation. Therefore patiently endure these tribulations which you yourself has chosen. Sow in the furrows of pain, and with your tears water the seeds that will mature in your lives to come; sow for others as well as for yourself, as others have sown for you! Go forth, immortal spirit, climb with a sure footing that steep path which leads to the heights from where the future will appear to you without a veil. The ascent is steep, and sweat will often flood your face; but from the summit you will see the great light emerge, and you will see on the horizon the sun of truth and justice."

The voice that we hear is the voice of the dead – the voice of the beloved spirits that have preceded us into the land of true existence. Far from lying asleep beneath a stone, they have been watching over us, from the depths of the unseen they have looked down and smiled upon us. Adorable and divine mystery, they unceasingly communicate with us! They are whispering to us: "Let there be an end to sterile doubting. Work and love, and some day, when your work is done, death will come and reunite us."

14

Objections

As we may see, many questions deemed unanswerable by most philosophies, have found their solution in the doctrine of successive lives. The terrible arguments of evil, pain, the disparity between human merit and human conditions, the apparent injustice of fate – all these objections, with which materialism and skepticism battered such a breach in the theological edifice, have been overcome by the philosophy of spirits.

There remains one point only, one last strong objection to demolish. If we have already existed in the past, if other lives have preceded this birth, why then have we lost all memory of them?

This seemingly formidable objection is easily disposed of. The memory of events experienced, of deeds accomplished, is not an essential condition of life.

None of us can recall the time spent in the mother's womb, nor even the later cradle days; and only few can recall the impressions and happenings of early childhood. Yet are not these integral parts of our actual life? Each morning that we awake, we lose all recollection of our dreams; although these dreams may have seemed very real to us at the time, there remain only the confused sensations experienced by the spirit as it returns to undergo the influence of matter.

Our days and nights resemble our terrestrial and spiritual lives, and sleep seems as incomprehensible as death. Both alternately transport us to varying conditions, and into a widely differing environment, which does not prevent our identity from existing and persisting throughout all these varied experiences.

During the magnetic sleep, the mind freed from the body recollects things that it will forget upon its return to the flesh, but of which it will recapture the sequence by returning to the lucid state.

This state of artificial sleep evokes special aptitudes in the somnambulists, which disappear during waking hours as though suppressed and stifled by the material envelope.

In these diverse conditions the psychical being may traverse two states of consciousness, two alternate phases of existence which are interwoven and intertwined, one with the other. Forgetfulness, like a thick curtain, separates slumber from wakefulness, secluding each earthly life from its antecedent lives as well as from the great life of eternity.

If the impressions which, in the course of this present life the soul freely receives, during either its natural or artificial sleep state, cannot be transmitted to the brain, one can readily see that it would be still more difficult when these proceed from an anterior existence. The brain is fitted to receive and register only such images as the spirit itself has received while linked to matter. Memory can only reproduce that which has been entrusted to it.

At each rebirth the cerebral organism represents a new book upon which are registered our sensations and experiences. On re-entering the flesh, the soul loses all recollection of what it has seen and done while in a state of freedom, which it will only recall by abandoning its temporary prison again.

The forgetting of past events is an indispensable condition to all human progress and trial. Each of our pasts is scarred with stains and blemishes. In our journeying through the series of vanishing times, in our stages through the bestial ages, we must have amassed many defects and various iniquities. Emerged only yesterday from barbarism, the weight of its memories would bear us down. The burdens of this Earth are sometimes very hard to bear. How heavy would they not seem if to our present ills was superadded the memory of the sufferings and the shames of the past?

Would the recollection of our own past not be linked to that of others? By going back to the chain of our existences, the screen of our own history, we would likewise be retracing that of our fellow-beings. All manner of unkind thoughts and deeds would thus be perpetuated; rivalry, hatred and discord would endure from life to life, from age to age. Our former enemies and victims, upon recognizing us, would vengefully pursue us.

It is good that the veil of oblivion hide us from one another, causing our mutual past for a while to disappear, thus sparing us painful remembrance and, perhaps ceaseless remorse. The knowledge of our faults and of their consequences, rising before us like a perpetual and fearful menace, would render our lives sterile and unbearable.

Without forgetting, the great culprits, the famous criminals would be marked for eternity. Are not living criminals who have served their term, ever greeted with universal distrust and repulsed with horror? By refusing to give them back a place in society, it literally obliges them to take refuge in the great army of evildoers. What would it be if the crimes of the distant past become patently alive to all eyes?

Almost all of us stand in need of pardon and forgetfulness. The shade that hides our weaknesses and our miseries relieves our spirit and renders our atonement less painful. After having drunk of the waters of Lethe we can more cheerfully face a new life. Vanished are the past and its phantoms. Transported into a fresh environment our being awakens to fresh sensations, is open to other influences and more readily abandons the evil and erring habits, which, in the past, had been stumbling blocks to its improvement. A guilty soul, being born in the shape of a little child, awakes to find itself surrounded by the tenderness and love necessary to its regeneration. In this weak and delicate little being, none would dream of seeking a vicious spirit returned to cleanse its stained past.

In some, however, the past is not totally obliterated. At the bottom of their consciousness there lingers a confused memory of what they once were. This is the fount of intuition, of innate sentiment, of vague reminiscence and mysterious presentiment that awakens within us the dim echo of the past. By consulting these impressions, it would not seem impossible to reconstruct the past, if not in detail, at least in its principal lines.

Towards the close of each life, these far-away memories slowly resurrect, and emerge of the shade of oblivion. We advance through life, step by step, and when death appears all becomes clear! The past expounds the present, and the future is lightened with a new ray.

The soul, returned to spiritual life, regains the plenitude of its faculties. Then begins a period of self-examination, of rest, of meditation, during which it has opportunity to measure and to estimate the distance that it has covered. To it are vouchsafed the advice and exhortations of more advanced spirits. Guided by these it will arm itself with strong resolve and, when the hour has come, choosing a suitable environment, the spirit enters into possession of a new body.

Upon its return into the flesh, the soul once more loses all recollection of its past existences and also that of the spiritual life, the only free and complete life, compared to which its earthly sojourn would seem unbearable. Long will be the struggle and painful the effort necessary to take again conscience of itself and to recover its hidden powers; but throughout all it will never quite lose its intuition, nor the dim recollection of the resolutions it made before it again re-entered the world of flesh; and, continuing the course of its existences, it will improve through work and the suffering.

Third Part
The Invisible World

15

Nature and Science

In the preceding pages we have stated the essential principles of the philosophy of successive existences. These principles, based upon the most vigorous logic, enlighten our future and supply a solution to many hitherto inexplicable problems.

It might, however, be objected that these conceptions, logical and rational as they may appear, are mere speculations – simple hypotheses deserving of no more credence than anything else of the kind.

Our generation is weary of vain imaginings, weary of preconceived theories and systems; it has grown skeptical, it requires a proof for every assertion, and the most logical reasoning no longer suffices. It demands facts, sensible and direct: facts that can be readily verified, to dispel doubt. Its skepticism is comprehensible: it is the inevitable outcome of the multiplicity of legendary lore, of fictitious and erroneous doctrines upon which for so many centuries the human being has been nurtured. Education has transmuted credulity into doubt, and each new theory is met with distrust, if not with open hostility.

We, however, should not find fault with this state of mind which is, after all, the unconscious tribute paid by human thought to truth. The philosophy of successive existences, at least, can only be the gainer thereby, since far from being a new and fantastic conception it is substantiated by an imposing array of facts whose soundness is attested by experimental proof as well as by universal testimony. To these facts we will devote the third section of this volume.

The advance of science, with its innumerable pauses, is comparable to that of an exploring party through a mountainous region. As the traveler ascends the arduous slopes, the horizon widens around him; the details of the lower plane are merged into a vast ensemble, while in the distance new perspectives are opened. The higher he ascends the vaster and the more majestic becomes his field of vision. Thus does science discover some new realm at each step of its unwearied progress.

We know how limited are our material senses and how small is their scope of action. Beyond the rays and colors that the eye perceives, there are still other rays and other colors whose existence chemical reaction reveals. The sound waves are only audible when they reach us between two keys. The sonorous vibrations that precede or follow are either too sharp or too deep, and produce no effect upon the auditory nerves.

If our power of vision had not been increased by optical discoveries, what would we know about the universe at present? Not only we would be unaware of the existence of that far-away empire of ether, where suns follow upon suns and where cosmic matter, in a state of eternal gestations, gives birth to stars by the myriad, but we would still not know anything about our neighboring worlds.

Gradually, from century to century, has our field of observation been extended. Thanks to the invention of the telescope the human being has been enabled to explore the heavens and to compare the puny Earth, his dwelling-place, with the giants of space.

More recently still the invention of the microscope revealed another infinitude of things. On every hand, encompassing us in the air, in the water, invisible to our feeble eyes, myriads of creatures swarm, rising and falling in alarming swirls. The study of the molecular constitution of the body has been made possible. We have found out that the corpuscles of the blood, that the cells and tissues of the human body are filled with living parasites, with infusoria: and that still other parasites live at the expense of these. No one can affix any limit to the ocean of life.

Science progresses and grows, and thought, emboldened, rises to new horizons. But after all how slight seems the sum of our knowledge as measured by that which still remains for us to acquire. The human mind has its limitations, whereas nature knows none. "With what we do not know of the laws of the universe," as Faraday reminds us, "the world might be constructed."

Our crude senses permit us to dwell in the midst of an ocean of marvels, of which we do not even suspect the existence; we are as blind people, bathed in torrents of light.

16

Matter and Force – The Sole Principle of All Things

Until now matter was known only in three conditions – solid, liquid and gaseous. Sir William Crookes, the learned English chemist, while endeavoring to create vacuum in a glass tube, discovered a fourth condition which he named the radiant state. The atoms, freed by rarefaction, assume in this relative vacuum vibratory motions on intense and incalculable rapidity. They ignite and produce effects of light and electric radiations which make it possible to explain the majority of the cosmic phenomena.[84]

Variously condensed, in its three first conditions, matter in the radiant state loses a number of its properties, such as density, shape, color and weight; but in this newfound realm, it appears to be more closely and intimately related to force. Can it be that this fourth aspect is the last which matter is susceptible of assuming? No, no doubt, for one can imagine many others. For instance the mind can picture a subtle, fluidic state, as superior to the radiant condition, as the radiant is superior to the gaseous, or the liquid to the solid. Future science will plumb these depths and will find in them an answer to such formidable problems as the unity of substance or the preponderating forces of the universe.

---
84 The X-rays are amongst the best known examples of this fact.

Already has the unity of substance been foreseen and admitted by most scientists. Matter, we have said, appears, in its principle, to be a fluid of infinite suppleness and elasticity, the endless combinations of which engender all bodies. In its primordial essence – invisible, impalpable, imponderable – this fluid, through successive transitions, becomes ponderable and capable of producing, by powerful condensation, those hard, opaque and weighty bodies that constitute the base of terrestrial matter. But, this state of cohesion is only transitory. Matter, re-ascending the ladder of its transformations, can as readily be disaggregated and so return to its primitive fluidic state; hence it is that the existence of the worlds is so ephemeral. Out of the oceans of the ether, they plunge again and dissolve there after having passed through their cycle of life.

It can be said that everything in nature converges towards unity. Spectral analysis reveals the identity of the constitutive elements of the universe, from the humblest satellite to the most gigantic sun. The displacement of the celestial bodies shows the unity of mechanical laws. The study of material phenomena leads us like an infinite chain, link by link, to the conception of one only substance, ethereal and universal, and to one only force, that of the principle of motion, of which electricity, heat and light are but the variants, the modes, the different aspects.[85]

---

[85] As to this (in his "*Origines de la Chimie,*" p. 320), Berthelot states: "The fluids – electric, magnetic, caloric and luminous – of which we were taught half a century ago, already have no more reality than the four elements of the ancients. By the advance of science these different fluids have been reduced to one, which is ether. And now, this ether of the physicians, like the atom of the chemists, disappears in its turn to make way for higher conceptions which promise to account for all things by the phenomena of motion." According to G. Le Bon ("*L'Évolution de la Matière*"; "*l'Évolution des Forces*"), matter and force are only two aspects of the same substance. The matter is only of the concrete force; the force of the disassociated matter.

Thus it is that chemistry, physics, mechanics, in their parallel advance, see more and more to establish the mysterious coordination of all things. The human mind is slowly, and at times unconsciously, gravitating towards the discovery of a unique and fundamental principle in which substance, force and thought are blended – of a Power whose might and majesty will some day overwhelm the mind with awe and admiration.

17

The Fluids – Magnetism

This fluidic world, which we see looming beyond the radiant state, has many surprises and discoveries in store for science. Innumerable is the variety of form that subtle matter may assume in order to fill the needs of a superior life.

Many observers are already conscious of the fact that beyond our perceptions, beyond the opaque veil, outcome of our gross constitution, which surrounds us like a fog, another world exists, no longer that of the infinitely little – but a fluidic universe which enfolds us, and which, also, is swarming with invisible multitudes.

Beings that are superhuman, but not supernatural, live near us – silent witnesses of our doings, who never make themselves manifest, save under predetermined conditions and within the action of natural precise and rigorous laws. It is important to penetrate the secrecy of these laws, because their knowledge would invest the individual with such power, that, if he chose to apply it, it would change the face of the Earth. This knowledge appertains to the domain of experimental psychology or – as some would say – to occult science.

The science of occultism is as ancient as the world. We have already spoken of the wonders worked in the sanctuaries of India, Egypt and Greece, and we will not dwell further upon this subject. There is, however, a kindred subject that we cannot ignore and this is magnetism.

Magnetism, which was secretly studied and practiced during all historical epochs, became more widely known from the end of the eighteenth century. The learned academies are still suspicious of it, and it is under the name of hypnotism that the masters of science have willing to discover it, one century after its final appearance.

> *"Hypnotism, says M. de Rochas[86] which has been up to now officially studied, is but the antechamber to a vast and marvelous edifice, a great part of which has already been explored by the ancient magnetizers."*

The most unfortunate part of it is that the official scientists – mostly doctors – who interest themselves in magnetism, or hypnotism as they prefer to term it, generally limit their experiments to the treatment of the sick – to hospital patients. The nervous irritation and morbid affections of these subjects can only result in the obtaining of incomplete and incoherent phenomena.

Some scientists seem to fear that the study of the same phenomena, obtained under normal conditions, might not demonstrate in the individual the existence of the animic principle. This much at least we gather from the commentaries of Dr. Charcot, whose competence is generally admitted.

---

86 See « Les Etats profonds de l'Hipnose, » by Col. De Rochas d'Ailgun (p.75).

Hypnotism, he writes, is a world in which one encounters, alongside of the palpable, material and gross facts that are always side by side with physiology, some other things that are absolutely extraordinary and thus far incomprehensible – things that seem to obey no physiological law and that are altogether strange and surprising. I shall consider the first only, and leave on one side the latter.

Thus do the most famous doctors acknowledge that this question is still very obscure to them. In their investigations, they content themselves with superficial observations, disdaining the facts that might lead them directly to the solution of the problem. Materialistic science hesitates to venture over the territory of experimental psychology; it seems to fear that it will find itself in the presence of psychical forces – that it will encounter that soul whose existence it has so obstinately denied.

Be this as it may, magnetism – which was long ignored by scientists – is now beginning under another name to attract their attention. But the results would be far more prolific, did they experiment on sane and sound persons instead of selecting the victims of hysteria. Magnetic sleep induces, in lucid subjects, new faculties and a surprising perceptivity. The most remarkable of these phenomena is perhaps the power of vision at a great distance without the assistance of the eye. A somnambulist is able to direct his steps, to read, write, and execute the most delicate and complicated tasks in absolute darkness.

Others have the power of seeing through the human body and of ascertaining both the ailment and its producing cause; they can read the thought that lies in the brain[87] and penetrate likewise, without the aid of their senses, into the most hidden recesses – even to the portals of another realm. They scan the mysteries of the fluidic life and commune with the invisible beings of whom we spoke, and transmit to us their advice and instructions. To this we will later return; but one point we may consider as established, it stands forth from the numerous experiments of Puységur, Deleuze, du Potet and their innumerable disciples: magnetic sleep, by immobilizing the body and deadening the senses, liberates the psychical being, greatly increasing its inner perceptivity, thus opening to it a world which is closed to corporeal beings.

And what may be this psychical being which, during the sleep of the body, thinks and acts without that body? Which asserts its independent personality by a peculiar individuality and by attainments superior to those shown in the waking state? What can it be, if not the soul itself enveloped in its fluidic form? The soul, which has ceased to be a resultant of vital forces, of organic creation, to become a free cause, an active will, which, temporarily liberated

---

87 "He (the subject) sees the brain cells vibrate under the influence of thought and compares them to stars that alternately dilate and contract" (*Les Etats profonds de l'hypnose*, by de Rochas – former manager of the l'École Polytechnique). More recently, Prof. Flournoy, of the University of Geneva, has written: "One need only to glance over the most recent medical literature, to be confronted by examples of the inner vision, cited by people who would never be accused of mysticism. Here we find cases of people, mentally unsound, who exhibited, a few days prior to their death, not only an improvement as marked as it was unexpected, but likewise a presentiment of their immediate demise; these cases are reported by French psychiatrists. Here again, we read the account of somnambulists who are endowed with a clear vision of the inner portions of their bodies, sometimes even of its most hidden recesses; this fact has just been admitted within the temple of science under the appellation of internal autoscopy (*autoscopie interne*), or the 'auto-representation' of the organism; by a droll irony of chance the godfathers of this newcomer happen to be none other than the disciples of a school which pretends to reject all psychological interpretation of these facts ("*Archives de Psychologie*," August, 1903).

from its prison, is roaming through nature, rejoicing in the entire possession of its inner faculties. Hence magnetic phenomena give evidence not only of the existence of the soul but also of its immortality; for if, during the corporeal life, this soul can be released from its gross envelop and can live and think outside of it, then, at death, it must all the more recover the fullness of its liberty.

The science of magnetism places marvelous resources at people's disposal. Fluidic action upon the human body is very great, and of varied and multiple properties. Numerous cases testify that the most intense suffering has been appeased by its intervention. Great missionaries healed by the simple laying on of hands: therein lies the secret of so-called miracles. The fluids, obedient to a powerful will and to an ardent desire to do good, penetrate into the debilitated system and gradually recall the ailing to health and strength.

One may well protest that a legion of charlatans have preyed upon an ignorant and gullible public by boasting of a fictitious magnetic powers! Such is the inevitable outcome of human's mental inferiority. We may, however, be sure of one thing: any person who is animated by deep sympathy and compassion for his suffering brother or sister, can alleviate their pains by giving himself up to a sincere and enlightened practice of magnetism.

18

Spiritist Phenomena

Of all proofs of the fact that the human being possesses a spiritual principle and its survival to the body, the most convincing are those furnished by the phenomena of experimental spiritualism or Spiritism.

Considered at first as pure charlatanism, Spiritist phenomena have now entered into the domain of critical observation; if there be scientists who still disdain, reject and deny them, there are others, no less eminent, who pay them the tribute of a most earnest investigation and research. In the United States and throughout Europe, societies for psychological research are the constant object of their investigations.

These phenomena, as we have seen, have taken place at all times. Formerly, they were shrouded in mystery and only the elect few could witness them. Now universalized, they are produced with a persistency and variety that confounds modern science.

Newton maintains that, *"It is folly to believe that everything is known, and wisdom requires that we investigate always."* It is the duty, not only of the scientist but of all sensible people, to investigate facts that open a door on an unknown side of nature, to seek their causes and the laws that govern them. Such investigation can but strengthen the mind and expedite progress by destroying superstition in its germ; because superstition is always prompt to seize the phenomena neglected by science, and to attribute them into a supernatural or miraculous seeming.

Most of those who scorn these questions or who have studied them only superficially, without order or sequence, are prone to accuse the spiritists of either misinterpreting their phenomena or of drawing hasty conclusions from them.

To begin with, we will point out that when the opponents of spiritist philosophy deny the interpretation of facts, instead of denying the reality of the facts themselves, it is already a step gained. The facts are, indeed, not disputed. Besides, as we shall see, the reality of spiritualistic phenomena is attested by people of the most undoubted veracity, by scientists of the greatest competency, distinguished as well for their research as for their discoveries. But learning is not needed to ascertain the existence of phenomena that are apparent to the senses and therefore ever open to scrutiny. Anyone endowed with a little perseverance and sagacity, by submitting oneself to the requisite conditions, can observe these phenomena and form an intelligent opinion concerning them.

It is true that out of this great mass of phenomena, some may be attributed to a state of auto-suggestion in the medium, to the exteriorization of forces, or to thought transmission; but after making all possible allowances for such causes there still remains a very considerable number of cases, the only logical explanation of which is the intervention of the departed.

We have elsewhere refuted objections of a similar character[88] and have produced a logical sequence of proof which establishes the reality of spirit-existence in such manner as must convince any seeker who is willing to discard the obstruction of preconceived ideas and prejudices.

---

[88] See Léon Denis, « *Dans l'Invisible,* » *Spiritisme et Médiumnité,* second part.

19

Scientific Testimony

It was in the United States, in 1848, that public attention was first attracted to spirit manifestation. In many places a sound of knocking made itself heard, of furniture being moved by an invisible agency, of tables displaced and violently banged upon the floor. One of the witnesses of these unusual occurrences conceived the idea of combining the letters of the alphabet with the number of knocks delivered, a kind of spiritual telegraphy was established, and thus a connection was established with the occult forces. The invisible being proclaimed himself the spirit of a person deceased in that immediate vicinity, and proffered a most minute account detailing the identity, life and death of that person, together with certain peculiarities of a nature to dispel all doubts.[89] Other spirits were invoked and responded with a like accuracy. All alike asserted themselves to be unsheathed by a fluidic envelope of material substance, although invisible to us.

Manifestations rapidly increased, successively spreading throughout all the United States. They occupied so much public opinion that a few prominent men, fearing they could become a menace to public reason, resolved thoroughly to investigate them and so demonstrate their absurdity. Hence it came to pass that

---
89 Fox's sisters

such men as Edmonds, Chief Justice of the Supreme Court of New York and President of the State Senate, and Mapes, Professor of Chemistry at the National Academy, were summoned to give their verdict in the matter. Their conclusions – formulated after a rigorous examination – were to the effect that these phenomena were genuine and could be attributed to none other than spirit action.

The spiritualistic movement increased to such an extent that in 1852 a petition hearing fifteen thousand signatures was sent to Congress, demanding an official proclamation asserting the genuineness of these phenomena.

Robert Hare, a well-known scientist and professor at the University of Pennsylvania, openly sided with the spiritists; his book, entitled *"Experimental Investigation of Spirit Manifestation,"* scientifically established spirit intervention, and created a sensation.

Robert Dale Owen, scientist, diplomat and writer, also rallied to this belief and published several books defending it. Of these his *"Footfalls on the Boundary of Another World,"* of 1877, met with considerable success.

Modern spiritualism numbers today over a million followers in the United States alone, and it is voiced by a large press.[90]

In recent years, the experiments conducted by a number of professors of the great American universities, with the help of the famous medium Mrs. Piper, have procured, in this milieu, important adhesions.

James Hyslop, professor of psychology at Columbia University, New York, said in his report on the mediumship of this lady:

"To judge from what I myself saw, I do not know how I could escape the conclusion that the existence of a future life is absolutely demonstrated."

---

90 NT: The principal organ is the *Progressive Thinker*, published in Chicago.

Dr. R. Hodgson wrote in his turn:

> "I believe without the slightest doubt that the spiritist communicants are indeed the personalities they say to be; that they survived the change we call death and that they communicated directly with us, the so-called alive, through the organism of Mrs. Piper asleep."

Dr. Richard Hodgson himself, who died in December 1906, communicated through mediumship with his friend Professor J. Hyslop. He entered into very extensive and precise details on the experiments and works of the Society of Psychical Research, of which he was president for the American section.

These messages, perfectly concordant with each other, were transmitted by different mediums who did not know each other. We find the words and phrases familiar to the communicant during his life.

It is, however, in England that spirit manifestations have been submitted to the most rigorous examination. Many English savants have devoted a persevering and minute attention to these phenomena, and it is from them that we have received the most formal proofs.

Since 1869 the Dialectic Society of London – one of the most prominent of all scientific bodies – named a committee of thirty-three members-scientists, literary men, clergymen, magistrates – of whom were Sir John Lubbock (Royal Society), Henry Lewes, physiologist, Huxley, Wallace, Crookes, etc., to examine and "destroy forever" these spiritist phenomena, which, they said, "are only work of imagination."

After eighteen months of exhaustive experimentation and research, the commission in its report recognized the reality of the phenomena and concluded in favor of Spiritism.

In its enumeration of the occurrences under observation, the record does not only speak of table turnings and of knockings, it also mentions:

> "The apparition of hands and shapes belonging to no human being, but which seem, by their action and mobility, to be alive. These hands were sometimes touched and grasped by the assistants, who were convinced that they were neither the contrivance of imposture nor of illusion."

One of the thirty-three, Alfred Russel Wallace, the worthy follower of Darwin, became, after the death of this last, the most eminent representative of evolutionism. He continued his investigations and consigned its results in a work: "*Miracles and Modern Spiritualism,*" which made a great stir in England. Speaking of the phenomena, he expresses himself as follows:

> "When I first did these researches, I was pre-eminently a materialist. In my mind there was no room for manifestation of a spiritual order. Nevertheless, facts are obstinate things; they proved victorious, and I was obliged to confess their existence long before I could admit their spiritist explanation. This came by degrees, under the constant influence of successive occurrences which were in no way to be explained nor set aside."

Among the English scholars of note whose testimony may be invoked in favor of spirit manifestation, we might name Stainton

Moses (*alias* M. A. Oxon), who published two volumes on this subject, entitled *"Psychography,"* which treat especially of the phenomena of direct writing, and *"Spirit Identity;"* Sir Oliver Lodge, Rector of the University of Birmingham, to which reference will be made later; Varley, engineer-in-chief of the telegraphic system, A. de Morgan, President of the London Mathematical Society, who strongly declared himself in his work, *"From Matter to Spirit;"* Challis, of Cambridge, and Barrett of the University of Dublin.

Taking precedence over these, comes a greater and more illustrious name, one that ranks high in the list of the partisans and the defenders of Spiritism; that of Sir William Crookes, of the Royal Society, he Academy of Sciences of England.

There is hardly a science which has not been indebted to his clever brain for some improvement or discovery. Crookes's discoveries in the mining of gold and silver, his application of sodium to the process of amalgamation, are used in the placer mining of America and Australia. At the Greenwich observatory he succeeded in taking the first photograph of the heavenly bodies, and his lunar reproductions are celebrated. His studies of the phenomena of the polarized light, on the spectroscope, are not less known. He likewise was the discoverer of thallium. But all this work is exceeded by his famous discovery of the fourth state of matter, which assured him and honored place in England's Pantheon, and of a still more enduring book in the memory of his countrymen.

Crookes devoted four years to the study of spirit manifestation, for the scientific observation of which he invented some wonderfully precise and delicate instruments. With the assistance of Miss Florence Cook, a very remarkable medium, and with the cooperation of a number of scientific people as methodical as himself, he pursued his investigations, using his own laboratory for his séances. He surrounded it with an elaborate system of electrical appliances, which rendered any attempt at connivance impossible of deadly for the conniver.

In his work on "*Spiritualistic Research,*" Crookes exhaustively analyses the different phenomena observed: the displacement of heavy bodies, the rendering of musical melodies without human intervention, direct writing, apparitions of hands in full light, appearance of forms and figures, etc. During several months the spirit of a young and beautiful woman, Katie King, appeared every evening to the assembled investigators, and for a brief period assumed all the outward semblances of a human person endowed with senses and organs. She conversed with Crookes, with his wife and their friends, submitting to all desired tests, even allowing herself to be touched, auscultated and photographed, after which, like a faint mist, she would fade away. Crookes, in his work, has related in detail these curious manifestations. [91]

Another scientific group, under the name of "The Society for Psychical Research," has been investigating spirit phenomena for thirty years. They have examined and recorded several thousand cases in their "*Proceedings*" and also in a work called "*Phantasms of the Living,*" by Drs. Myers, Gurney and Podmore, who explain these occurrences by telepathy, or influence at a distance between human beings. It is noteworthy that these apparitions almost invariably took place at the time of the death, and in some instances even after the death of those that appeared.

On the contrary, their objectivity and reality is evident from the very terms of the "*Proceedings,*" and the testimony gathered during the investigation. In some cases, animals were affected by the apparitions:[92] terrified dogs hid themselves or ran away; horses,

---

91 Note from SAB: For further reading about Crookes and the spirit of Katie King, see the book "*Evidence for a Future Life*" of Gabriel Delanne.
92 "*Proceedings,*" pg. 151

trembling in every limb and covered with sweat, backed and could not be induced to advance.

Of these apparitions, some were not only visible, but likewise audible and tangible. Phantoms are mentioned that were successively witnessed by different persons from the several floors of the same house.[93] In the "*Phantasms of the Living,*" frequent allusion is made to the physical effects produced by phantoms: such as noises, knockings, opened doors, objects displaced, etc.; even of voices predicting events to come;[94] photographs were obtained of some of these apparitions.[95]

The identity of the deceased was established with greater precision by the method followed in the experiments instituted by this same society with the assistance of the mediums Piper and Thompson, experiments which we have described elsewhere.[96]

A most important work on the subject is that by Professor Myers, of Cambridge, entitled "*Human Personality and its Survival of Bodily Death.*" It contains a substantial and methodical synopsis of all manner of spiritist occurrences, ending with a philosophical and religious synthesis deduced from these facts.

Professor Flournoy, of the University of Geneva, albeit a skeptic in such matters dwells nevertheless upon the importance of this work, of which he says:

> "*The reasoning and proofs advanced by Myers in favor of psychical phenomena of a supernormal order, constitute by their very bulk and weight a case too formidable to be altogether ignored – which would be impossible save*

---

93 "*Proceedings,*" pg. 102, 107.
94 "*Proceedings,*" p. 305; "*Phantasms of the Living,*" pg. 102, 149.
95 « *Annales des Sciences psychiques,* » pg. 356, 361.
96 See Léon Denis, « *Dans l'Invisible,* » Spiritisme et Médiumnité, chap. XIX.

through willful blindness. Indeed it would be a foolish silliness to discard the evidences as a whole, under the false pretense that such matters cannot be scientifically investigated." [97]

Sir Oliver Lodge, vice-chancellor of the University of Birmingham, expressed himself in this manner in a speech he gave, as chair of the British Association of Sciences, on September 10th, 1913:

"Although I speak as an ex-professor, of the representatives of orthodox science, I will not abstain from a personal note, summarizing the thirty year result of my experiments in psychic investigation, an investigation that I started without any predilection for these studies, and with the usual hostility (...) the occult phenomena, from the scientific point of view, convinced me that the memory and the affections are not limited to this combination with matter by which only they can appear here and now, and that the personality persists beyond the death of the body," (Annales des Sciences Psychiques, June 1914.)

On November 22nd, 1914, in a conference realized at the Settlement Browning, in Walworth, Sir Oliver Lodge was even more affirmative:

"... We will certainly continue to exist after death. I say it because I know that some of my deceased friends still exist, since I talked with them. "The communication is possible; but one can only obey the laws, by seeking, first of all, the required conditions. I do not say that this

---
[97] Flournoy, « Archives de Psychologie, » No. 7, June, 1903.

is easy, but rather, that is possible. I talked with my late friends exactly as I could talk with anyone in this audience. Being men of science, these friends provided the proof of their individual identity, the proof that they were truly themselves, and not some personification or some other thing emanating from me. We occupy ourselves to publish some of this evidence" I say to you, with the force of the conviction of which I am capable, that we do persist after death, that the departed continue to be interested in what occurs on Earth, and that they know much more on this subject than we ourselves are aware of. ("Annales des Sciences Psychiques," January 1916).

Very personal facts came out, thus further increasing the number and the importance of the evidence that sir Oliver Lodge could give in support of his convictions. His son Raymond, an engineer, who had volunteered during the war, was killed in Flanders on September 14th, 1915, at the age of twenty-six years. Spiritualistic communications began to occur between father and son, and it is following these communications that Sir Oliver Lodge published the beautiful book: "Raymond - Life and Death," a book that has thrown a new light on the details of the life in the other world. This work, that the unfortunate father wrote, not with his expertise of a scholar but with his heart, will certainly cause many conversions among those which were cruelly struck by the current war, feel germinating within themselves the salutary hope and will not longer be able to declare that death is an end that involves with it eternal separation.

The spiritist movement has spread through the Latin nations. Spain has in each of its principal cities a society and a journal of psychic studies. The most important nucleus is "Centro Barcelones." A federation joins together all the groups and circles of Catalonia, in a number of around fifty.

Italy, too, has had its striking spiritist manifestations. Passionate debates have stirred the learned circles of Italy, following upon the experiments of Professor Ercole Chiaia of Naples and his medium Eusapia Paladino. Chiaia successfully reproduced all of the most remarkable phenomena of Spiritism – apports, materialization, levitation, etc., as well as the imprint of faces, feet and hands, made in melted paraffin placed in receptacles, sealed against all possibility of human contact.

The notoriety that followed these experiments called forth a sharp criticism from Professor Lombroso, the distinguished criminologist and anthropologist. Mr. Chiaia then offered to reproduce them in his presence, and, at the end of 1891, several séances were held in M. Lombroso's apartment in Naples. Lombroso, assisted by Tambourini, Virgilio, Bianchi and Vizioli of the University of Naples, witnessed these spirit manifestations, of which he published an account.[98]

L'Italia del Popolo, a political newspaper of Milan, published (November 18th, 1892) a special supplement, giving an official account of seventeen séances held at Mr. Finzi's house in Milan with the same medium, Eusapia Paladino. This document was signed by the following eminent scientists of many countries: Schiaparelli, Director of the Astronomical Observatory of Milan; Aksakof, Russian Counselor of State and Director of the *Psychische Studien*, published in Leipzig; Dr. Karl du Prel, of Munich; Angello Brofferio,

---

98 See Gabriel Delanne's « *Le Phenomène Spirite, Témoignage des Savants* » page 235.

Professor of Philosophy; Gérosa, Professor of Physics at the High Scholl of Portici; Ermacora and G. Finzi, Doctors in Physics; Charles Richet, Professor of the Paris Medical Faculty, director of the scientific Review (for five terms); Lombroso, professor of the Faculty of Medicine of Turin (for two terms).

In this official report we find a narration of the following phenomena, which took place in the dark, the medium's hands and feet being constantly held by two of the audience:

> "Diverse objects, chairs, musical instruments, etc., moved without human contact; the imprint of fingers on clay; the apparition of hands against a luminous background; the apparition of phosphorescent lights; lifting of the medium on a table; chairs and their occupants being lifted; touches experienced by the spectators." Finally in a half light: Apparition of living human hands over the medium's head. Contact with a bearded face." (These last facts obtained in half-light)

In conclusion, the aforementioned witnesses declare that thanks to the precautions taken, no fraud was possible. They furthermore declare that, from what they had witnessed, there resulted "the triumph of a truth which had been rendered unjustly unpopular."

Concerning supernormal psychical manifestations, Professor Lombroso has more recently published in the Roman supplement, *Revista d'Italia*, the following important declaration: [99]

> "Among these demonstrations, one can quote levitation, i.e. the rising of the body without any effort on behalf

---
[99] Reprinted in Paris, 1904, March number of the "*Revue d'Etudes Psychiques.*"

of the person who lifts or of the one who is lifted; the motion of inanimate objects; and still more singularly, the manifestation of beings who are certainly in possession of a will and of a thinking capacity – bizarre and capricious as it may be – seemingly as though they were living human beings – sometimes they are even gifted with a prescience of future events. Having denied these, before I witnessed them, I found myself obliged to submit to evidence, when, in spite of myself, the most manifest and palpable demonstrations took place before my eyes. I do not deem myself obliged to deny what I cannot explain. Besides, as the laws governing the Hertzian waves very largely account for telepathy, thus the new discoveries on the radioactive properties of certain metals, especially radium, destroy the most serious objections of the scientist to mysterious spiritualistic manifestations. These discoveries certainly tend to prove that there may not only be short manifestations, but also a continuous development of enormous energy, of light and heat, without apparent waste of matter.

Professor Milesi, of the University of Rome, one of the most notable champions of the young Italian psychological school, known in France by his lectures on Auguste Comte at the Sorbonne, goes still further. He affixed his signature to the official records of the spirit materializations at which he assisted, among which was that of the apparition of his own sister, deceased some three years before, in Cremona.[100]

---

100 Read the "*Revue d'Etudes Psychiques,*" Paris, March, 1904, pg. 80.

More recently, professor Lombroso, while giving an account of his experiments in the Italian magazine "Arena," reported the following facts:

"After the transport of a very heavy object, Eusapia, in a state of trance, said to me: "Why do you waste your time with these trifles? I am able to show you your mother; but it is necessary that you concentrate intensely on her." Dominated by this promise, after half an hour of meeting had transpired, I was drawn by an intense desire to see it achieved. The table seemed to give its approval, with its usual movements of successive risings, to my intimate thought. Suddenly, under a half reddish light, I saw a short leaning form leaving from within the curtains, as had been that of my mother, covered by a glazed veil. She came around the table until she approached and stopped next to me, murmuring words that several people heard, but that my own particular hearing deficiency did not enable me to receive. Then, as if under the influence of a sharp emotion, I begged her to repeat their words. She then said to me: "Cæsar, fio mio!" what, I acknowledge that it was not her ordinary way of saying it. Indeed, being Venetian, she would have said: mio fiol; then, drawing aside her veil, she gave me a kiss."

Lombroso then points out the communications, written or spoken, in foreign languages, the revelations of unknown facts as well of the medium and of the assistants, and the facts about telepathy. And further states:

"It is advisable to add that the cases of haunted houses, in which, for many years, appearances or noises had been reproduced, concordant with the account of prior tragic deaths and observed by many without the presence of mediums, pleads against the exclusive action of those and in favor of the action of the departed"

20

Spiritism in France

France could not, like England, produce three members of the Academy who were believers in Spiritism. More than elsewhere the French scientists have shown themselves either indifferent or prejudiced where psychical manifestation is concerned. There are, however, some brilliant exceptions. Foremost amongst these stands the astronomer Camille Flammarion, whose enchanting style has popularized the science of the universe. His interest in occult science was shown in his discourse over the grave of Allan Kardec and later by his book on *"The Unknown and its Psychical Problems,"* which narrates 187 cases of apparitions and telepathic phenomena, most of which were coincidental with death.

Since 1887, Dr. Paul Gibier, a pupil of Pasteur, who later became a director of the institute of New York for the suppression of Rabies, has published two works – *"Spiritism, or Western Fakirs,"* and *"The Analysis of Things,"* in which he conscientiously studies and courageously asserts the reality of spirit manifestations.

Dr. Gibier, assisted by the medium Slade, has made a special study of direct writing on slates, to which he consecrated thirty-three séances. Numerous messages in several languages have been obtained on the inside of double slates, which the experimenter himself provided and sealed, one facing the other.

"We have observed these phenomena; he writes[101] so many times over and under such varied forms that we may state that we can no longer believe in anything of that which we see in every-day life, if we are not allowed to trust to our senses in this particular case."

In 1900, this same scientist dedicated to the International Official Congress of Psychology, assembled in Paris, a monograph relating the numerous materializations of apparitions observed in his own laboratory in New York, in the presence of several witnesses, in particular of the preparers who usually assisted it in his studies of biology.[102]

It is above all in the artistic and the literary world that we shall encounter a number of followers and defenders of the spiritual phenomena and of the doctrines connected with them. Among its many literary supporters we will mention the following writers: Eugène Nus, author of *"Les Grands Mystères and Choses de l'autre Monde;"* Vacquerie, whose tendencies are revealed in *"Miettes de l'Histoire;"* Victor Hugo, Maurice Lachâtre, Théophile Gautier, Victorien Sardou, C. Fauvety, Ch. Lomon, Eug. Bonnemère, Alexandre Hepp, etc.

Spiritist experimentation, in France, has almost invariably been conducted without support of the Academy, which doubtless accounts for the small encouragement it has received. From 1850 to 1860, table turning, to be sure, was in high favor, and no entertainment, great or small, was complete without it. But among all who frequented these assemblies and amused themselves with

---

101 « Le Spiritisme ou Fakirisme Occidental, » p. 340.
102 See the official report of the Fourth International Congress of Psychology (Paris, ed. P. Alcun, 1901, p. 675), reproduced *in extenso* in the *"Annales des Sciences Psychiques"* of Dr. Dariex, February, 1900).

the phenomenon, how few sought its scientific side or foresaw its great importance to humanity? People soon tired of consulting the spirits concerning trivial questions. The fashion of table turning lasted no longer than other fashions, and after a certain noted trial, Spiritism was discarded.

However, in the absence of official scientists in France, there has been at least one Frenchman who was to play a considerable and universal role in the advent of Spiritism.

Allan Kardec devoted ten years to experimentation, which he shrewdly and patiently conducted, following the positivist method. After collecting the data and depositions that poured in from all over the world, he classified this mass of evidence, deducing thereafter the general principles from which he formulated a body of doctrine that filled five volumes, the success of which has run, in some cases, into thirty editions.[103] Among these are: *"The Spirits' Book"* (philosophical), *"The Mediums' Book"* (scientific), *"The Gospel According to Spiritism"* (ethical), *"Heaven and Hell,"* and *"Genesis."*

Allan Kardec founded The *Spiritist Review* (La Revue Spirite), which became the representative organ and bond of the spiritualistic world and in which it is easy to follow the slow, progressive evolution of this scientific and ethical revelation.

Allan Kardec's work is therefore, and above all, a synopsis of what people, scattered over all parts of the world, have learned in the space of twenty years from the spirits.

In this teaching there is nothing supernatural, since spirits are beings similar to ourselves, who have lived on this Earth and will, most of them, return here to live again – beings who are governed by the same natural laws: who like us have a body, except that it is

---

103 Editor's Note: Over 100 editions until the year 2001

more ethereal than ours, and becomes tangible to us only under certain conditions.

As a writer, Kardec is both admirably clear and extremely logical. His deductions are invariably founded upon positive events, for which multitudes of witnesses can vouch. At his call, philosophy descends from the abstract heights of its domain, becoming simple, popular, and accessible to all. Stripped of its pompous robes, setting within the range of the humblest minds, it brings hope and comfort to those who seek and to those who suffer, by showing them that the grave is not the end of life.

This doctrine which Allan Kardec extends to us – a doctrine born, as we cannot too often repeat, of methodical observation and careful experimentation – cannot, however, be deemed a final and unchangeable system, beyond and above the future conquests of science. A blend of the knowledge of two worlds, the product of a fusion of two humanities, both imperfect and both struggling towards truth and the unknown, this doctrine of the spirits is ever changing with progress and knowledge, and however superior it may already be to all the philosophies of the past, it nevertheless stands ever open to receive the amendments and the enlightenment which the future must bring.

Since Kardec's death, Spiritism has already made a considerable advance by assimilating the fruit of forty years of research. The discovery of radiant matter, the cathodic rays, the subtle analysis to which English and American scientists have submitted the fluidic bodies, those perispiritual envelopes of forms in which the spirits are enveloped when they reveal themselves to the human beings – all this progress has opened new horizons to Spiritism. And into these Spiritism, boldly venturing, has made a profound study and having penetrated into the inner nature of the fluidic world, and can now struggle equally against any adversary upon this personally acquired field of science.

The spiritist congresses which met in Paris in 1889 and 1900 bear witness to the vitality of a doctrine which might well have been buried under an avalanche of irony and ridicule. Its meetings were attended by hundreds of delegates from all parts of the world; eighty papers and reviews were there represented. People of great learning and high standing – doctors, magistrates, teachers and even churchmen – of all nationalities – French, Spanish, Italians, Belgians, Swiss, Russians, Germans, Swedes – took part in the debates.

The members of the different schools that were represented in theses congresses – Spiritist, Theosophical, Occult, Swedenborgian, etc. – all unanimously agreed, without a single dissentient voice, to assert the two following principles:

(I) "The Persistence of the conscious Ego after death";
(2) Communication between the Living and the Dead."[104]

The spiritist congress of 1889, while arousing public interest, had already instilled the spirit of critical analysis, thus giving rise to a fresh impulse in scientific research and experimentation. A *Society of Psychical Research* was founded in Paris by Professor Charles

---

[104] The following declarations of faith were unanimously ratified by the International Spiritist and Spiritualist Congress, met in Paris in the year 1900: An acknowledgement of the existence of God, the Supreme Intelligence and First Cause of all things. The plurality of inhabited worlds. The soul's immortality; the succession of its corporeal lives upon this Earth and the other worlds of space. The experimental demonstration of the survival of the human soul, by means of the mediumistic communication with spirits. The happy or unhappy conditions of the human estate, as proceeding from the past episodes of the soul; its merits or demerits and the progress which it has achieved. The being's infinite progression. Universal and brotherly solidarity.

Richet, of the Academy of Medicine, and by Colonel de Rochas, then administrator of the Polytechnic School. His first care was to establish an investigating committee that would examine all apparitions and occurrences of an experimental psychological order that might be reported in France. A special magazine, "*Les Annales des Sciences Psychiques,*" under the direction of Dr. Dariex, has recorded its investigations, as well as those of foreign societies.

At Mr. Charles Richet's house, in the island of Roubaud, some séances, with the medium Eusapia Paladino, were held in 1894; while those held at M. de Rochas' home at Agnélas in 1895 obtained results identical with those of Milan, three years before.

The International Congress of Experimental Psychology, which met in London in 1892, showed what a profound modification this science had undergone in the past few years.

Mr. Charles Richet went straight to the heart of the new psychology, which includes spirit phenomena, telepathy, second sight, etc. In his prelude the eminent professor first proposes the following question:[105] "Has this occult psychology any true reality?" and then goes on to say:

> "*For us the matter is not questionable. It does exist! It is not possible that so many of the distinguished men of England, America, France, Germany, Italy, etc., should have erred so grossly and so completely. They had already weighed and considered every objection which has since been brought forth to weaken their conclusions; and in suggesting chance, or fraud, nothing has been suggested against which they were not already on their guard. It*

---

[105] In his monograph reprinted in the "*Annales des Sciences Psychiques,*" December, 1892.

appears to me highly improbable that their learned labors should all have proved sterile, or that their meditations, reflections and experimentations should have been wasted on vain illusions."

Mr. Richet reminded the Congress how frequently scientific academies have had cause to regret that they had denied, à priori, some of the greatest discoveries. He asked them not to commit once more the same mistake. Then he went on to show what powerful results, whether scientific or philosophic, might arise from the study of this new psychology, which is founded on fact.

In an article of the *Figaro*, 9th October 1904, entitled: *"Beyond Science,"* Mr. Richet went even further in his assertions:

"The occult world exists," he wrote. *"In spite of taking the risk of being considered by my contemporaries as a fool, I believe that there are phantoms."*

Since then some remarkable works have appeared in France concerning Spiritism and related matters; the works of Colonel de Rochas, Dr. Geley, Dr. Duphony and of Mr. Maxwell, Prosecuter at the Court of Appeals of Paris.

A psychological institute has been founded in Paris. Its first president was Dr. Duclaux, who was succeeded by M. D'Arsonval, Professor at the Collège de France. Its objects are the study of telepathy, suggestion and all mediumistic phenomena. Societies of psychical research have been founded at Nancy, Marseilles, Nice, Montpellier, Toulouse, and at many other places.

The psychic wave extending from town to town has now swept over the entire country. It is felt now in the highly educated environment. Certain representatives of the advanced science include all of its importance. Mr. Boutroux, professor with the Faculty of Arts of Paris, member of the Institute, wrote recently:

> "A broad, complete study of psychism does not offer only an interest of curiosity, even considering its scientific aspect, but also an interest directly related to the life and destiny of individuals and of humanity."

Dr. Duclaux, director of the Pasteur Institute, in a conference given at the Psychological General Institute, said:

> "I do not know if you are like me, but this populated world of influences which we undergo without knowing them, penetrated of this quid divinum that we guess without having the details of it, eh well! This world of psychism is a world more interesting than that in which our thought was confined up to now. Let us try to open it with our research. There are immense discoveries to be achieved, from which humanity will profit."

21

The Perispirit or Fluidic Body

In denying the soul's existence, materialists have often argued the difficulty of conceiving of a formless being. The spiritualists themselves could not well understand how an immaterial and imponderable soul could be closely united to, and command, a material body whose nature was essentially different. These difficulties have been solved by the discoveries of Spiritism.

As we have already state, the soul, during the life of the flesh as well as after its death, is ever enveloped in a fluidic envelope, which is more or less subtle and ethereal, and which Allan Kardec has denominated the "perispirit," or spiritual body. The perispirit acts as a mediator between the body and the soul; to the latter it imparts the impressions received by the senses, while to the body it transmits the will of the spirit. At the moment of death it detaches itself from tangible matter, abandoning the body to the decomposition of the grave; but being inseparable from the soul it ever remains the exterior form of its individuality.

The perispirit is therefore a fluidic organism – the pre-existent and surviving form of the human being; the general mold upon which the fleshly envelope is modeled, as an invisible garment, made of a quintessential matter that penetrates into all bodies, however impenetrable they may appear to us. [106]

Gross matter, which must be incessantly renewed by the vital circulation, is neither the stable, nor is it the permanent part of the human being. It is the perispirit that assures the maintenance of the human structure and of the physiognomic features, and this during the whole term of life, from the individual's birth to his death. It is the compressible and expansive mold upon which earthly matter is incorporated.

This fluidic body is not, however, immutable; it is uplifted and purified by the spirit. It follows the soul through its innumerable incarnations: with it, it ascends the rungs of the hierarchic ladder, becoming ever more diaphanous and brilliant, at last to shine with that dazzling brightness of which the Scriptures tell and which history has sometimes recorded concerning certain apparitions.

The perispirit preserves all that the living being has acquired. It is in the brain of this spiritualized body that knowledge is stored and imprinted in phosphorescent lines; and it is after this plan that, at reincarnation, the child's brain is formed. Thus the spirit's intellectual capital, far from being lost, is accumulated and increases with each of its lives. This accounts for the extraordinary aptitudes that some gifted and precocious beings display at an early age.

High thinking, pure living, a constant striving after the noble and the good, a patient endurance of trials and sufferings, all these things tend to refine the perispirit and to extend and multiply its vibrations. As if by chemical action, the grosser particles are thereby consumed, and only the more tenuously subtle are suffered to endure.

---

106 The existence of this subtle condition of matter has been scientifically demonstrated by the experiments of Le Born, Curie, Becquerel, etc., upon the radioactivity of matter.

Inversely, material appetites and all low and base cravings react upon the perispirit, weighing it down and rendering it denser and darker. Inferior worlds, such as the Earth, exert a strong attraction upon such organisms as they still partially preserve some of the cravings of the body, which they are unable to satisfy. When this is the case, incarnations follow one upon another in rapid succession until the progress through suffering mitigates their passions, shields them from terrestrial influences, and opens them the access of better worlds.

A close correlation unites the three constituent elements of the being. Proportionately to the elevation of the spirit, the perispirit becomes subtle, light and brilliant; the more exempt is the body from passion, the more marked are its moderation and asceticism. The soul's dignity and nobility are reflected in the perispirit, which becomes ethereal and assumes a more harmonious contour; it is even noticeable in the body, and the human countenance is illuminated by an inner radiance.

It is by more or less subtle fluids that the perispirit communicates with the soul and connects itself to the body. These fluids, though invisible, are powerful cables which connect the perispirit to matter; their action is exerted from birth till death, and even, in the case of sensual organisms, until complete dissolution has take place. The final agony represents the sum of effort required by the perispirit to emerge from its carnal bonds.

The nervous or vital fluid, of which the perispirit is the source, plays a considerable part in human's economy. Its existence and mode of action may supply the key to many a pathological problem. Acting as a transmitting agent, both for external sensations and for inner impressions, it resembles in this the telegraphic wire, which is a thought transmitter with a double current.

The existence of the perispirit was known to the ancients. *Ochémà* and *Feroe* (*férouer*), so the Greek and Oriental philosophers designated the envelope of the soul – lucid, ethereal, aromatic. According to the Persians, when the hour of incarnation has sounded the Feroe attracts and condenses about such material molecules as are necessary to form a body; then at death it gives them back to the elements, and in other surroundings gathers the materials for other carnal envelopes.

Christianity likewise shows indications of this belief. In his first Epistle to the Corinthians, Saint Paul says: *"It is sown a natural body; it is raised a spiritual body."* And again *"As there is a natural body, so there is a spiritual body."*

Although the fact of the existence of the perispirit has at various epochs been maintained, it was left to Spiritism to determine its precise nature and parts. Thanks to the experiments of Crookes and others we now know that it is through the perispirit that the phenomena of magnetism and Spiritism are accomplished. The spiritual body is a veritable reservoir of fluids that the soul sets in motion by the will. This same perispirit during sleep, whether natural or artificial, frees itself from the body and travels over great spaces with the power to hear and to observe, in the darkness of night as well as in the brightness of day, many things of which the body could not of itself be cognizant.

Thus it is evident that the perispirit possesses senses, which are akin to those of the body, only far superior. It sees, by a spiritual light unlike that of the stars – one which is imperceptible to the human vision, although the universe is filled with it.

The permanence of the fluidic body, after as well as before death, likewise solves the riddle of apparitions, and spirit materialization. In the free life of space the perispirit is in virtual possession of all the forces that appertain to the human organism; but it does not utilize them. As soon as the spirit is placed in the necessary conditions, that is, so soon as it can borrow from the medium the needful fluidic matter and vital force, it assimilates these and slowly assumes the outward appearance of earthly matter. The vital current begins to circulate and under the action of the borrowed fluid, the physical molecules group themselves according to the laws of the body – laws reproduced by the perispirit in all its essential features. Thus is the human body reconstituted and the organism fitted to fulfill its functions.

Photographs show us that this reconstructed body is identical with that which the same spirit animated during its earthly life. This, being an abnormal life, is perforce brief and evanescent; after a short cooperation, the elements that produced it must return to their respective sources.

22

The Mediums

The faculties of the perispirit, its possibilities of perception and liberation, though developed in certain subjects, can never be fully exerted during the period of incarnation – that is, during this earthly life, when the perispirit is too closely knit to the body. A prisoner in this dark and dense envelope, it can only move away from it at certain moments and under special conditions, its resources remain in a latent state, hence the feebleness of our memory, which is powerless to retrace the course of our past lives.

Returned to the spiritual life, the soul regains complete self-possession, and the perispirit recovers the fullness of its perceptions. The soul and the perispirit are henceforth free to exercise a combined action upon the fluids, and through these upon the human brain and system. Herein lies the secret of spirit manifestations; the magnetizer's influence over his subject is powerful enough to free the perispirit from the body and to suspend material life: in like manner, spirits, or disembodied souls, may, through the exercise of their will, direct magnetic currents upon human beings, influence their organism, and using them as intermediaries, establish a connection through them with other people. These intermediaries, who are especially adapted to spirit manifestation by the delicacy and sensitiveness of their nervous systems, are called *mediums*. Their aptitudes are many and various.

They are the sensitive, the clairvoyants, whose sight pierces the dense fog that for us obscures the ethereal world: who, as through a rift, perceive some faint glimpse of the heavenly life. To some is it even given to see spirits, and to hear their revelation of the higher laws.

It is true that we are nearly all of us mediums, but in a very varying degree. Many who are do not know it. There is no one in whom the good or evil influence of the spirits is not at work. We live in the midst of a vast and invisible multitude, silent and attentive witnesses of every least event of our lives, participating in spirit in our labors, our sorrows and our happiness. In this crowd are most of those that we have known on Earth, whose poor, worn, fleshy raiment we sorrowfully followed to its last resting-place. Relatives, friends, acquaintances, and enemies – all are present, attracted, whether by habit or memory, to the places and people with which they were familiar. This unseen multitude is forever observing, influencing, inspiring or advising us, without our knowledge; sometimes indeed, they persecute us, following us with their hatred and their vengeance.

Every writer has had his inspired hours, when thought would suddenly seem to glow with an unexpected radiance, when the words quickly flow from the pen. In hours of sorrow and despondency, which one of us has not felt himself comforted and sustained by some mysterious inner force? Inventors, those pioneers of progress, and all who struggle for the betterment of humanity, have they not likewise experienced the benefit of that invisible assistance which our precursors are able to render in the hour of need? These suddenly inspired writers and suddenly gifted inventors, are they not so many intuitive mediums, unconscious of their faculty? With others, the faculty of spirit communication is more clear-cut and pronounced. Some perceive that their hand is being directed by a strange agency and that the paper is being covered with advice and admonition: others, who abound in vital fluid, find that the table is stirring beneath their fingers, and obtain, by the resonance of the inanimate wood, communications which, albeit slower, are more precise and more impressive to the incredulous.

Others again, plunged by spirit influence in a magnetic sleep, abandon all control of their faculties to these invisible hosts, who use them to converse with their friends in the flesh, just as they would do during their own incarnation. Nothing is stranger or more awe-inspiring than to see those departed spirits in momentary possession of the delicate body of a woman or of a young girl. Spirits of the most diverse personalities – a priest, a servant girl, a working man – incongruously follow one another through this frail abode of borrowed flesh, each assuming the language and attitudes that characterized them during their earthly existence. [107]

Quite often, spirits that were near and dear to some in the audience will come to assert their reality and immortality and to impart encouragement and advice to those who still linger in this troublesome world, striving to fit them for the higher life, by showing them the supreme goal. Who will paint the emotions, the tears, the transports of those to whom has come, from the nethermost depths of space, a father, mother or wife, with loving words of comfort and encouragement!

Some mediums facilitate by their presence the phenomena of apparitions, or rather of spirit materialization, to use the recognized term. The spirits proceed by borrowing from the perispirit

---

107 See Léon Denis' « *Dans l'Invisible,* » *Spiritisme et Médiumnité,* first part.

of the medium a sufficient quantity of fluid which they assimilate by an act of will, condensing their own more tenuous fluidic body until it becomes visible and sometimes even tangible.

Some mediums have served as intermediaries in order that the spirits may, through them, transmit to the sick the magnetic effluvia that relieves and sometimes cures. This is one of the most useful and beautiful features of mediumship.

Many apparently inexplicable sensations arise from the occult action of the spirits. The presentiments, for instance, which warn us against misfortune or loss, are caused by fluidic currents directed by disincarnated beings upon their friends. Our body perceives these spirit tides, but seldom do we seek to analyze them. There is surely a rich harvest of high knowledge to be garnered in the field of mediumistic study and practice.

It is erroneous to consider the mediumistic faculty as a gift or privilege. Each of us, as we have said, bears within him the rudiments of mediumship which can be developed by practice. In this as in most other things, the will plays a large part. The capacities of certain celebrated mediums arise from the particularly flexible nature of their fluidic organization, which admirably lends itself to spirit action.

Almost all of the world's great missionaries, the reformers and the founders of religions, were powerful mediums in constant communion with the invisible ones, from which they received fertile inspiration. The entire life of such individuals bears witness to the existence of a spirit world and of its relationship with terrestrial humanity.

This explains the number of historical facts described as supernatural and marvelous which have been deemed fictitious or legendary. The existence of the perispirit and the laws of mediumship indicate the means by which, during a succession of ages, spirit action has been brought to bear on the human beings. Numa's Egeria, the dreams of Scipio, the familiar spirits of Socrates, of Tasso, of Jerome Cardan, the voices of Joan of Arc, the inspired folk of the Cevennes, the seers of Prévorst, and a thousand other similar instances lose, in the light of modern spiritualism, all of their mysterious and supernatural attributes.

These events, moreover, disclose to us the great law of solidarity that unites the humanity of the Earth to the humanities of space. Liberated from the restrictions of the flesh, the superior spirits find themselves free to lift the heavy curtain that hides the great truths. To them the eternal laws appear, released from those shadows that the miserable sophistry and self-seeking of the world have created. Inspired by a lofty ambition to quicken human's desire to rise, they have condescended to our level so that some communication might be established through those who are fitted by their perceptive and sensitive organism to serve as mediums. Thanks to these intermediaries they are enabled to collaborate, by their wisdom and counsel, in the moral progress of humanity.

Still, we fell compelled to remark, in a general way, that mediums, in our day, do not seem to be sufficiently impressed with the necessity of leading pure and blameless lives, if they would hold communion with the higher beings of space. In olden times the subjects – women preferably – were chosen at a tender age and carefully nurtured within the temples and sacred enclosures, far from all contamination, surrounded only by that which might inculcate a love for the good and the pure. Such were the Roman Vestals, the Sibyls of Greece and the Druidesses of the Isle of Sein. Through their intermediacy the gods and higher spirits were consulted, and the responses vouchsafed were generally precise.

Joan of Arc was also a medium of this description, directly receiving celestial inspiration. Nowadays, the conditions of purity and moral elevation are harder to realize. Many mediums are subjected to material, even to gross, influences and are inclined to use their faculties to a vulgar end. Hence the inferior character of certain manifestations, the lack of efficacious protection, the intervention of backward spirits.

23

The Evolution of the Soul and of the Perispirit

The secular interchange existed between spirits and human beings, confirmed and elucidated by recent spiritist experimentation, effectually demonstrates the survival of the being in a more perfect fluidic form.

This indestructible form, this companion and slave to the soul, this witness of its sufferings and struggles, participates in all its wanderings and with it rises and is purified. Formed in the nether regions, the perispiritual being slowly ascends the ladder of existences. At the beginning it is but a rudimentary creature, an unfinished sketch. Having attained to humanity it begins to show evidence of higher feelings; the spirit shines brighter and the perispirit glows with a new radiance. From life to life, as the faculties are enlarged, as the aspirations are clarified, the horizon of knowledge broadens and its wealth is enhanced by the acquirement of new senses. At the close of each incarnation the spiritual body spurns its fleshly tatters, like a butterfly speeding away from its chrysalis. The soul, whole and enfranchised, once more finds itself in its entirety, and on beholding the fluidic mantle which surrounds it, according to its appearance - whether radiant or bedraggled - it is enabled to compute its own condition.

As the oak preserves within itself the mark of its annual growth so does the perispirit, beneath its present aspect, keep an inner reckoning of the former lives, and of the transformations that it has successively undergone. These often forgotten vestiges rest in us: but as soon as the soul awakens them the hidden memories start into life, like so many witnesses that were scattered along the road over which we came.

The fluidic bodies of backward spirits are coarse, and impregnated with material emanations. Even after death they experience earthly wants and cravings. Cold, hunger and pain are still perceptible to the most materialistic of them. Obscured by human passions, their fluidic organism can vibrate but weakly and their perceptivity is proportionally limited. They know nothing of the life of space; all is steeped in darkness within and about them.

The pure soul, detached from bestial attractions, transforms its perispirit and makes it similar to it. The more subtle this spiritual body, the more intense will be its vibrations and the larger the scope of its perceptions and sensibility. It will then be ready for a life the like of which we can barely conceive. Into this it will enter with an ineffable joy and vibrate in unison with the majestic harmony of the infinite. This is the duty of the human spirit, and such its reward. By long and weary labors it must create new senses of unlimited delicacy and power; it must subdue the brutal passions; it must transform its gross envelope into a diaphanous and luminous form. This is the task that has been allotted to all beings and which all must pursue through the innumerable stages of the marvelous highway of eternal progress.

24

Ethical and Philosophical Consequences

The evidences of Spiritism are full with philosophical and ethical consequences. Fully and clearly do they meet those questions which have perplexed the cleverest brains of all ages; they solve the riddle of our mysterious and impenetrable inner nature and with it that of our destiny. Survival and immortality, hitherto a mere hope - aspirations towards a better state or brain concept - these may now be considered as established facts, as also that other fact of the communion between the living and the dead which follows as a logical consequence. Doubt is no longer possible; the human being is indeed immortal, and death is but another condition of life!

From this certitude, and from what the spirits have revealed, we moreover acquire the assurance of the plurality of our terrestrial existences. This evolution which persists through the ever renascent lives of a being who, whether struggling in inferior existence or partaking of the felicities of happier humanities, remains, throughout all, the artisan and builder of his own destinies; the identity of origin and purpose of all people; the gradual improvement, fruition of work accomplished and of ordeals encountered - these all exemplify the eternal principles of justice, order and progress which rule the world, and ordain the destiny of the soul according to wise, profound and universal laws.

Spiritism is then, at once a moral philosophy and a positive science. It can satisfy both reason and heart. It reveals itself to the world at the very hour when the religious conceptions of the past are tottering upon their pedestals - at a time when humanity, having lost the simple faith of olden days and with skepticism gnawing at its heart, is aimlessly wandering in the gloom, blindly groping his way. The advent of Spiritism, is, let us not be blind to the fact, one of the greatest events in the world's history.

Some nineteen centuries ago, upon the ruins of a foundering paganism in the bosom of a corrupt society, Christianity, lifting a supplicating and despised voice, brought as a gift to the worthless world not only a new morality and a new faith, but likewise the revelation of two principles hitherto unknown - charity and human fraternity. Similarly today, in the face of doctrines weakened and petrified by material interest and powerless to enlighten the human mind, a rational philosophy starts into life bearing a germ of social transformation, a means of regenerating humanity by ridding it of the elements of a decomposition which is fast debasing it and rendering it impotent. It brings to faith a solid basis: to morality a sanction: to virtue, an inducement. It makes progress the goal of life and the higher law of the universe. It puts an end to the reign of favoritism, of arbitrariness, of superstition, by showing that the elevation of the human being is the product of that being's individual efforts. In teaching that an absolute equality and a close solidarity unite people throughout the course of their collective lives, it strikes a vigorous blow at pride and selfishness - those tow monsters that nothing, so far, had seemed able either to subdue or to crush.

25

Spiritism and Science

The phenomena of Spiritism, so significant because of its scientific results and ethical consequences, have not attracted all the interest it deserves. As we have remarked before, the individual, so often misled, has become skeptical and suspicious. However, this reception can appear strange as it may seem proceeding from those very scientists whose mission consists in studying all the phenomena and to ascertain their law and cause, will not surprise those who have studied human nature and remember the lessons of history.

The new is always alarming; it undermines cherished theories and revered systems that cost much to construct; it blasts established reputations and causes much disquietude, compelling a research and observation now grown irksome.

Scientists are people, and as such have their prejudices and failings. It takes true heroism to remain impartial respecting matters that inflict a denial to the work of a lifetime and to blast a hardly won fame.

Like all discoveries, Spiritism was to receive the baptism of trial and humiliation. Almost all new ideas, and especially the most fertile, have been scorned, reviled, and rejected as utopian at their inception. The discoveries of steam and electricity were long deemed fallacious, and even so was it with the making of railroads. Initially, the Academy of Medicine pushed back Harvey's theory of the circulation of the blood, as it pushed back magnetism later. While the Paris Medical Academy was asserting that there was no such thing as magnetism, the Vienna Academy was prohibiting its practice as dangerous. With what ridicule did the learned men, but a little time ago, assault the discoveries of Boucher de Perthes, the creator of prehistoric anthropology, today a recognized science which sheds a bright light upon the origin of Human societies?

All who have striven to rid humanity of its shackles of ignorance, by disclosing the secrets of natural forces and moral laws – all the pioneers of progress have had a Calvary for their reward, and upon them have gall and abuse been thrust. Galileo was thrown into prison; Giordano Bruno was burned; Watt, Fulton and Papin were reviled; Salomon de Caus was locked up for a madman. People nowadays are no longer imprisoned, burned, nor judicially pursued for a matter of opinion, but irony and sarcasm still remain a favorite mode of torture. Some ideas have required a tremendous fund of vitality that they might prevail despite the plotting of priests and scientists. But ideas, like people, thrive on suffering. Sooner or later, despite all anathemas, truth will prevail.

After having evoked these painful memories and to have considered the successive probing of the thought, by recalling us to the reception made in the past to ideas, related to the discoveries which centuplicated the power of the human, assured his triumph outer blind nature; after having recalled the reactions of the spirit of a routine being drawn up against the innovators, aren't we in the position to request from the detractors of Spiritism a little reflection before condemning without thorough examination, we will not say ideas, free speculations of the spirit, but of the facts about the observation and the experiment?

Each step shows the individual how little he knows. Our scientific conquests are but provisional glimpses, superior, it may be, to the science of our fathers, but which in their turn will be supplanted by new discoveries and fresh knowledge. The present epoch is but a stage in the great journey of humanity, a speck in the history of the generations. The utopia of yesterday becomes the reality of tomorrow. One may glory in having contributed to the intellectual acquisitions of the past, but one must never say: *"That which I do not know will never be known."* Let us compare the modest realm of science to the great infinite, to the limitless fields of the unknown, that still are spread before us awaiting discovery. This comparison may teach us to become more circumspect in our conclusions.

26

The Dangers of Spiritism

Among the experimenters of Spiritism there are those who, with an aim of control, undertook to regulate the conditions under which the phenomena were to occur; so much so, that by heaping objection upon objection, they made it impossible to obtain satisfactory results and thereupon became hostile to this order of phenomena.

We would remind such persons that spirit messages cannot be treated like experiments of chemistry and physics, though even these are subject to certain rules outside of which no result is possible.

In the case of spirit manifestations we stand in the presence not of blind force, but of intelligent beings who are both free and willful, and who, reading our minds and finding them perchance inimical, may feel but little inclined, if they be truly superior spirits, to become the sport of our fantasies.

The study of the spiritual world demands much wisdom and perseverance. It is only after years of reflection and observation that we learn to know people, to judge of their characters, to avoid those ambushes with which the world is strewn; still more difficult is it to know that invisible humanity which is around and above us. The disincarnated spirit is, after death, what it made of itself in its earthly sojourn – neither better nor worse. More than one lifetime is often necessary to curb a passion, to correct a defect, to eradicate a vicious tendency.

It is therefore natural that the serious minded and thoughtfully disposed should be in the minority – in the spirit as in the earthly world – and that the thoughtless, who are forever busy with vain and puerile things, should constitute the immense majority. The invisible world is then the reproduction, on a vast scale, of the terrestrial world. There, as here, truth and science are not a universal heritage. Moral and intellectual superiority are acquired at the price of slow and unremitting labor, by the accumulation of the improvement amassed in the course of a long sequence of centuries.

We know, however, that this occult world constantly reacts upon the corporeal world. The dead influence the incarnates, guiding and inspiring them; though the incarnates know it not. Souls attract one another by reason of their affinity. Those who have shed their garments of flesh come to the assistance of those that are still encumbered with them. They encourage them in the path of righteousness; but often also do they lead astray.

The superior spirits manifest themselves only when their presence may be useful and conducive to our amelioration. They avoid all noisy gatherings and communicate only with the pure of heart. They dislike our dark atmosphere, and return, as quickly as possible to regions less charged with coarse fluids; still, regardless of distance, they continue to keep watch over their wards.

The inferior spirits, who are incapable of high aspirations, feel at home in our atmosphere. They mingle with our lives, and solely preoccupied with that which captivated their thoughts during their bodily existence, they take part in the pleasure and labors of those people to whom they feel drawn by similarity of habit or character. Sometimes even they subjugate and dominate weak people, who are unable to resist their influence. In some cases their empire has been such as to drive their victims to crime or madness. Such cases of obsession and possession are more common than we think. Herein must be sought an explanation of many of the terrible crimes of history.

It would be dangerous to yield oneself unreservedly to spirit experimentation. The person whose heart is pure and whose reason is sound and enlightened can gather in them ineffable consolations and precious teachings. But the one who seeks only material benefit or amusement would undoubtedly become the object of endless mystification, the toy of perfidious spirits who would, by subtle flattery and alluring promises, gain his confidence, then overwhelm him with taunts and disappointments

It is therefore necessary to use much prudence before entering into communication with the invisible world, in which good and evil, truth and error, are mingled – to discern between which, all revelations and all teaching must be sifted through the fine sieve of criticism. In this region we can proceed but step by step. That evil influences may be driven away, that the troop of frivolous or malignant spirits may be set to flight, it suffices to remain master of oneself, never resigning the right to analyze and examine, seeking always and above all to grow more perfect through the study of the higher laws and the practice of virtue. The one whose life is pure, and who seeks truth with a sincere heart has no cause to fear. The spirits of light see into him, read his intentions and come to his assistance. Treacherous and lying spirits fly from righteousness, as troop of partisans disperse before a well-defended citadel. The spirits of obsession seek their prey in the frivolous people who shun morality in their quest after pleasure and amusement.

Almost invariably, there are ties, formed in previous existences that unite the obsessed to their invisible persecutors. Death does not wipe out our misdeeds, nor does it deliver us from our enemies. Our iniquities revert to us for centuries, and those that have suffered from them, pursue us beyond the tomb with their hatred and vengeance. Thus ordains sovereign justice. Everything may be redeemed and expiate; that which, in cases of obsession and possession, appears monstrous and iniquitous, is often only the consequence of some act of infamy and barbarism perpetrated in a remote past.

27

Charlatanism and Venality

The perfidiousness of malevolent spirits is not the only peril that besets Spiritism; it encounters other dangers, and these proceed from the human being. Venality and charlatanism, more redoubtable than the most pronounced hostility, may overwhelm and stifle the new doctrines, as they have overwhelmed most of the faiths that the world has held. Spontaneous and morbid products of a corrupt society, they grow and flourish almost universally, and their growth is favored by the ignorance of the masses. Many false mediums and all manner of impostors, have already sought to make capital out of Spiritism. Magnetism, as we have seen, is no longer safe from these charlatans, and this is undoubtedly one of the reasons for which scientists have so long distanced themselves from the study of these phenomena.

Still the very fact that there are imitations should rather tend to demonstrate the existence of the genuine product. Because conjurers call themselves physicians, should one argue physics unworthy of study? Trickery and knavery are the inevitable accompaniments of an inferior human society. Ever watchful for an opportunity of profiting at the expense of credulity, these ubiquitous rascals compromise the noblest enterprise and cast suspicion upon the purest intentions.

Most perilous is the tendency of some to trade in mediumship – to enrich oneself by the exercise of real faculties, but of a variable character. As the occurrence of phenomena arises from the voluntary action of spirits, we cannot count on their permanent and regular intervention, nor can high spirits lend themselves to stoop to such sordid motives. The least therefore that one may expect in such cases is to fall beneath the influence of frivolous and trifling spirits. The paid medium, in the absence of genuine phenomena, will inevitably be induced to simulate it.

To allow the notion of money to enter into the realm of such high ideas is to lessen their moral value, for the love of gold corrupts the most steadfast. Catholicism has lost many followers since the humble disciples of the Gospel were transformed into followers of Plutus. If Spiritism were to become mercantile and distribute its consolations at a price, how speedily would its influence weakened, how slow and individual would its progress become, instead of being rapid and universal as it actually is?

But ignorance is not a lesser evil. Many who seek and obtain manifestations, devoid of exact notions, lacking in all essential knowledge on the questions of fluids, of perispirit, of mediumship, confound and misrepresent all things by their false interpretations. By dint of their misinterpretation, everything becomes confused and distorted with the result that spiritist research is brought into disrepute, and the skeptical are convinced that it is altogether illusory and vain. It is hard to overcome ignorance, whose errors and blunders often strike deeper than truth itself. There is no doctrine or principle that ignorance has left unscathed, nor a truth that it has not falsified and obscured.

In spite of prejudice and ignorance, in spite of the hostility that it has encountered, Spiritism, born of yesterday, has already made giant strides. Fifty years ago he scarcely stammered his first words; today its voice resounds over the whole world, and its followers are counted today by millions, among them are several of the undisputed masters of science. Such progress denotes an unprecedented vitality, and, faced with the accomplished facts, indifference is no longer appropriate.

Notwithstanding all this, if we look closely into the matter we shall find not only the germs of these diseases, but likewise some incipient division, such as differences of opinion and rivalry between the different groups. Quite often do we meet with antagonism and internal discord instead of that harmony and order which we should expect. Nineteen hundred years ago, Christ warned us: *"I am come not to bring peace but a sword."* Thus has it ever been here below. Everything in contact with human weakness becomes infected with contention and disaffection.

While deploring this state of affairs it is comforting to see that in the face of rivalry and controversy the fundamental idea still continues to develop and advance. Human beings, the tools of a day, may pass away and with them their interests and ambitions and all such vain and fugitive things: but truth, the divine spark of which they were vouchsafed a distant glimpse, will expand into a mighty flame. Ever glowing, ever mounting, it will ultimately become a dazzling star whose light will descend with beneficent force upon this backward and hesitating humanity.

28

The Utility of Psychological Research

Considering the essentially rational character of Spiritism, the accusations of "supernaturalism" and "empiricism" seem puerile.

We cannot too strongly emphasize this point. The genuineness of spirit manifestation has been vouched for as we have seen, by individuals of undoubted competence. Their decision has been given only after much patient research. The effects being unquestionably proven, it becomes imperative to ascertain their cause; if this cause has been found to proceed from spirit intervention, we may rest assured that it is because the very nature of these phenomena has not allowed of any other interpretation. But it does not therefore follow that these occurrences must be classed in the realm of the supernatural – nothing, indeed, would be more contrary to common sense. The supernatural does not, and cannot, exist. Law governs everything in the universe.

To demonstrate the existence of a phenomenon is to class it in the permanent order of things – to subject it to natural law. In this vast universe, where all beings and every created thing are interdependent and united, like the links of an endless chain, there is space neither for the supernatural nor for the miraculous. Laws, as rigid and inflexible as those that govern matter, rule the invisible world. To understand the admirable mechanism of these laws there is but one way, the patient study of them.

What indeed could be more prolific than this study of the spirit world, in spite of all the difficulties that attend it? It discloses to the mind a thousand unexplored paths: teaching us to know ourselves, to probe into the most hidden recesses of our being, to analyze our sensations, to measure our faculties, and therefore the better to apply them. But, above all, it is the science of life —of the life of the soul, not only in its earthly state, but also in its successive transformations through time and space.

Experimental spiritualism may become a means of reconciliation, a bridge, between the two hostile systems of metaphysical spiritualism and materialism, which have been fruitlessly bickering and fighting for so many hundred of years. For Spiritism has adopted the principles of the first, shedding light upon them and giving them a solid basis; it conciliates the second, by proceeding according to scientific methods and by showing the perispirit, a fluidic semi-material body, to be the cause of numerous physical and biological phenomena. It goes still farther, it provides science with the philosophical synthesis and ethical point of view that materialism lacked, and without which it was powerless to affect social life.

Science, or rather the sciences, devote themselves to a partial or fragmentary study of nature. The progress in physics, chemistry and zoology is immense, their achievements are worthy of all admiration; there is, however a noticeable lack of unity and cohesion between the several branches of science. Knowing of only one side of life, the gross external side, and from this attempting to formulate a conception of the laws of the universe, the science of our day, which is after all only a cut and dried classification of material facts, concludes in a purely mechanical theory of the world, since, by its logical deductions, it is forced ultimately to decide that, nature force reigns supreme.

Hence it is that science has been powerless to exert any salutary moral influence. So far, deprived of any comprehensive or universal outlook, it has been unable to deduce from its accumulated store of learning, that superior conception which alone is able to affirm the destiny of the human being, to designate his duties and to supply him with the principle of individual and social improvement.

But this new conception which coordinates the branches of special knowledge, which cements its divergent elements, imparting to them harmony and unity; this moral law, so necessary to social life and progress – Spiritism brings them to science with the philosophical synthesis which must centuplicate its power.

The mission of Spiritism is tremendous and its moral consequences are incalculable. It is born of yesterday, yet with what treasures of hope and comfort has it not already endowed the world? To how many cold and sad hearts has it not brought warmth and cheer, how many desperate wayfarers has it not halted upon the road to suicide! When rightly understood, its teachings will alleviate the keenest affliction, and strengthen the heart against the direst onslaughts of adversity.

Spiritism is therefore not only a powerful synthesis of the physical and moral laws of the universe, but also a means of regeneration and progression; unhappily it is known to too few as yet. Most people spend their lives in a frantic race after imaginary wealth. Onward they hurry and flurry, fearing to waste time over subjects they deem superfluous – whereas, in reality, they are wasting it in the pursuit of vain and ephemeral things. The human being, in his blindness, disdains that which would bring to him all the happiness this world affords: the happiness of benefiting others and of surrounding himself with an atmosphere of peace and meditation.

Fourth Part
The Hereafter

29

Know Thyself

The human being, as we have seen, is a complex being. In him three elements combine to form a living unity. These three are:

The *body*, a temporary material envelope, which at death we discard like a worn-out garment.

The *perispirit*, a permanent fluidic envelope, imperceptible to our actual senses, that accompanies the soul in its travels and with it is ameliorated and purified.

The *soul*, the intelligent principle, center of force, and seat of conscience and individuality.

These three elements – matter, fluid and intelligence – closely united within us to constitute life, are to be found at the base of the universal order, of which they are the component parts, the fundamental substance. Thanks to them the human being is a compendium of the universe; a microcosm containing like forces and submitted to like laws. Thus we are led to believe that a perfect knowledge of our being would bring us, by analogy, to the comprehension of the superior laws of the universe; but a perfect understanding of the human being has so far eluded the most perspicacious minds.

The soul, disengaged from the material body and encased within its subtle envelope, constitutes the spirit: a fluidic being of human form, enfranchised from earthly restrictions, invisible and impalpable in its normal state. The spirit is therefore only a disincarnate person; each of us, at his hour, again becomes spirit. Turn by turn, death takes us back to the life of space; them comes birth to restore us to this material world, again to resume the battle of life, a struggle essential to our improvement. The body might be compared to the armor that a knight wears before battle and which he removes when the fight is over.

The fact of the survival being experimentally established by spirit manifestations, it remains for us to learn what manner of life the soul leads after death and what is its position in the realms of space. To this great problem, we consecrate the fourth part of this volume, drawing our inspiration from preceding works and from those innumerable spirit communications that, coming to us from all quarters of the world, have revealed the happiness and sorrows of the life beyond the grave.

This exposition is therefore by no means to be mistaken for the conclusions of some imaginative theory or for the lucubration of a more or less plausible hypothesis, but as the veritable outcome of genuine revelations given by the spirits. Thanks to them, the future life, hitherto full of uncertainty and obscurity for the human being, becomes enlightened and becomes a reality; all of us can see, by the example of those who have preceded us, the respective positions that we are likely to occupy.

The scope of this revelation is great indeed. It imparts to all our acts a fresh impulse. In the different positions allotted to the spirits, according to their merits, we see the enactment of the law of justice, a law that we may no longer question. In its secret way and by a sublimely simple arrangement of all things, it rules the entire universe and everything that is therein. The knowledge of this satisfies our reason and renders more bearable the woes of this life by strengthening our faith in the life beyond.

30

The Last Hour

What occurs at the moment of death, and how does the spirit free itself from its prison of the flesh? What impressions and what sensations await it at this dread time? This is what we should all like to know since we must, each one of us, undergo this ordeal. Tomorrow, life may desert us, from death none of us can escape.

Happily, spirits in great numbers have come to enlighten us, where religion and philosophy had left us in ignorance. They teach us that the sensations which precede and follow death are infinitely varied, and depend, above all, upon the character, merits and moral elevation of the departing spirit. The separation is almost invariably slow and the extrication of the soul takes place very gradually. Sometimes it begins a long while before death sets in, and is only complete when the last fluidic ties that unite the body to the perispirit are sundered. The impression experienced by the soul is the more painful and prolonged as these ties are stronger and more numerous. The soul, permanent cause of life and sensation, experiences all the commotion and all the rending of the material body.

Painful to some and full of anguish, to others death comes like a sweet slumber followed by an enchanting awakening. Disengagement is quick, the crossing is easy, to him who is already detached from the things of this world, who has fulfilled his duties and aspires to spiritual life. On the other hand, a prolonged agony and struggle await the spirit attached to the things of the Earth that has courted only material pleasure, neglecting to prepare for its irrevocable journey.

In any event, however, the separation of soul and body is followed by a period of trouble, brief for the righteous and good spirit, who soon awakens to all the beauties of the heavenly life but which is very long - sometimes spanning years - for the culpable souls, impregnated with coarse fluids. Long after death many of these still deem themselves to be living the life of the body. They mistake the perispirit for another carnal body, subjected to the same habits and sometimes even to the same physical sensations as during the earthly life.

Other spirits, of an inferior order, awake to find themselves steeped in darkness; alone, in the deepest gloom, they are overcome by terror and uncertainty. Criminals are tormented by the awful and constant vision of their victims.

The hour of separation is a cruel one for the spirit of him who believes in annihilation. He clings desperately to this life which is slipping away from him. At the supreme moment doubt overwhelms him; he sees fearful world opening like a abyss at his feet, and would like to delay the beginning of his fall. Out of this there arises a terrible struggle between failing matter and the soul that is desperately bent on retaining its hold upon its miserable body. Sometimes, as if riveted to it, it hangs on until decomposition has entirely set in: and feels - to borrow the expression used by a spirit - "the worms gnawing at its flesh."

Peaceful, resigned and joyful is the passing of the just spirit; it is the departure of a soul which, having greatly striven and suffered much here below, leaves the Earth, full of faith and trust in that which awaits it. Death, the deliverer, comes like a pledge against further trial. The feeble bonds that still unite this soul to matter are readily cast off: its only sensation is of a slight numbness, like sleep.

The spirit, purified by pain and sacrifice, sees its past recede, and sink further and further into remoteness with all its bitterness and vain illusions, until finally it vanishes, like the mists that crawl on the ground at dawn and fade away with the coming of the sun. The spirit then finds itself in suspense between two sensations: that of the material world, which is vanishing, and that of the unknown life which is arising before it. This new life it already perceives, dimly, as through a mist – full of mysterious charm, dreadful yet desirable. Soon the light grows greater – not the familiar solar rays, but a spiritual, omnipresent radiance. Slowly it bathes and penetrates the spirit, and with it comes a sensation of happiness, a blending of youth, strength and serenity. The spirit joyfully plunges into this rejuvenating flood, and in it leaves all fear and uncertainty. Soon thereafter, it feels able to detach its gaze from the Earth; from the weeping friends who surround its deathbed, and to look upwards. Above it are the vast heavens and in them other beloved beings, the friends of yore– younger, more beautiful and more alive than ever on Earth – who are come to greet and to guide this spirit through the realms of space. With these it speeds on and ascends, until it has attained such ethereal regions as its degree of purity allows. Here its troubles are at an end: new faculties awake and its happy destiny begins.

The entrance into the new life evokes a great variety of sensations which are graduated according to the degree of excellence of the spirit. Those, and they are many, whose life has gone undecided, marked neither by misdeeds nor by merits, at first find themselves overcome by a state of torpor and of profound depression; then comes a shock that violently perturbs their being. The spirit slowly leaves its envelope. Finally it discovers itself to be free; but timid and hesitating it dares not make use of its freedom, and remains, rooted by fear and by habit, in the spot where it had dwelt. It continues to weep and suffer with those who shared its life. Time passes, unmeasured by the outcast spirit, until other spirits come to soothe and advise it, when it finally manages to separate from its last earthly bonds and to rise into brighter regions.

In a general way the liberation of the soul is less painful after a long illness, which has the effect of gradually loosening the carnal bonds. Sudden and violent death, occurring when the organic life is in full flow, causes a painful rending of the soul and casts it into a state of prolonged commotion. Suicides fall a prey to horrible sensations. For years they endure the anguish of the last hour, and discover with terror that they have exchanged their earthly sufferings for others that are worse.

The knowledge of the spiritual future and the study of the laws that govern disincarnation are of much benefit in preparing us for death. They may render our last hours easier, facilitate our liberation and enable us to place ourselves more readily in that new world which opens to us.

31

The Judgment

A law as simple in principle as it is admirable in effect presides over the grouping of the souls in space.

The more subtle and rarefied the constituent molecules of the perispirit, the quicker the disincarnation and the broader the horizons that are opened to the spirit. By reason of its fluidic weight and affinities, it rises to meet those celestial groups which are similar to it. Its very nature and degree of purity determine its level and the place where it belongs. The relative elevation attained by the spirits has been quaintly compared to balloons which, being inflated with gas of varying density, rise, proportionately to their specific gravity, to different elevations. But we must hasten to add that the spirit, far from being condemned to remain in one spot, is free to move and to traverse, within certain limits, the ethereal regions. It is freely empowered to modify its tendencies, to transform its nature, by suffering and trial, and consequently to elevate itself as it wills in the scale of beings.

It is then a natural law analogous to those of gravitation and attraction, which decrees the destiny of the soul after death. The impure spirit, weighed down by material fluids, remains confined to the lower strata of the earthly atmosphere; whereas the virtuous soul, whose envelope is purified and subtle, joyfully speeds, rapid as thought, into the infinite azure.

The recompense or chastisement of the spirit proceeds from its own conscience; it comes from within and not from without. The spirit is its own judge. When the vestment of flesh has fallen away, the light penetrates and the soul is laid bare; then within it there appear, clear-cut as a living picture, all its deeds, thoughts and desires. Truly a solemn moment: an introspection full of anguish, often of disillusion. Memories in throngs start forth as the entire life slowly unrolls, with its train of errors, weaknesses and pain. From infancy to death, everything – thoughts and words and actions – springs forth from out of the fostering shadow, becomes animate and lives again. The being sees himself and reviews, one by one as they occurred, his past existences – his falls, his ascents, his innumerable faults. He computes the stages accomplished measures the distance covered, compares the good and the bad done.

At his call, like so many phantoms from out of the depths of an obscure past, arise the forms that his soul had assumed in the course of its successive lives. His memory sees the long vista of the past ages which now appear as clear as a startling vision; he stands appalled before the many gloomy, bloody, passionate and sad scenes of crime and sacrifice they display. In it he discovers the reason for such progress as he has accomplished, for the atonement he has made, for the condition in which he now finds himself. He perceives his past lives as rings upon an endless chain that continuously unwinds through successive centuries. The past, to his understanding, explains the present and the present forecasts the future. This is the spirit's hour of great moral torture.

This evocation of the past entails the dread sentence: the judgment of his own conscience, which is, in a manner, the judgment of God. Painful though this self-examination may be, it is necessary, for it may form the basis of a new resolve which will lead to regeneration.

The soul's degree of purification, the position it occupies in space, represent the sum total of its progress and give the measure of its value. Such is the unerring sentence that decrees its fate, beyond appeal. Profound harmony! Marvelous simplicity, which no human institution could reproduce; the principle of affinity ordaining all that is in the heavens, and assigning to each his place! There is neither judge nor jury; nothing but immutable Law executing its own just sentences through the natural play of spiritual forces, and according to the use to which they are put by the free and responsible soul.

As we will explain later, every thought has a form, and this shape created by the will is photographed in us, as in a mirror, in which reflections would imprint themselves. Our fluidic envelope reflects and preserves like a register, all the facts of our existence. This register is closed during life. The flesh is the thick cover which hides its contents from us; but at death, it slowly opens, and its pages are spread before our eyes.

The disincarnate spirit thus bears within it, visible to all, its heaven or its hell. The undeniable proof of its elevation or degradation is written on its fluidic body. Our deeds and intentions are the harsh or kindly witnesses that justify or condemn us, and nothing can still their voices, which are raised to the confusion of the evil minded who thought his unclean desires and ignoble deeds securely hidden, and who now sees them plainly revealed to all. Hence his remorse, when before him ceaselessly defiles the procession of his wasted and barren years, of the hours given over to sin and debauchery, or the victims of his brutal instincts. Hence also the happiness of the pure spirit, who had subjugated passion and consecrated his life to the service of others.

To distract himself from his worries, from his moral preoccupations, the person has work, study, and sleep. The mind no longer has these resources. Once liberated from the bonds of the body, he finds himself ever face to face with the truthful and living picture of his past. The bitter and continual regrets which most often arise from this contemplation, soon awaken in him the desire again to enter into a human body, that he may once more struggle and suffer and finally atone for this accusing past.

32

The Will and the Fluids

The knowledge the spirits have imparted to us concerning their condition after death, gives us some notion of the manner in which the fluidic body is transformed and of the progress of the soul.

As we have already stated[108] the same force that impels the being, likewise incites it through a parallel and similar action to perfect its faculties and to create new methods of action, appropriate to its fluidic, intellectual and moral capacity.

The fluidic envelope of a purified spirit is lightened or darkened according to the refined or gross nature of the thoughts which are reflected in it. Every act and every thought makes itself felt by the perispirit and is imprinted within it. This causes inevitable modifications in the condition of the spirit itself. The spirit exerts a continuous action upon its envelope, the condition of which it is able to alter by an effort of volition.

The will is the sovereign faculty of the soul – the supreme spiritual force above all others. It is the very foundation of individuality. Its power over the fluids is unlimited and increases with the elevation of the soul. In earthly surroundings its effect on matter is limited, because the human being, ignoring himself, does not know

---
108 See Chapter XXIII

how to utilize the powers that are in him; but in the more advanced worlds the being who has learned to desire, commands the whole of nature, directing at his pleasure the material fluids and having the power to effect astounding transformations. Through space and upon these higher worlds, matter exists in a fluidic state of which only the recent discoveries in radio-activity can give us a notion. As certain chemical combinations are produced on this planet by the mere influence of light, so in those other far-distant worlds the fluids are united and held together by an act of the will of superior beings.

The action of the will on matter now belongs to the domain of experimental science, thanks to the study of magnetic phenomena pursued by a number of physiologists under the names of hypnotism or mental suggestion. By a direct act of volition, the experimenter has caused wounds and stigmas to appear on the body of the subject, and blood and matter to flow – afterwards healing the subject by a contrary volition. Thus is the will of the individual empowered to destroy and to heal living tissues; it can even modify material substances so far as to impart new properties to them, to the point of provoking drunkenness with clear water, etc. It exercises the same action upon the fluids, creating objects that those in a hypnotic state can see, smell and touch, and which moreover possess for the hypnotized a positive being, obedient to all the laws of optics. This is clearly evidenced by the researches of medical men, such as Charcot, Dumontpallier, Liébault, Bernheim and of professors such as Liégeois, Delboeuf, and others, whose monographs have appeared in all medical journals.

If then the will obtains such influence over brute matter and rudimentary fluids, we can all the better comprehend its power over the perispirit and the benefits or perturbations it may confer upon the latter according to the nature of its action – during this life as well as after death.

Every act of the will, we have stated, assumes a fluidic form or appearance, and imprints itself upon the perispiritual envelope. It is evident that if these acts are inspired by material passions, their form will be gross and material. The perispirit, impregnated and saturated with such forms and pictures, is materialized by their contact, and grows ever denser. The same causes being reproduced, the same effects are accumulated; the condensation is accelerated, the perceptions are weakened, and the vibrations diminish in force and length.

At death, the spirit finds itself enveloped by opaque and heavy fluids that no longer permit the impressions of the exterior world to enter, and which become the prison and the grave of the soul. Such is the punishment that the soul has brought upon itself. This condition is indeed its own handiwork; it will only cease when higher aspirations, repentance and a determination to amend, return freedom to him.

If brutish and passionate instincts darken the fluidic system, generous thoughts and noble deeds exert a contrary action, refining and dilating the perispiritual fluids. We know that as matter is purified, some of its properties are increased. Crookes' experiments have demonstrated that the rarefaction of atoms converts them to a radiant state. In this subtle state matter becomes inflammable, luminous and imponderable. Even so is it with the perispiritual substance which is a degree more quintessential than matter. It gains in elasticity and sensitiveness in the process of rarefaction; its power of radiation and its vibratory energy are in a like measure increased; thus is it enabled to escape terrestrial attraction. The spirit then enters into possession of its new faculties, through which it gains access to a purer and more ethereal environment. These faculties, which are the key to the happy regions, any human soul may acquire and cultivate, for their undying germs are contained in the soul. Our successive lives, so full of labor and effort, have indeed no other object than the fruition of these germs.

This parallel evolution of matter and spirit by which the being obtains dominion over its senses and faculties —becoming in a sense its own creator and unremittingly adding-on to itself – gives us further evidence of the intercommunion that underlies all the forces of the universe, connecting the world of the spirit with that of the flesh. More especially does it show that wealth and power may arise from a logical and persevering application of the will; then does the will become the supreme force; it is the soul itself exerting its might over the inferior forces.

According to the manner in which we employ our will, our progress is regulated, our future is prepared and our strength or weakness increases. There is no such thing as chance or fate! There are laws! To utilize and direct some of these, to obey the others; therein lies the secret of all greatness and all elevation. The achievements that the will has already encompassed astonish the most scientific minds; but these are very little compared to those obtained in the high spheres where at the spirit's command all forces unite in action. And if, to pursue this line of thought, we directed our attention still higher, should we not, analogically, perceive how the divine will acting on cosmic matter can create the suns, trace the orbits beyond which the moving worlds may not stray, and give birth to the universe?

Yes, the will exerted in the direction of the good and in accordance with the eternal laws can carry out great things, as it may likewise work much evil. Our wrong thoughts, our evil deeds, our impure desires, corrupt by their very reflection the fluids that surround us; and these, by contact, convey an uneasiness and produce an unwholesome impression upon all who approach us; for every organism is subject to the influence of ambient fluids. In like measure, generous sentiments, kindly thoughts and earnest exhortation, penetrate, help and sustain those who approach us. This explains the power that the great missionaries and superior minds have wielded over the people; it also explains the opposite influence of the evil minded, which we can always admittedly entreat by an energetic resistance of our will.

A more precise knowledge of the powers of the spirit and of the way to apply them will entirely modify our tendencies and determinations. When we are convinced that every deed and every intention is being recorded within us to testify for or against us, we shall consider them more carefully. To begin with, we should strive to develop our latent resources, so as through them to influence the special fluids in such manner as to purify and transform these to the common good, surrounding ourselves with a pure and beneficent atmosphere, impervious to all vicious emanations. The inactive spirit, content to drift upon the tide of every material influence, is weak and unfitted to perceive the subtle sensations of the spiritual life. After death, it wakens to find itself in a state of complete inertia; to its clouded senses the great fields of space seem to contain naught but darkness and void. The active spirit, whose constant care has been the continual exercise of its faculties, acquires new forces, its sight embraces vaster horizons, and the circle of its perceptions gradually broadens.

Thought, utilized as magnetic force, might set many disorders aright and attenuate many evils. Proceeding by continuous will, by resolutely and constantly projecting our will-power towards our weak, suffering and erring brothers and sisters, we might do much to help and comfort them. In exercising this power we should not only accomplish unexpected results for others, but also our own minds would attain an extraordinary degree of strength and penetration.

Thanks to a strong combination of the wholesome fluids that flow out of nature's inexhaustible reservoir, and with the aid of the invisible spirits, it is possible to restore compromised health strengthen and to encourage and animate those who have ceased to hope. It is even possible, by a regular and persevering impulse of the will to exercise an influence through space – a distant influence upon the incredulous, the skeptical and wicked-minded – weakening their obstinacy, lessening their hatred, causing a ray of light to shine in the most hostile heart. Here we stand in the presence of an unknown form of mental suggestion, of formidable though often misused power, which if purposely and rightly applied could regenerate social morality.

The will, fluidically exerted, defies even the most acute observation. It works in darkness and in silence, crossing all obstacles and penetrating into the deepest recesses; but that it may produce its utmost effect, energetic and powerful effort, and unwearyingly patience are required. As a drop of water gradually wears away the hardest granite, so will persistent and kindly thought finally work its way into the most refractory mind.

If isolated will has the power to work much social good, what might not be accomplished by the cooperation of many strong spirits, by the combination of many sturdy wills? The forces of the intellect, now divergent, work against and annul one another.

This gives rises to the doubt and confusion of modern ideas; but when the human mind, becoming cognizant of its powers, will concentrate the scattered will-forces into one common effort of will to project them in the sense of Righteousness, Beauty and Truth, then truly will humanity begin to scale the eternal heights, then shall the face of the world be glorified.

33

The Life of Space

Were we to believe certain religious doctrines, the Earth would be at the exact center of the universe, while over our heads the sky, like a round roof, would be spread. In the upper part, we are told, Heaven is located, while the gloomy viaducts of Hell bore into the entrails of the Earth.

But modern science and spirit revelation have destroyed such theories by revealing to us a vast universe with countless inhabited worlds. Heaven is omnipresent; on every side we are met with the incommensurable, the infinite. Turn where we will, there are suns and spheres innumerable, huge bodies beside which our Earth is but a feeble unit.

In all the great infinitude of space there are no longer any confined dwelling-places for spirits. The purer they are the freer they become. They move through this vast infinitude and travel to where their affinities or sympathies call them. The inferior spirits, weighed down by their fluidic density, remain, as if attached to it, close to that Earth on which they have dwelt, circulating through its atmosphere and mingling with its humankind.

The perceptions and happiness of the spirit do not depend upon its environment; they are the outcome of its inner state, the resultant of acquired perfections. A backward spirit, whose perispirit is dense and full of darkness, may come in contact with some radiant soul whose subtle envelope responds to the most delicate influences as well as to the most intense vibrations. Each bears within itself its glory or unhappiness.

The soul's condition in that life which lies beyond the grave, its elevation and its degree of happiness, depend upon its faculty to feel and perceive, which are proportional to the more or less advanced state of the spirit.

Even on Earth, we find that intellectual enjoyment is proportionate to inner culture. Art and literature, the best achievements of civilization and the highest flights of genius, are alike beyond the appreciation of the savage – and indeed beyond that of many of our own fellow-citizens. Thus the spirits of a lower nature, like blind people surrounded by the daylight or deaf persons in a concert, remain indifferent and insensitive in front of the wonders of the infinite one.

The spirits enveloped by dense fluids, are subject to the laws of gravitation, and are attracted by matter. Under the influence of their gross appetites, the molecules of their fluidic body are closed to external perceptions, and they remain slaves to the same material forces that dominate humanity. One cannot lay too much stress upon this fact, which is the very foundation of universal law and justice. Souls group and station themselves in space, according to the degree of purity of their envelopes; the rank of the spirit is directly proportionate to its fluidic constitution, which itself is of the spirit's own making, the direct resultant of its past and of all its works. This is what determines its position; in this does it find its reward or chastisement. While the pure spirit is freely moving through the vast and radiant heavenly spaces, visiting the worlds and tarrying in them as it lists – encountering scarce any limits to its freedom – the impure spirit is constrained to stay in the vicinity of material worlds.

Between these two extreme states there are numerous intermediate degrees in which similar spirits can come together, forming veritable heavenly societies. The community of thought and sentiment, the similarity of taste and tendencies, unite these souls in great families.

The life of the advanced spirit is essentially active and fatigue is unknown to it. Distance does not exist for the spirit, which moves with the rapidity of thought. Its envelope, which resembles a light haze, becomes so subtle as to be entirely invisible to inferior spirits. It sees, hear, feels and perceives – no longer by those material organs which are interposed between nature and the human being and which intercept, in transit, the greater number of sensations – but directly and without intermediacy, through every portion of its being. Hence its perceptions are incomparably clearer and more varied than our own. The superior spirit would seem to be bathed in an ocean of ineffable sensation. Ever changing pictures unroll before it, and wonderful harmonies ceaselessly resound. Color has a perfume and scent becomes audible. But, however exquisite its impressions may be, it can escape from it and collect itself at will, by enfolding itself in a fluid veil, isolating itself in the midst of thronged space.

The advanced spirit is freed from all bodily needs. Food and sleep are no longer necessary. On leaving Earth, it has forever left behind it the vain worry, fear, and all the evil illusions that prison the human being's life. The inferior spirits carry away with them, beyond the grave, their material habits, needs and preoccupations. Being unable to rise above the Earth's atmosphere they return to share in the life of people and to take issue in their battles, their labors and their pleasures. Their instincts and desires, which are still alive, quickened by continual contact with human beings, overwhelm them, and the material impossibility of satisfying these becomes a new source of torture.

Spirits do not require speech in order to make themselves understood. Every thought is reflected in the perispirit, like the image in the mirror; they exchange ideas without effort and with vertiginous rapidity. The superior spirit can read the mind of the person and discern his most secret intentions. Nothing is hidden from it. It scans all of nature's mysteries, and can, if it chooses, pursue its explorations to the entrails of the Earth, or to the bottom of the sea, there to ponder upon the remains of submerged civilizations. It passes through the densest bodies, and kingdoms inaccessible to the vision of people are as an open book to the spirit.

34

Errant Souls

While the souls that are liberated from terrestrial influences, having formed themselves into sympathetic groups of which affection and comprehension are the component elements, live in a state of perfect equality and absolute happiness, the spirits that have been unable to master their passions lead an errant and idle life, which, although not in itself a cause of suffering, makes them restless and uncertain. This is what errant spirit implies, and this is the condition of the majority of those that have lived on Earth; of the spirits which are neither good nor bad, but merely weak and inclined towards material things.

One meets in the errant state an immense crowd, always in search of a better condition, which flees them. There are innumerable spirits that float uncertainly, hesitating between righteousness and unrighteousness, truth and error, light and shadow. Others are plunged in loneliness, darkness and sadness, or wander, begging for a little kindness and sympathy, here and there.

Selfishness and ignorance and all manner of defects rule in this aimless state where the influence of matter still prevails. Good and evil are there, side by side. It is an antechamber to the luminous spaces, to the happier regions. All pass through; all abide there awhile, but only to rise higher presently.

The teaching of spirits concerning the life beyond the grave teach us that in it there is no room for sterile contemplation or idle beatitude. Every region of the universe is peopled with busy spirits. Everywhere swarms of souls are ascending, descending, ever actively engaged – whether in the spaces of light or in the darkest regions. Here is a vast audience gathered together to receive the teaching of some superior spirit. Beyond, groups are forming to welcome some newcomer. Further on, are spirits engaged in combining fluids, in a thousand shapes and a thousand colors, according to the subtle ends to which they are destined.

Elsewhere, are multitudes surrounding the revolving planets and following their revolutions; these are dark and somber gatherings; that influence, unknown to themselves, the atmospheric conditions. Luminous spirits, speedier than light, likewise traverse these terrestrial atmospheres, bringing help and comfort to needy mortals. Each plays its part and contributes to the great work, in the measure of its merit and degree. The whole universe evolves. Worlds and spirits alike pursue their eternal course, consecrated to diverse works and ever drawn towards a higher state.

Some progress to realize, some science to acquire, some sorrows to extinguish, some remorse to calm, some errand of human love, atonements, devotion or sacrifice – all these motives, stimulate, urge and impel them on the path of duty. In this shoreless and limitless immensity, motion and life incessantly reign. Inaction and immobility are equivalent to retrogression, to death. Under the impulse of the great Law, beings and worlds, souls and suns, all gravitate, following the stupendous orbit traced by the Divine Will.

35

The Higher Life

When the virtuous soul has conquered its passions, and discarded its miserable body – instrument of suffering as of glory – it takes its flight through space and rejoins its immortal brothers. Transported by an irresistible force it passes through regions in which all is beauty and harmony. What it sees, human speech is too poor to describe. But above all what a relief, what an entrancing joy to have broken those chains which held it to the Earth – to be conscious of the freedom of space, to plunge into limitless vacancy, to float in the ethereal ocean which overlaps the uttermost orbits of majestic worlds! Here, at last, the body is no more – the ailing, infirm body, heavy with the heaviness of a lead cover; here, the spirit is no longer shackled with a material ball to drag along painfully. Liberated from its terrestrial bonds the spirit radiates; it becomes intoxicated with light and space. Earthly hideousness, wrinkled and decrepit age make way for the fluidic body, gracefully shaped, an idealized human form which is both radiant and diaphanous.

The soul has finally rejoined those who on Earth were near and dear – those who had preceded it into the new life; those who were its heart's elect, the close companions of its trials and toil. They have come to welcome the liberated spirit, as though it were a home-faring traveler from a distant land. Freely together do they commune and the joy of their communication is still further enhanced by the recollection of the Earth's sad memories, by the contrast of the present with that distressing past. Other spirits, fellow-workers and earthly companions of long-spent ages, who had vanished during the past incarnation, are come to mingle with the first. All who had ever shared in its happy or evil days, all those with whom it had lived, are present to complete the glad reunion.

How can one summarize the impressions of the mind in the radiant life that opens before it? The thick garment, the heavy cloak that oppressed its every sense has suddenly been rent asunder, and its perceptions were multiplied.

No more limits, no more bounded horizons. The deep, luminous infinity is unfolded, with its dazzling wonders, with its millions of suns, multicolored beams, sapphires, emeralds, great gems hung in space, and their sumptuous processions of spheres. These suns, which to the human being appear as mere sparks, the spirit now sees in their magnificent and colossal splendor; far superior to that which enlightens our feeble plane. It sees how the force of attractions binds each of these great worlds to its appointed place and distinguishes, in the distant depths, the formidable stars which preside over their evolutions. Thus before him all of these gigantic torches of eternity revolve, gravitate, and, bent upon their eccentric courses, intertwine like live balls of fire, manipulated by some invisible juggler.

We who ceaselessly tormented by the disturbed murmurs and mutterings of the human tribe cannot conceive the solemn peace, the majestic silence of space, which fills the soul with an august reverence, with a wonder that borders on fear. The good and pure spirit is, however, inaccessible to fear. This infinitude, which appears so silent and deathlike to the inferior soul, soon awakens, and to the quickened perceptions there comes the sound of a powerful voice. The dematerialized soul gradually learns to discern the melodious vibrations of the ether, the delicate harmonies of the celestial colonies, the imposing rhythm of the spheres. Then, entranced, the spirit listens to the chant of the worlds, to the voice of infinitude that echo throughout the majestic silence. Enraptured with a holy ecstasy, overcome by a deep and grave religious feeling, and an endless admiration, steeped in the sea of ether, the spirit is absorbed in quiet contemplation of the sidereal depths, while before it legions of spirits flit past, light and graceful shapes that presently disappear like shadows melting in the light. The spirit assists at the genesis of new worlds; it is present when life awakens and struggles to manifest itself upon the surfaces of these worlds; it follows the growth of the human races that people them and, throughout all this great vision, it notes that everywhere life, activity and motion are in harmony with the order of the universe.

Whatever its state of advancement may be, the spirit that has just departed from Earth could not aspire to continue endlessly to lead this higher life. It is still subject to reincarnation, for to it this life is only an interlude of rest, a compensation for hardships; it is strengthened for future struggles. But in that future which awaits it, it will not again encounter the suffering and distress that attended its earthly life; for the more advanced spirits are called upon to be reincarnated in better worlds than this of ours. The great ladder of the universe has innumerable rungs that are spaced in view of the gradual ascent of the souls; each soul scales these one after the other.

In the higher worlds the empire of matter is less, and the evils that arise from it are attenuated as the soul progresses, until they gradually disappear. The being moves freely; no longer constrained to crawl painfully upon the ground, overwhelmed by the weight of a too heavy atmosphere. Bodily wants are few, and heavy labor is unknown. The term of life, which is longer than ours, is present in study and in the furthering of a more perfect civilization, founded on a purer morality, on the observance of universal rights, friendship and brotherhood. The horrors of war, plague, pestilence and starvation are there unknown, and the coarser interests, cause of so much strife, are no longer subjected to division.

Indeed these revelations concerning the habitability of the stars have been confirmed by science. With the spectroscope science has analyzed their constituent elements, established their powers of attraction and measured their density. Astronomy shows us that the seasons vary in length according to the angle of a globe's inclination upon its orbit. We are told that Saturn's density is equivalent to the maple; Jupiter's to water, and that on Mars a body weighs half of what it would upon the Earth. The organism of living creatures being the resultant of the active forces of its environment, we can imagine the variety of form arising from this cause and from the infinite variation of the types of life upon the innumerable worlds of the universe.

A time finally comes when the spirit, having achieved the cycle of its planetary lives and being purified by its rebirths and migrations through the worlds, sees the end of its series of incarnations, and finally sees the dawning of the spiritual life; the soul's real life, in which evil, darkness and error are banished. There, the last vestiges of material influence have finally disappeared. Calm serenity and absolute security have taken the place of anxiety and sorrow. The soul has reached the end of its tribulations, and now rests in the sublime assurance that no further trials await it. With what keen emotion it reviews its lives, dispersed through the cycle of time, its long ascent, the slow crowning and award of its merits! What a lesson do we not read in this ascending march during which the unity of its nature and its immortal individuality are fulfilled and confirmed!

From the recollection of far distant alarms, anxieties and sorrows, it reverts to its present felicity, the blessedness of which is thereby rendered more appreciable. What a blessing indeed to feel oneself for evermore surrounded by enlightened, patient and beloved spirits, to form ties with them which will be truly indissoluble, to share in their aspirations, occupations and pursuits; to feel oneself truly understood, uplifted and beloved, free from the yoke of suffering and death; young with a youth over which the centuries to come shall have no power! Then to be able to ponder, to admire, to glorify the divine work and to enter ever more deeply into its mysteries; everywhere to meet with justice, beauty and heavenly goodness; to identify oneself with them, to eat and drink of them, to follow the high spirits on their work and missions, to know that some time one is to be their equal, to know that one is to attain ever higher, that always and forever fresh joys, fresh work and fresh progress await us! Such is the eternal, magnificent and superabundant life; such is the life of the spirit that suffering has purified.

The high heavens are the abode of the ideal and perfect beauty from which all art seeks inspiration. The superior spirits possess the sense of beauty to an eminent degree, and from it derive the purest satisfaction; they are all masters and their works would shame the best that human mind ever conceived. Every time that genius has manifested itself on Earth, each time that art has revealed itself in a new guise – one may well believe that a spirit from the regions on high has been incarnated on Earth to initiate humanity into the splendors of eternal beauty. Art in its many aspects is, to the superior being, an homage, a prayer, breathed to the eternal Principle.

The spirit being fluid itself, acts on the fluids of space. By will power it combines them, disposes of them as it pleases and arrays them in the shape and color that serve its purpose. It is by means of these fluids that works, incomparable and beyond analysis, are executed.

It is in ethereal dwellings that spiritual rejoicings take place. The pure spirits, dazzling with light, group themselves in families. Their brightness and the varied tints of their fluidic envelopes portray their attributes and the degree of their elevation. Heavenly harmonies resound, compared to which earthly music would seem but as discordant noise; the setting is the infinite space with the worlds revolving in its immensity and uniting their notes to the celestial voices in the universal hymn which ascends to God.

All these spirits, in innumerable crowds, know each other and love one another. The affection and family ties that united them in the material life, and which death severed for a while, are now reconstituted forever. They gather together from far parts of space and from the higher worlds to communicate the results of their missions and works, to rejoice over each success and to assist one another in their difficult enterprises. No jealousy and no afterthought can arise in these pure spirits. Love, faith, and sincerity preside over these reunions. There, the instructions, conveyed by divine messengers, are received, and new tasks allotted, which are to further the advancement of those that undertake them. Some agree to watch over the progress and development of worlds and nations; others accept to be reincarnated on some planet of space, to fulfill missions of devotion and to instruct the dwellers in them in science and morals; others still, the spirit-guides or protectors, devote themselves to some incarnated soul, sustaining it along life's rugged path, following it from birth till death, through several successive lives, meeting it at the end of each, on the threshold of the invisible world. At all degrees of the spiritual hierarchy, each spirit has its allotted share in the great work of progress, and contributes to the realization of the divine laws.

The purer the spirit becomes, the more ardent and the more undeniable its need to love and to draw to its own serene level, in regions where pain is unknown, all that suffer, struggle and vegetate in the nether depths of immortal life. When one such spirit has adopted a humbler brother, constituting itself the other's guide and protector, with what loving care it watches over his steps, with what joy it marks his progress, with what sorrow it notes the backslidings it is powerless to prevent! As the child from the cradle takes its first uncertain steps under his mother's fond eyes – thus does the weak spirit encounter the struggles of life, shielded by the invisible protection of its spiritual guide.

We all have one of these tutelary spirits, who comes to our assistance in the difficult hours and sets our feet once again upon the straight path. This is the origin of the poetic Christian legend of the Guardian Angel; there is no sweeter and more consoling conception. To feel that we have a faithful friend who is ever ready to help us – whether by exerting his influence from a far distance or by standing close to us in the hour of trial – ever counseling our intuition, ever heartening us by his affection; such an assurance is of incalculable moral assistance. The thought that kindly and invisible witnesses see all our actions, by which they are gladdened or afflicted, inspire us to act with greater wisdom and circumspection.

It is this occult protection that strengthens the bonds of solidarity that unite heaven and earth – the enfranchised spirit to man, that captive of the flesh. This never-failing helpfulness must in the end bring forth deep sympathies and lasting friendships. The love that animates the superior spirit is little by little extended to all beings, while constantly reverting to God the father of souls, the center of all the affective powers.

We have spoken of hierarchy. There is indeed a spiritual hierarchy, but virtue and such merits as arise from suffering and work are its sole constituents. We know that all spirits are equal in principle, that they differ only by their state of advancement, being destined to the same great end. The degrees of the spiritual hierarchy take their root in the very depths of the lower life, from where they rise until they attain such heights, as we cannot even conceive of. It is a marvelous progression of power, light and virtue, growing greater from base to summit, if indeed there be a culminating point.

It is a spiral of progress that winds on forever. It is divided into three major phases – material life, spiritual life, and heavenly life – each of which reflects and reacts upon the others; the whole constituting the complete evolution of the being, a true Jacob's ladder. All beings upon this wonderful ladder are united by invisible bonds; each being is attracted and sustained by some more elevated being. Those higher spirits that have revealed themselves to the human being appear as sublime beings, and yet, they assure us, there are others as superior to them as they are to us. Thus the degrees rise innumerable, until they disappear in a mysterious profundity.

The superiority of a spirit is apparent in its fluidic clothing. It is like a cloak woven with the merits and virtues acquired in the succession of its many existences. Somber and dull with an inferior being, progress purifies and clarifies it. Radiant already in the case of an elevated being, upon the superior spirit it shines with unbearable brightness.

Each spirit is a center of light; a light which may be, for a long while, veiled and invisible, but which develops with the intrinsic worth of the spirit; slowly increasing, it augments, both in intensity and in the circle of its radiance. At first it is like a fire hidden under ashes, emitting a faint glow; presently it is a timid and flickering flame; one day it will become a halo! Then it grows and expands until the whole glorified spirit is as refulgent as the sun or as one of those wandering stars that traverse the darkness of the immensity of space, tracking in it a luminous pathway. Such a degree of splendor is only obtainable by an accumulation of good works, wrought through a succession of lives that would seem as an eternity to us human beings.

By rising higher up, to the summits which thought cannot measure without faint and giddy, could one not perceive by intuition that God, the soul of the Universe, is a prodigious center of light? The direct sight of God, we are told, is bearable only to the greatest spirits. The divine light expresses the glory, might and majesty of the Eternal; it is the very vision of truth. But few spirits can gaze upon it unveiled, for to withstand its splendor absolute purity is necessary.

Earthly life suspends the radiant properties of the spirit. While it lasts, the light of the soul is hidden beneath the flesh, like a torch burning solitary in the bottom of a vault. We can, however, assure ourselves of its presence within us; our good deeds, our generous impulses, maintain and animate it. A whole crowd can feel the warmth of an enthusiastic soul. In our moments of expansion, of pity, of love, we feel that within us which is like a flame, a beam emanating from our deepest being. It is this inner light that electrifies audiences, rouses nations, causing them to perform great deeds. The strength of the spirit then becomes apparent to all eyes, and shows what psychical force may effect when set in action in the cause of righteousness and justice. The strength of the soul is greater than all material forces. It can uplift a world, and this strength is light.

We have endeavored, by faithfully following the description imparted by spirits, to convey an idea of the ultimate and heavenly life. It is the end towards which all souls are tending – the place where all happy dreams are realized, where noble aspirations are satisfied, where hope disappointed, blighted affection and generous impulses repressed by the material life, will blossom to full perfection till they meet and blend in one great love which includes all beings, uniting them in a perpetual communion in the boundless bosom of universal harmony.

However, to reach these almost divine heights, it is necessary to have given up, on the slopes that lead to it, the appetites, passions, the desires; it is necessary to be torn by brambles, and purified by the water descended from the glaciers. One must have acquired sweetness, resignation and faith, one must have learned to suffer uncomplainingly, to have wept in solitude, to have scorned the world's ephemeral treasures and joys, to have centered all desires in such things that do not pass away. One must have buried in earthly graves many pain racked affections; one must have suffered many privations and meekly accepted much sorrow and humiliation; one must have tasted of the poisoned fangs of evil and endured the weight of loneliness and sadness! One must have emptied many times the deep and bitter chalice. For suffering alone, by developing the virile forces of the soul, can steel it against the inevitable struggle and prepare its elevation. It is suffering that purifies, matures, elevates, and finally throws open the gateway to the happy life.

Immortal spirit, whether free or incarnate, if you want to quickly traverse the magnificent sequence of the worlds, and gain the ethereal regions, you must cast far from you all that weighs you down and delays your progress. To the earth returns that which proceed from the earth; then covet only the treasures that are eternal. Work, pray, console, help, and love! Ah, love! Love to self-abnegation, to immolation! Fulfill your duty even at the price of sacrifice and death! Thus you will sow the seed of your future happiness.

36

Inferior Spirits

The pure spirit carries within its own light and happiness. They are ever with it and form an integral part of its being. In like manner the guilty spirit wearily carries along its darkness, its chastisement, its self-censure. The sufferings of perverse souls, though not material, are not less lively. Hell is only a fictitious place, a product of the imagination, a scarecrow that might have been useful in keeping childish peoples within bounds; but which has not the least reality. Quite other is the teaching of the spirits concerning the torments of the future life; hypothesis has nothing to do with this.

These sufferings have been described to us by those who are actually enduring them, just as others have depicted their own happiness. They have not been imposed by an arbitrary will. No sentence has been passed. The spirit undergoes the natural consequences of its actions which fall upon it, glorifying or crushing it. The being suffers in the life beyond not only from the harm that he has brought, but likewise from his idleness and weakness. In a word, this after life is his work; it is just what he made it, with his own hands. Suffering is inherent to imperfection; it diminishes with the being's progress and disappears when the spirit has overcome matter.

The punishment of the wicked spirit is continued, not only in the spiritual life but also throughout the successive incarnations which bind it to inferior worlds, where life is precarious and where pain has reigns supreme. These are the worlds that might truly be called hells. The Earth, in some respects, might be classed among these. Around these worlds, real penitentiaries that revolve through space, somber legions of imperfect spirits glide, awaiting their hour of reincarnation.

We have seen how painful, prolonged and full of trouble and anguish is the ordeal of corporeal disintegration for the spirit that has been a slave to its passions. The illusion of the terrestrial life continues in him throughout the years. Incapable of realizing his condition or of breaking the ties that bind him, the weak spirit continues to live as prior to death; a slave to his habits and tastes, indignant that his friend seem neither to see nor hear him, sadly wandering without aim or object among the scenes that are familiar to him. These are the "lost souls," whose presence in some houses has long been suspected, and whose reality is being daily confirmed by numerous and noisy manifestations.

The spirit's condition after death depends solely upon the aptitudes and tastes that it has cultivated. Here again appears the inexorable law of seed and harvest. The one who has placed his whole happiness in the things of this world suffers acutely when they fail him. In each passion lies the germ of its own punishment. The spirit that has not freed itself from gross and brutal desires becomes their toy, their slave. The punishment of the spirit lies in that it can do nothing to lessen the eternal pricks of desire.

Great is the despair of the miser who witnesses the squandering of the treasure he has so painfully amassed. And in spite of all, he still loves it; in the throes of a terrible anxiety he gives himself up to paroxysms of unspeakable fury.

Almost as pitiful is the case of the proud and powerful – of those who have squandered their fortune and titles, living for luxury and glory alone, despising the poor and oppressing the weak. They find in the kingdom of silence neither obsequious retinue, sumptuous suits. Stripped of all that composed their earthly grandeur, solitude and penury now await them in space.

Still more lamentable is the condition of cruel and rapacious spirits, of criminals of all degrees – of all who have shed blood and derided justice. The moans and curses of their victims re-echo in their ears for a seemingly endless period; ironical and menacing shades pitilessly surround and pursue them; they can find no retreat that is deep and secret enough to hide them, and vainly do they seek rest and oblivion. Their reincarnation in some obscure form, their subsequent misery, humiliation and lowly drudgery can alone attenuate their evils.

Nothing can equal the shame and terror of the soul which is perpetually confronted with the spectacle of its own guilty lives with their train of spoliation and murder; it feels as if it had been laid bare and was being probed through and through by a merciless light which was constantly detecting its most guilty secrets. Memory, that ardent spur, is continuously scourging and rending the guilty spirit. When one has experienced this suffering, one can understand and bless the divine foresight that has spared us so much during this earthly life; thereby giving us, through a mind at peace, some chance of self-improvement.

Selfish people, those who are exclusively taken up with their own pleasures and interests, are preparing for themselves a painful future. Having loved only themselves – having neither helped, sustained nor consoled any other soul in need – they now find in this new life neither sympathy nor aid. Lonely and abandoned, time flows from them monotonously and slowly. A dull bore embraces them. The regret of lost hours, of a wasted life, a hatred for the miserable interests that once absorbed them, torments and crazes them. They suffer and wander on until some charitable thought at last occurs to them, glowing in the darkness of their night like a heaven-born ray of hope; but the dawn does not finally appear until, acting on the advice of some enlightened and kindle spirit, they sever, by an act of will, the fluidic network that enmeshes them, and resolutely determine to undertake a better path.

The fate of the suicide has much in common with that of the criminal; sometimes it is even worse. To commit suicide is a cowardly act, a crime of which the consequences are terrible.

To borrow the expression of a spirit, *he who commits suicide evades suffering only to encounter torture.* Each of us has duties and a mission to fulfill on Earth; trials to endure for our own good and improvement. To seek to evade these and to liberate ourselves before our time from human suffering is to violate natural law; and every violation of this law brings down a terrible reaction upon the guilty.

Suicide is not a way out of physical suffering. The spirit remains bound to the carnal body that it thought to destroy; slowly it suffers from every phase of decomposition, and its painful sensations are multiplied rather than diminished. Far from shortening its trial, it indefinitely prolongs it; the disturbance and the uneasiness endure long after the destruction of the material envelope itself. And more than this, the spirit will be obliged to again undergo the self-same trials from which by death it thought to escape, and which its past had occasioned. It will have to endure these under worse conditions, to retrace step by step the rocky path, and for that, to still undergo a more painful incarnation than that from which it wanted to flee.

The after-death sufferings of those who have been executed are terrible, and the depositions made by some noted criminals might well melt the hardest hearts, and convince human justice of the terrible effects of the death sentence. Most of these unfortunate creatures find themselves a prey to the most acute state of excitement and to the most maddening sensations. The horror of their crimes, the gaze of their victims, which seems to pursue and to transfix them, dreadful visions and hallucinations; such is the fate that awaits them. Most of them, striving to find an escape from their pain, seize upon the incarnated ones with similar tendencies and push them into the road of crime. Others, devoured by remorse as by an inextinguishable fire, seek without ceasing, a shelter they cannot find. Beneath them, overhead and everywhere around, their gaze encounters nothing but ghastly corpses, malignant countenances, pools of blood.

Evil spirits, upon whom the burden of their faults heavily weighs, are unable to foresee any brighter future. They have no inkling of the higher laws; the fluids that overlay them prevent all communication with the superior spirits who would take them away them from their lethargy and rescue them from their evil inclinations. This they are unable to do because of the gross, almost material essence, as well as by the limited perceptiveness of these unfortunates. Consequently these spirits remain absolutely unwitting of their ultimate destiny and believe in the eternal nature of their sufferings. Such of these as are still imbued with the Catholic teachings, therefore believe and declare themselves to be in hell. Distraught by jealousy and hatred, many seek relief in making sport of weak and evilly inclined people. They are ceaseless in their persecutions and remitting in evil suggestion; but gradually these new excesses engender new sufferings. The reaction of the evil they cause enmeshes them in a still denser fluidic web. The darkness becomes blacker, the narrow circle contracts and a painful and dolorous reincarnation awaits them.

Calmer are those who have found repentance; resignedly they await the advent of fresh trials, resolved to satisfy eternal justice. Remorse, like a pale gleam, dimly illuminates their soul, allowing the good spirits to make themselves understood so that their advice and encouragement no longer fall on unheeding ears.

37

Hell and its Demons

Basing its judgment upon cases of obsession and upon the noisy manifestations of trivial spirits, the Church has pronounced all spirit phenomena demoniacal, and condemned them as useless or dangerous. Before disproving this assertion, it is well to recall the fact that Catholicism has treated all great discoveries, many of them epoch-making, in precisely the same way. There is hardly any of the conquests of science that were not, at first, considered diabolical.

The invisible world is, as we have stated, is a counterpart of the human world. Spirits are only the more or less perfect souls of people, deprived of their bodies, and our relations with them must be as prudently ordained as with our fellow-beings.

To see nothing in Spiritism beyond the manifestation of inferior spirits is equivalent to perceiving nothing but evil in humanity. The teaching of the higher spirits has opened a new path in life, it has solved the problems of the future, it has vivified a waning faith and restored justice upon an adamantine pedestal. Thanks to it a crowd of atheists and unbelievers have been brought back to a belief in God and immortal life; thousands of ignorant and vicious persons have returned to the ways of righteousness and truth. Can this be demoniacal work, and would Satan, if he existed, be blind enough to work against his own cause?

Some perspicacity is needed in order to detect the nature of a spirit and to discern in our communications with them what may be accepted and what should be rejected. Jesus has told us *"a tree is known by its fruits."* The language and instructions of a superior spirit are always marked with dignity, wisdom and charity. Their only aim is the spiritual progress of the human being; they care little for the material side. The communications of the lower spirits show an opposite tendency; they abound in contradiction and generally treat of vulgar things, devoid of all moral interest. The trivial or inferior spirits more readily lend themselves to physical manifestation.

Spiritism brings to humanity a teaching proportioned to its needs. They have corroborated the teaching of the Scriptures in their primitive and pure form; expounding and completing their doctrines, stripping them of all speculative ideas and cast interests, and restoring them to their true sphere of action, which is their influence over the soul of the human being.

The Christian religion has been altered in consequence of the ages, and currently it exercises only an enfeebled and insufficient action upon morals and characters. Spiritism has now come to take up and to carry on the task that was allotted to Christianity. Upon the invisible spirits has devolved the mission to set all things straight, to enter into the humblest as well as into the proudest dwellings and – innumerably strong – to undertake the regeneration of humanity. Any sensible person can no longer entertain the notion of demons and of a place of endless torment. Satan is a myth, and no creature is eternally doomed to evil.

38

The Action of the Human Being over Unhappy Spirits

Our indifference concerning spirit manifestation would deprive us not only of the knowledge of a future state, but would likewise render it impossible for us to influence the unhappy spirits and to lighten their condition by making it easier for them to atone for the faults that they have committed. Backward spirits, having more affinity with people than with pure spirits, because of their still gross fluid constitution, are thereby more accessible to our influence. In entering into communication with them, we may do good work by instructing and improving them, while at the same time we shall clear and purify the fluidic atmosphere that surrounds us all. The unhappy spirits are amenable to our appeals and evocations. Our sympathetic thought plays upon them like an electric current and draws them to us, permitting us, through a medium, to communicate with them.

Thus is it with every soul that departs this world. Our evocations attract the attention of the deceased and facilitate their corporeal liberation. Our ardent prayers that are like luminous rays of harmonious vibrations enlighten them and dilate their being. It is well for them to know that they are not abandoned to themselves in space; that there still are beings on Earth who take interest in their fate and desire their happiness. Even if this happiness is beyond the power of such prayers, they at least are welcome to the departed spirits whose despair they relieve, imparting to them the fluidic force required to fight against pernicious influences and to progress.

We must, however, bear in mind that all communication with inferior spirits demands clearness of mind, besides much firmness and tact. In this respect all could not hope to succeed. True moral superiority is necessary in order that such spirits should be dominated, kept in order and on the right road. This superiority can only be acquired by a life exempt from material passion. In this case, the purified fluids of the dialoguer easily control the fluids of the backward spirits.

A practical knowledge of the invisible world is likewise necessary so that one should not be led astray by the errors and contradictions in which the communications of trivial spirits abound. Because of their imperfect nature, they have very limited knowledge. They see and judge things differently. Many retain their opinions and prejudices of the earth.; hence are wisdom and perspicacity indispensable guides to navigate through this maze.

The study of spirit phenomena and the communication with the invisible world present many difficulties and sometimes with real danger for him who is frivolous and ignorant and who cares little for the ethics of the question. He who has neglected to study the science and philosophy of spirits and would suddenly penetrate into the secrets of the invisible kingdom, unreservedly, yielding himself to its manifestations, will find himself, from the start, in contact with thousands of beings whose deeds and speech he has no means to control.

His ignorance will deliver him defenseless into their power, for his weak and undecided will would be unable to cope with the suggestions to which he is exposed. Weak and passionate, his own imperfections will attract similar spirits; they will take hold of him and unscrupulously deceive him. Knowing nothing of the occult laws, standing alone on the threshold of a world where illusion and reality are intermingled, he has all to fear – deceit, derision and obsession.

The role played by inferior spirits in spiritist manifestations was considerable at the start, and not without its utility. In a world as materialistic as ours has become, noisy manifestations and phenomena of a physical order were best calculated to impress people, and to turn them from that indifference which they commonly display for all that is not to their immediate advantage. This is what justifies the table turning, rappings, haunted houses, etc. These vulgar phenomena, the contribution of spirits that are yet under the dominion of matter, were appropriate to the general attitude and mental condition of those whose attention was desired. Under no circumstances could they be attributed to superior spirits, who manifest themselves only later and in finer ways, especially by writing, by audition and trance mediums.

After this display of material facts, which were chiefly aimed at the senses, the spirits addressed themselves to the intellect, sentiment and reason. This gradual improvement of the means of communication shows the extent of the resources available to the invisible powers, and what varied and profound combinations they know how to put into play, in order to stimulate the human being in the path of progress and the knowledge of his destiny.

39

Justice, Solidarity, Responsibility

Everything in the universe is interlinked and interdependent, so the spirits teach us. In the physical world a law governs every fact, complex or simple; each effect arises from a cause, and every cause generates an effect identical to itself. Thus we find in the moral domain the principle of justice, the sanction of good and evil, and the distributive law, which renders to each according to his work. As sun-gathered mists inevitably return to Earth in the form of rain, so do the consequences of acts accomplished revert to their author. Each deed and each effort of our will following the given impulse accomplishes its mission and returns with its good or bad consequences to the source that has produced them.

In this manner punishment and recompense are allotted according to a natural distribution. Both good and evil return to their starting-point. There are evils whose consequence is manifest even during this life. Others, and graver ones there are, the consequences of which are only revealed in the life of the spirit, and sometimes even not before ulterior reincarnations.

The law of retaliation is not absolute. It is nonetheless certain that human's passions and misdeeds invariably produce identical results, from which it is impossible for him to escape. The proud individual prepares for himself a future humiliation; the egotist, a coming void and indifference; difficult privation awaits the sensualist. Such is the inevitable punishment, the radical treatment which is to extirpate the evil at its root. These punishments impose themselves, automatically as it were, and neither judge nor executioner is required.

Only repentance and an earnest appeal to the divine clemency can, by putting us in touch with the higher spirits, provide us with the necessary strength to persevere on this dolorous way which our past has made necessary; but nothing short of atonement can wash our faults away. Only pain, the great teacher, can rehabilitate us. only the fulfillment of the universal moral law, and its punishments and penalties are only the reaction of nature, outraged in its eternal principles. The forces of the universe are interdependent, acting and vibrating in unison. Every moral force reacts upon its violator, proportionately to the violation. God chastises no one. He has simply ordained that in the course of time every cause shall produce its inevitable effect.

The human being is therefore his own executioner, since, according to the good or bad use he makes of his freedom, he will be happy or unhappy. The consequences of his acts are sometimes slow in coming. In this world we may witness many things; we may see the guilty stifle their consciences, scoff at the law and finally sink into honored graves; and again we may see many a just man a perpetual strike to calumny and all manner of adversity. Such are the things, amongst many, that necessitate other lives to come – that the principle of justice may find its application, and the being's moral status its equilibrium. Without this necessary complement, this present life would be devoid of meaning and most of our acts would be senseless.

Ignorance is, in truth, the sovereign evil out of which all ills arise. If the person could clearly foresee the consequences of his actions, his conduct would be greatly altered. Cognizant of the moral law and of its inexorable consequences, he would no more seek to violate it than he would rebel against the laws of attraction or gravitation.

~~

These facts still more strengthen the ties that unite us to the great family of souls; for, incarnate or disincarnate, all souls are kin. Given birth to by their common father who is God they continue towards a like destiny. All spirits owe one another a common debt of helpfulness. Protected or protector, turn by turn, they help each other on the way; by services performed, by trials endured together they are unconsciously sowing the seed of that fraternal love whose blossoming is one of the conditions of the superior and happy life.

The bonds that unite us to our brothers in space bind us still more closely to those on Earth. All people, be they savage or civilized, are spirits kindred to us by their origin and ultimate destiny. Taking them as a whole, they form a body of which all the members are united, and of which every individual, while working for his personal advancement, must participate in the general progress and welfare. The law of justice being only the resultant of all acts performed, the sequence of cause and effect will explain why so many ills afflict humanity.

The history of the earth is but a tissue of murders and iniquities. All the past centuries of bloodshed, violent lives and wicked deeds are united in the present, as tributary streams unite in the main river. The spirits that compose the actual society are but the people of the past, returned to atone the consequences of their former lives, together with their derivative responsibilities. Being compounded of such elements – how could humanity expect to be happy? The solidarity of generations extends through time; the mist of their passions enwraps and follows them until entire purification. This consideration makes us still more keenly realize the necessity for improving the social atmosphere, by enlightening our fellow-being as to the origin of our common afflictions, and by creating about us, by our combined effort, a healthier and purer atmosphere.

The individual must at last learn to estimate the consequences of his acts, the extent of his responsibilities, and to shake off that indifference which has dug the ditch of social misery and morally poisoned this earth on which he may have to be born many times again. A new breath must quicken the nations and kindle in them those convictions which give rise to a strong and steadfast determination. It is necessary that all should at last learn that the reign of evil is not eternal and that justice is not a vain word. Justice alone governs the universe, and under her powerful leveling hand all souls bow to the future world and all resistance and rebellion are crushed.

From a lofty conception of justice, rise equality, solidarity and mutual responsibility. These principles are linked into one compact unit, in a single law that rules and dominates the universe, the title of which is: progress in freedom. Does not this harmony, this mighty coordination of laws and beings, supply an infinitely grander and more consoling conception of the life and destiny of the human being, than any that the nihilist theories offer? In that immensity in which everything is ordained by profound and wise laws; in which equity is made manifest in every least detail; in which no useful deed is without profit, no fault without chastisement, no suffering without compensation, - there, only, can the being feel himself to be truly at one with all that exists. Working for himself, and simultaneously for others, he freely develops his forces, and assists at the expansion of his understanding and the increase of his happiness.

Compare these views with the cold materialistic theories; this universe, with the dreadful one in which all human beings suffer and disappear without ties, purpose or hope, living their evanescent lives, like so many pallid shadows, sprung from nothingness, only to relapse into the silence of an endless night! Let it be submitted as to which of these conceptions is fitter to sustain the human being in his troubles, to strengthen his character and to serve as his guide upon the uplands of Divine Truth.

40

Providence and Free-Will

The problem of free-will has proved to be a grave stumbling block to both philosopher and theologian. It has seemed all the more difficult to reconcile human's will and freedom with the demands of a natural law and of a divine will, since, to most people, the intervention of blind chance seems to further complicate the problem. The revelations of the spirits have elucidated this point for us. The seeming fatality that is forever placing obstructions in the path of our endeavor is in reality but the inevitable outcome of our past sins. It is the effect that reverts to its cause; it is the fulfillment of the program in which we acquiesced before we were reincarnated, following the admonition of our spiritual guides or our greater good and our elevation.

In the lower strata of creation, the being is not yet self-conscious. Instinct, a species of incipient fatality, is its sole guide; it is not until the higher types of animal life appear that we discover rudiments of the first faculties – pale forerunners of the glories to come. In humanity, the soul awakens to spiritual freedom. Its discernment and conscience acquire ever-greater powers as it advances on its immense career. Placed between good and evil it is free to discern and to choose between them. Grown wise through its mistakes and consequent sufferings, its experience is the outcome of trial, whence also arises its spiritual strength.

The human soul, once in possession of conscience and freedom, can never again relapse into an inferior life. Its incarnations follow one upon the other through the prescribed chain of worlds until it has acquired the three imperishable gifts to the attainment of which its interminable quest has been directed; these are wisdom, science and love. The possession of these forever frees the soul from the yoke of rebirth and death, and opens to it the gates of the heavenly life.

By making use of its free-will, the soul settles its own destiny and prepares its sorrow or happiness. But never – be it in the full tide of progress, in the bitter hour of trial or in the midst of a passionate struggle against evil – will the help that descends from on high be refused to it. Let the soul remain true to itself, no matter how unworthy it may appear, as soon as it manifests an intention to regain the straight and blessed road, then will Providence sends assistance and support to it.

Providence is the superior spirit; it is the angel that watches over the unhappy; it is the unseen consoler whose inspiration warms the heart upon which despair had laid an icy finger; it is the bright beacon whose rays guide the mariner adrift upon turbulent seas. Providence is still, above all, divine love flowing over its creature. What solicitude and what foresight does not this love encompass? Was it not for the soul, to frame its struggles and to crown its achievements that these worlds have been hung in space, that these suns were lighted, that rolling sea and fruitful land were created? For the soul alone this great work is carried on, natural forces combined, and universes hatch within nebulas.

The soul was created to happiness; but that it should prize and appreciate this happiness it must first deserve it; in order to know its value, it must conquer it itself and, for that purpose, freely develop the powers which are in it. Its liberty of action and responsibility increase with its elevation; the more enlightened it becomes, the more it should and must subordinate personal force to the laws that govern the universe.

The freedom of the individual is, therefore, restricted to narrow limits; firstly, by the requirements of natural law, which allows of no infringement and no disturbance in the order of the world; secondly, by its own past, the consequences of which must recur until complete reparation. In no case can the exercise of human liberty be allowed to interfere with the fulfillment of the divine plan, else the harmony of the universe would be continually interrupted. Far transcending our circumscribed and fickle views, the immutable order of the universe is maintained, and serenely progresses. We are almost invariably poor judges as to what constitutes our ultimate good: and if the natural order of things were to yield to our wishes, what a terrible upheaval would not ensue!

The first use to which the individual would put his absolute freedom would certainly be the elimination of all pain from this life, and to contrive that it should be one all of happiness. Unquestionably there are evils which it is our duty to extirpate and destroy – those, for instance, which proceed from material causes – but there are others, inherent to our moral constitution, that pain and repression alone can master and subdue; of these are our vices. In this case suffering is the school, or rather the one indispensable remedy, and the trials decreed are only those equitably discerned by an infallible justice. The outcry we raise against the laws and justice of the world arises, therefore, from our ignorance of the ways of God. If we criticize, it is because we perceive not the hidden motives.

Destiny is the final resultant, evolved from our successive lives, of our deeds and free resolutions. More enlightened, when disincarnated, as to our imperfections and seeking the means of improvement, we accept material life in the form and under the conditions that appear best fitted to attain this goal. The phenomena of hypnotism and of mental suggestion finally show, under the influence of our spiritual protectors, what occurs in such cases. In the state of somnambulism the soul, at the suggestion of the magnetizer, agrees to do such and such a thing in a specified time. Being restored to a waking condition, and having apparently retained no recollection of this promise, the soul nevertheless scrupulously fulfills the required task. In a like way, the person seems not to remember the resolutions that he made before his reincarnation; but, when the time comes he eagerly anticipates the inevitable, and acts as his progress dictates – or as the fulfillment of the inexorable law commands.

41

Reincarnation

We will not close this study into the life of space without outlining in a general way the laws that govern reincarnation. All souls that have not freed themselves from terrestrial influence must be born again into this world to work out their improvement; thus is it with the immense majority. Reincarnation, like all other phases of life, is subject to law. The degree of refinement of the perispirit and the molecular affinity that determine the spirit's position in space likewise regulate the conditions of reincarnation. Like attracts like; it is by virtue of this law of harmony and attraction that spirits of the same order, character, and of similar tendencies, are attracted one to another, follow each other through their multiple existences, are reincarnated together, and form homogeneous families.

When the hour for reincarnation has arrived the spirit feels itself drawn by an irresistible force, a mysterious affinity, towards the environment that suits it. This is an hour of anguish, more terrible than that of death. Death is, in truth, only the liberation from corporeal ties, the entrance into a freer and more intense life. Incarnation, on the other hand, means the sacrifice of the free life, the diminution of self, the transition from open space to dark confinement, the descent into an abyss of blood, mud and misery, where the being will be subjected to innumerable tyrannical exactions. Therefore is it more painful and more distressing to be born again than to die; the spirit's disgust, fright and extreme dejection on the threshold of this world of darkness is readily conceivable.

───⁂───

Reincarnation takes place by a gradual coming together, by a slow assimilation of material molecules by the perispirit, which progressively is reduced and condensed, adding to its own weight, until such time as, by sufficient adjunction with matter, it shall have made for itself a freshly covering, a human body.

The perispirit thus plays the part of a fluidic, elastic mold which lends its shape to matter. Hence arise the physiological conditions of rebirth. The qualities and blemishes of the mold appear in the physical body, which is usually only a coarse and ugly copy of the perispirit.

From the beginning of the process of molecular assimilation which is to procreate a body, the spirit is overcome by confusion; it is gradually overpowered by a species of torpor, of semi-annihilation. Its faculties, one after the other, are clouded, its memory fails, and its conscience slumbers. The spirit is as if embedded within a thick chrysalis.

Once launched in the terrestrial life, the task of the soul for a long time will be to prepare this new organism and to adapt it to its necessary functions. It is only after twenty or thirty years of experimentation and of instinctive effort that it will regain the use of its faculties, although blurred by matter, and will be enabled to pursue with some degree of assurance the perilous undertaking of the voyage of life. And yet the person ignorantly weeps and laments over a grave, that open door to space, while were he familiar with the higher laws, it is over a cradle that he would lament! Is not the first cry of the newborn child like the complaint of the mind before the sad prospects of life?

The inexorable laws of nature, or rather the resultant effects of a being's past, determine the conditions of that being's reincarnation. The inferior spirit oblivious of these laws and careless of its destiny, mechanically submits to its fate and returns to take its place on Earth, under the compulsion of a law which it does not even try to understand. The advanced spirit seeks inspiration from the examples that surround it in the fluidic life; it treasures the advice of its spiritual guides, weighs the good and bad conditions that attend its reappearance on Earth, foresees the hindrances and difficulties that it will be likely to encounter; it makes to itself a plan, and arms itself with strong resolve, that this plan may be carried out. It does not achieve its new descent into the flesh until it has made sure of the help of the unseen powers, who will sustain it in the accomplishment of its new undertaking. In this case the spirit is not entirely subject to the pressure of fate. Its choice may be exerted within certain limits, so as to accelerate its progress.

This explains the enlightened spirit's preference for a laborious existence, a life of struggle and abnegation; for it is aware that, thanks to such a life, progress will be more rapid. Earth is the real purgatory. In order that the crimes and faults of the past may be effaced, and that vice should be eradicated, it is necessary to be born again and to suffer. This accounts for the cruel infirmities, the long and dangerous maladies, and for the loss of reason, we see on every side.

The abuse of the high faculties of the intellect, as well as pride and selfishness are atoned by rebirth in incomplete organisms, in deformed and sickly bodies. The spirit therein acquiesces in this temporary immolation, seeing there in the price of rehabilitation, the one possible means to acquire modesty and humility; it consents therefore to be deprived for a short time of the knowledge and talents in which it gloried, and to descend into an imperfect body of faulty parts; thus becoming an object of pity and derision.

Let us therefore reverence all mentally impaired, cripples and mad; and may all suffering be sacred to us! In these fleshly sepulchers, a spirit watches and suffers; for, in its inner consciousness, it is cognizant of its misery and abasement. Let us rather fear our own excesses, because we may incur in a like fate. However, these intellectual gifts, which the soul resigned for self-humiliation, it will once more regain in death – for they are the property and possession of the soul, and nothing that it has acquired by its own efforts can ever be lost or diminished. The soul will regain them, and with them those new qualities and virtues that it has obtained through sacrifice and which in space will be to it as a crown of light.

Hence everything must be accounted for, and everything likewise may be redeemed. Wicked thoughts and guilty desires have their aftermath in the fluidic life, and the faults committed in the flesh must be atoned by the flesh. All of our existences are linked together; good and evil reverberate through time. If those who are false and wicked depart in seeming peace and ease, we may be sure that an hour of justice will sound when the sufferings they have caused shall react upon them.

Therefore, one must resign oneself and patiently endure the inevitable but indispensable trials that will wash one's faults away and prepare one for a better future! Take example from the ploughman, who goes ever straight before him, indifferent both to the scorching sun and to the winter's blast; who by his sweat waters the ground – that excavated the soil which, like your heart, is seamed by the iron prong, but out of which the gilded harvest of happiness shall likewise spring.

Beware of those moments of weakness that would treacherously bring you back under the yoke of matter, and would weigh on your future happiness. Be good, be virtuous, in order to avoid being drawn into the labyrinth of evil with all its consequences. Flee the degrading joys, the sterile discussions, and the vain rivalry. It is not in the pursuit of honors and wealth that you will find wisdom and self-approval, but rather in work, charity and right doing; in solitary meditation, in the study gathered, in front of your own conscience and nature, this admirable book that God Himself has set His seal.

Fifth Part
The Straight Way

42

The Moral Life

In every human being, somewhere – in mind or conscience – are engraved the rudiments of the moral law – which, even in this world, is not without sanction. The one who performs a good deed, experiences an innate satisfaction, a pleasant sensation of warmth and expansion, whereas our sins are usually attended by bitterness and remorse. This consciousness of self-approval, which is moreover experienced in varying degree, is far too incomplete to right the scales of justice. Therefore has religion allotted to the rewards and penalties of a future life the final adjustment of our claims. To many minds, however, this speculative future is too illusory; it exercised a very considerable influence over the Middle Ages, but today they no longer suffice to remove man from the paths of sensuality.

Prior to Golgotha's dark tragedy, Christ had announced the coming of another consoler, the Spirit of Truth, which was to confirm and to complete His teaching. The Spirit of Truth has come and has spoken to people; everywhere it made his voice heard.

When, eighteen centuries after the death of Christ, free speech and free thought had been granted to most of the world, science having ventured to probe even the high heavens, and the human intelligence having developed – the hour was deemed propitious.

Legions of spirits drew near to instruct their earthly brother in the law of infinite progress, to realize Christ's promise, by reiterating his doctrines and commenting upon his parables.

Spiritism provides us with a key to the Gospel. It expounds their obscure or hidden sense; it gives us that superior and final morality whose beauty and grandeur reveal a superhuman origin.

That truth might reach all nations at once, so that none should pervert or deny it, it was not, this time, confided to any one individual or group of apostles. Spirit voices proclaim it from every part of the civilized world, and thanks to its permanent and universal character, this revelation will withstand all persecution and antagonism. It is possible to set aside the teachings of a single individual and to falsify or annul its fruits, but who can reach or push back the revelations imparted by the dwellers of space? They are well able to cope with all opposition, and to sow the precious seed in the remotest regions. Hence arises the power and rapid increase of Spiritism and its superiority over the doctrines which preceded it and prepared its advent.

It is therefore on the deposition of millions of spirits who, through mediums have testified throughout the world, giving an account of their personal experiences of happiness and suffering, that the morals of Spiritism are founded.

Independent morality, such as that which the materialists have attempted to construct, is at the mercy of every passing gust, being without solid basis. The chief motive power in churches is fear, the fear of hell; a wrong sentiment assuredly, and one which is certainly depresses and destructive. The spiritist philosophy offers humanity a higher incentive and a far noble and more generous ideal. Eternal torment is abolished; in its place we have the righteous consequences of misdeeds visited upon their perpetrator.

The spirit is ever and universally what it has made itself to be. When it violates the moral law it befogs its own conscience and faculties, it becomes materialized, it forges its own chain. By practicing the law of righteousness, by dominating its brutish instincts, it grows lighter, and hence draws ever nearer to the higher and happier zones.

Thus considered, the moral life imposes itself as an undeniable obligation upon all who take thought as to their future destiny. Hence the necessity of a hygiene of the soul, by the light of which our every deed will be weighed, and our spiritual forces will be maintained in a state of perfect harmony and equilibrium. If it be deemed wise to subject the body, that mortal envelope and perishable tool, to such observances of the physical law as it will ensure its maintenance and proper working, it is far more important that we should be solicitous of the soul, that imperishable entity upon which hangs our entire future estate. Spiritism will provide us with proper directions for this hygiene of the soul.

The knowledge of life's true aim is of incalculable service in furthering our elevation and amelioration; once we know whether we tend, our step becomes firmer and our every motion is quickened into a vigorous impulse towards the ideal conceived.

The doctrines of nothingness make this life an impasse and logically lead to sensualism and disorder. Religion, by considering life as a very questionable means of personal salvation, imparts to it a narrow and selfish aspect.

With the spiritist philosophy, the outlook immediately changes and the perspective widens. What we must seek is no longer of mere earthly enjoyment – on this Earth happiness is rare and precarious – but of unceasing improvement, the means to which lies in the observance of the moral law in its every aspect.

With such an ideal, society becomes indestructible; it defies all vicissitudes, all events; it thrives on misfortune and adversity, and it finds in adversity the means of rising above itself. Any society lacking in idealism, seeking its nutriment in the sophistry of sensualism, becomes perforce debilitated and corrupt; his faith in progress, in justice, is extinguished with his virility, and soon it will be but a soulless carcass and will fall an easy prey to its enemies.

Happy is the one who in this life of darkness and pitfalls steadily proceeds towards a chosen elevation which he unswervingly keeps in view. Happy, too, is the one who feels himself sustained by some heaven-born inspiration. To him pleasure is indifferent, and neither the temptations of the flesh nor the allurements of wealth possess any reality. A traveler on the march, the goal calls him; and he rushes to reach it.

43

Duty

Duty is the set of prescriptions of the moral law, the rule of conduct of the human being in his relations with his fellow-beings and with the whole universe. Noble and holy, he hovers over humanity, inspires great sacrifices, pure devotions, and beautiful enthusiasms. Smiling at some, formidable to others, always inflexible, he stands before us and shows us that scale of progress, the degrees of which are lost to immeasurable heights.

Duty is not invariably one and the same for all people; it varies according to our learning and position. The more elevated our thoughts, the broader and greater our duty appears. But to the wise duty's service is ever light, and our obedience to its mandates ensures such inner happiness as nothing else can provide.

No matter how obscure the person or how lowly his standing, duty still remains the ruling power, the ennobling factor of his life. It alone can bestow that serenity of mind, that inner peace, more precious than all the riches of the world, and which we may continue to enjoy, even in the stress of trouble and reverse. We cannot change that which is to be, our destiny must rigorously follow its preordained course; but we can always, even in the midst of thunderstorms, retain that peace of conscience that accompanies a sense of duty filled.

The sense of duty has deep roots in every elevated mind, hence their road is an easy one to travel. Their natural inclination – the outcome of acquired habits – prompts them to avoid all that is vile and directs every impulse towards the pure and the noble. Duty then becomes the care of each passing instant, the very condition of existence; a power to which one feels indissolubly bound, in life as in death.

The forms of duty are many. There is the duty we owe ourselves, which abides in self-respect, in a wise government of our willful nature, in the desire to do only that which is consistent with dignity, utility and beauty. There is a professional duty which requires us scrupulously to fulfill all the tasks that have been committed to us. There is a social duty which invites us to love our fellow-beings and to work for them; as faithfully to serve our country as humanity. There is our duty towards God. Duty has no limits. One can always do better, and it is in the sacrifice of self that the being finds the surest means of purification and elevation.

Honesty is the very essence of the moral person. So soon as he strays from it he is unhappy. The honest person is righteous for righteousness' sake, without thought of approval or reward. Being himself incapable of hatred or vengeance, he forgets that he has been offended and heartily forgives. Kindly to all, to the weak he is boundlessly helpful. In every person he sees a brother, regardless of his antecedents or faith. Full of toleration he respects a sincere belief, and respects the faults of others in seeking their good qualities; never does an ill-natured comment arise to his lips. He partakes with moderation of the good things that life has brought him, consecrates his wealth to the general good; in poverty he is without envy or jealousy of others.

Worldly honesty is not always the same thing as divine honesty. Public opinion has its value; it makes merit easier by its recognition, but it is far from being regarded as infallible. The sage does not disdain her, no doubt; but when it is unjust or inadequate, it passes over and measures its duty to a more precise standard. Merit and virtue often go unrecognized in this world; the opinion of the multitude is as frequently directed by its material passions and its interests. The honest person will, before all, seek to merit his own self-esteem and the approbation of his own conscience.

He who has comprehended the higher ethics of spiritual philosophy has a still nobler conception of duty. He knows that responsibility is a corollary of knowledge and that the possession of the secrets of another world obliges him to work the harder towards his own improvement and that of his fellow-beings. The voices from the unseen world awaken strange echoes within him and make forces to vibrate which are dormant in most people; these urge him strenuously onward in his ascending conquest. A noble ideal stimulates and torments him at once, at which the wicked sneer, but which he would not renounce for all the wealth of an Empire. The practice of charity has now become a lightsome task, for his generous and affectionate impulses have greatly expanded. Sympathizing and righteous, he is moved by all the sorrows of humanity. To his companions in misfortune he would gladly impart the hopes that inspire him; he would like to shoulder their sorrows, heal their wounds, and remove their pains.

The constant observance of duty conduces to perfection; to speedily attain which one must first carefully study one's own individuality, while keeping strict watch over every action; for it is impossible to cure an unknown evil.

One can study oneself in others; If any vice, some unfortunate defect, shocks us in them, let us seek carefully whether there is not in us an identical germ, and if we discover it, we must spare no pains to eradicate it.

Let us think of our soul as it really is, an admirable but most imperfect work, whose constant embellishment and adornment is our concern. The realization of our imperfection will render us more modest and will keep us free from presumption and foolish vanity.

Let us submit ourselves to a rigorous discipline; as the growing shrub is trained to follow a given shape and direction, so may the tendencies of the moral being be regulated. The habit of righteousness renders its application easy. The first are the only painful efforts. We must above all acquire self-control; impressions are fleeting and fickle things and the will is the only solid reliance of the soul; we should then learn to control this will and to master our impressions, else they will master us.

The human being should not isolate from his siblings. It is important however to choose his relationships, his friends, to attempt to live in an honest and pure environment, where only good influences, calm, and beneficial fluids reign.

Let us avoid idle and frivolous conversation, which leads to slander. Come what may, we must always unflinchingly speak the truth. Let us often have recourse to study and meditation, for in them the soul gathers new strength and light. May we be able to end each day by saying: I have accomplished some useful thing – I have won some victory over myself; I have comforted or assisted some needy person; I have enlightened my brothers and worked for their good; I have fulfilled my duty!

44

Faith, Hope and Consolation

Faith is the confidence of the human being in his destinies, it is the sentiment that leads him toward the infinite Power; it is the certainty of being on the path that leads to truth. Blind faith is the lantern whose red glare cannot overcome the fog; enlightened faith is a powerful beacon that brightly illuminates the road ahead. One cannot possess this faith until one has experienced all manner of doubt, that painful perturbation that often besieges the earnest seeker.

Many, indeed, end in a wretched state of uncertainty, and drift for a long period at the mercy of contrary winds. He who believes, knows, sees and progresses, with assured tread, and is happy, for his faith is deep, unshaken and so robust as to overcome all opposition. In this sense has it been said that faith is powerful enough to move mountains; the mountains being figuratively the innumerable obstacles of passion, prejudice, ignorance and interest which stand in the way of the innovator.

Faith is generally held to designate the mere uncritical acceptance of religious dogmas. But it should also apply to other convictions susceptible of awakening and stirring the person. There is a faith in oneself, a political faith, a faith in one's country, etc. For the artist, poet or thinker, faith is a conception of the ideal; it is the vision of a sublime fire which some divine hand once kindled upon the mountain-top to guide humanity towards the Beautiful and the True.

The religious faith, which excludes reason and relies upon the judgment of others, which accepts an entire doctrine, be it true or false and unquestioningly obeys it, is a blind faith. In its spasms of intemperate impatience it readily resorts to coercion which in turn are conducive to fanaticism. But even at its worst, faith remains a powerful influence. It has taught the human being to be humble and to suffer. Perverted by the spirit of domination it has been the cause of many crimes; but still we must bow down to the power that is in it.

If blind faith can produce such results: what might not an intelligent, discerning and comprehending trust achieve? Some theologians ask us to deny and stifle our reason. They object to all the errors into which it has fallen, and seem to forget that it is reason itself that has helped us to correct them. Should we deny it even while it reveals to us so much that is good and lovely?

Reason is a superior faculty whose mission is to enlighten us upon every subject; like all our faculties it can be developed by use. Human reason is a reflection of the eternal Reason: *"It is God within us,"* as Saint Paul said. To misunderstand its value and utility is to misapprehend human nature and to slight one of God's gifts. To use faith instead of reason is to ignore the fact that the two are interdependent and inseparable, that they strengthen and vitalize one another. Their union opens to thought a wider field, harmonizes our faculties and grants us inner peace.

Faith is the procreator of noble sentiments and great deeds. The one who has perfect faith will be unshaken by the direst peril as by the cruelest trial. Above the seduction, flattery, threats and even desire, a voice echoes in the person's conscience and urges him on to the righteous fight, and sustains him in the dangerous hours.

To attain such results faith must rest on the solid basis of free examination and liberty of thought; instead of dogma and mystery it must recognize those principles that depend upon direct observation and the study of natural laws. Such is the nature of the spiritist faith.

The philosophy that the spirits have brought us is a belief which is as robust as it is rational. The knowledge of the invisible world, the confidence in a higher law of justice and progress, impart to faith a dual character of peace and conviction.

What indeed remains to be feared when one knows that the soul can never die; that after the storms and struggles of life, beyond that dire blackness in which everything seems to be submerged, we shall behold the enchanted dawn of those bright days which shall be without end!

When the old age advances, putting its mark on our face, extinguishing our eyes, stiffening our members, curving us under its weight, then with it sadness, the dislike of all and the great feeling of tiredness come, a need for rest, like a thirst for nothing. Oh! At this hour of trouble, in this twilight of life, how delightful and comforting is the small light that shines in the heart of those who believe, who have faith in the infinite future, faith in Justice, and faith in the Supreme Goodness!

Once we have thoroughly grasped the fact that life is but a moment in our immortal existence, we shall patiently bear the ills that it brings us. The vista revealed by this conception will permit us readily to master our actual distress and to place ourselves above the fluctuations of fortune; then shall we feel confident and ready for any adversity. The spiritist knows the cause of his suffering and understands their necessity. He knows that suffering is legitimate, and uncomplainingly endures it. To his vision death sunders nothing, the bonds of sentiment still persist in the life beyond, and all who have loved on this Earth will meet again, emancipated from every affliction, in regions far remote from this planet of sorrowful sojourn, there where separation does not exist, except for the wicked and imperfect. This assurance is in itself a fund of comfort unknown to the indifferent and the skeptical. Were this belief universal, reaching from end to end of the world, history's greatest moral transformation would be effected.

Unfortunately too few, as yet, possess this faith. The Spirit of Truth has spoken, but the world has turned a deaf ear. It is not the powerful who have listened to it, but rather the humble, the small, the disinherited, all those who thirst for hope. At first this spiritist revolution encountered a lively opposition from religious and scientific circles. This opposition is gradually diminishing. Many people, however, lack the courage to reconsider their statements and to frankly acknowledge their error; they would rather continue to deny a truth which might compromise their intellectual standing and reputation. Others secretly admire the grand beauty of this doctrine, but are intimidated by its ethical requirements. Fond of pleasure and desirous of living according to their tastes, without heed for the life to come, they thrust aside every thought that might interfere with their pleasant but pernicious habits, a decision which will some day be a matter of bitter regret.

Our feverish and intemperate civilization is very little concerned about moral teachings. Too many contradictory and conflicting opinions are involved in this chaos; the human being himself, swept away on the whirlwind of materialism, seldom pauses and more seldom reflects.

Still, every mind in quest of faith and truth will find them in this new revelation. A superior influence will descend upon such, directing it towards that kindling light which, some day, will enlighten the whole world.

45

Pride, Wealth and Poverty

Of all vices, pride is the most dangerous, for it leaves in its wake the seeds of most of the others. It is the monstrous, ever-begetting hydra whose offspring are monsters like her. As soon as it has access to a soul then it takes complete and arrogant possession, spreading and fortifying itself therein until it has become inexpugnable.

Woe to the person who has allowed himself to be thus taken by surprise! He may only be rid of this tyrant at the cost of exhausting struggles, many painful attempts, obscure lives and a lengthy future of lowly humiliation; for such is the sole remedy for the evils of pride.

Pride is the greatest plague of humanity. From it all the slashes of social life, all clashes of class and rank, all intrigue, war and hatred proceed. Inspirer of the insane ambitions, it has covered the Earth with blood and ruin. Pride is still the originator of our sufferings in the life beyond the grave; for its consequences reach beyond death, and attain even to our far destiny.

Not only does pride withhold us from the affection of our neighbors, but it renders improvement impossible, by misleading us as to our value and blinding us as to our defects. It is only by a rigorous examination of our thoughts and actions that we can hope to reform. How can the proud person submit to such an analysis? Of all people he is the last to know himself. Infatuated with his personality, nothing can open his eyes since he is careful to avoid those who might enlighten him; he cannot brook contradiction and is only happy when surrounded by flatterers.

As the worm eats into a fine fruit so pride corrupts the most meritorious works, even to turning them against the one who accomplishes them. Charity ostentatiously bestowed, with a secret desire for approval and notoriety, turns against the donor. In the spiritual life, our intentions, those hidden impulses that inspire us, suddenly appear like so many living witnesses; they overwhelm the proud, and reduce their illusory merit to dust.

Pride obscures all truth from us. That the study of the universe and its laws may be fruitful, simplicity, sincerity and straightforwardness of heart and mind are above all necessary – all of these qualities are unknown to the proud one. The thought that so much transcends us is intolerable, and pride promptly discards it. The opinion of the vain person encompasses the limits of the possible, and it is difficult for him to admit that his knowledge and understanding can have any limit.

He who is simple and humble of heart will attain to truth, in spite of his possible mental inferiority, more quickly than the presumptuous person who is vain of his earthly knowledge and rebels against the law that lessens his importance.

Spirit communications have shown us the real position of the proud in the life beyond the grave. Those that were humble and meek in this world are greater in the next; whereas the proud and powerful are lowered and humbled. Some have brought with them that which constituted true superiority, the virtues and qualities they acquired through sufferings: whereas the others, on dying, left behind them their titles, wealth and vain knowledge; all that constituted their pride and happiness vanished like smoke. Thus, poor and destitute they make their entrance into eternity, and this sudden destitution contrasting with their past splendor, increases their sorrow and vain regret. It is with profound bitterness that they recognize in the light that transcends them, those whom on Earth they had scorned and disdained. The same thing takes place in future reincarnations. That pride and grasping ambition may be gradually lessened and finally disappear, one requires many troubled lives – lives of work and renunciation, during which the vain soul retires within itself, discovers its weakness, and, little by little, becomes capable of conceiving worthier sentiments.

A little thought and wisdom will preserve us from these evils. How indeed could we allow pride to invade and dominate us, when we need only to examine ourselves in order to realize how little we are? Is it our body, our physical pleasures that inspire us with vanity? Beauty is short-lived; one single illness may destroy it. Time is daily at its task; still a few more steps in life and all these charms will be faded and wrinkled, and our body will have become a repulsive thing. Is it of our superiority over nature? Let the strongest and cleverest of us be transported into a desert and there left to his own resources; let him fight the elements single-handed or be exposed, alone, to the mercy of the sea: in the midst of the great storm, the huge waves and the raging wind, and his weakness will be revealed!

In the hour of danger all social distinctions, titles and wealth are estimated at their just value. We are all equal before danger, suffering and death. All people, from the highest to the lowliest, are made of the same clay. Whether attired in silk or rags, their bodies are animated by the same kind of spirit and all will meet in the future world. Then only, and by their moral value alone, will they be distinguished. The greatest here below may become a beggar in space, and the beggar can put on a dazzling robe. Let us despise no one, and let us not draw vanity from favors or from temporary advantages – for no one knows what tomorrow may bring forth.

⁓

If Jesus promised that the poor and lowly should be admitted into the kingdom of heaven, it is because wealth and power too often engender pride, whereas an obscure and laborious life is the surest factor of moral progress. In the fulfillment of his daily task, the worker is less frequently affected by temptation and unwholesome desire, he has frequent opportunity to meditate and to develop his conscience; the worldly person, on the contrary, is absorbed by the frivolous pursuits of pleasure or speculation.

Wealth binds us to Earth by so many and such insidious ties, that death seldom suffices to break them and to liberate us; hence the rich person's anguish in the life beyond. It is, nevertheless, easy to see that nothing on this Earth is really ours. These goods, to which we attach so much value, belong to us only in appearance. A hundred others, a thousand before us, thought they possessed them; a thousand others will, after us, deceive themselves with the same delusions, which sooner or later all must abandon. Our body itself is a loan from nature, and she knows how to reclaim it when it so pleases. Our sole lasting possessions are our intellectual and moral acquisitions.

From the love of material goods envy and jealousy are often born, and when one falls a prey to these vices one may bid farewell to peace and rest. Life then becomes a perpetual torment. The wealth and success of another awaken in the envious person a feverish and consuming desire for possession. He dreams of attaining unrivalled glory and of amassing such treasures as lie beyond his capacity to enjoy. Is this not a pitiful life? Endlessly to pursue a visionary happiness, to set one's heart upon vanities, the loss of which causes us bitter regret – is it not to provide ourselves with an unnecessary fund of self-torment?

Wealth, in itself, is not necessarily an evil; it is evil or good according to the use we make of it. One must, above all, guard against the pride and hard-heartedness which its possession frequently instills; one must be the master and not the slave of wealth, one must be superior to it, remaining generous and unselfish. On these terms the perilous test of wealth becomes easier to bear. It does not soften the characters; it does not awaken that sensuality which seems to be the almost inseparable from well-being.

Prosperity is dangerous because of the temptations it offers and of the fascinations it commands. It may nevertheless be a source of great good, if rightly and wisely applied.

Wealth empowers its possessor to contribute to the intellectual progress and social improvement of humanity, by establishing colleges and charitable institutions; by sharing with the needy the benefits of science and the revelations of eternal beauty in its many aspects. But, above all, wealth must come, in the form of work and help, to those that are in need.

Exclusively to consecrate one's means to the gratification of the senses or of vanity is to waste this life and to create heavy shackles for the next. The rich person must render an account of the deposit which was placed in his hands for the common well. When the stern voice of law and the accusing tones of conscience are lifted against him in that blessed world where gold can purchase no influence, what then shall he plead against the accusation of having applied to his own selfish ends that which was destined to satisfy the hunger and needs of others?

When the spirit does not feel strong enough to resist the glamour of wealth, it will act wisely in avoiding this severe test and in electing, in its place, a simple life far from the lure of fortune and greatness. If fate destines it, in spite of its wishes, to fill a high place in this world, it should not rejoice, for its duties and responsibilities will be proportionately increased. But placed in the lowest ranks of society, let him never blush, for the role of the humble is the most meritorious. It is them which support all the weight of civilization, and it is upon their work that humanity lives and is fed. Poverty should be held sacred by all people, for it is in poverty that Jesus elected to live and die; it is poverty which was chosen by Epictetus, Francis of Assisi, Michael Angelo, Saint Vincent of Paul and so many other noble spirits that have lived in this world. They knew well that work, privation and suffering strengthen the virile forces of the soul, while prosperity softens and loosens them. In the detachment from mundane things, some have found sanctification and others the power that constitutes genius.

Poverty begets tenderness for the sufferings of our neighbors, by bringing them to us. It makes us one with all who suffer; it imparts a value to a thousand things, of which the rich are indifferent. Those who have not known his lessons will always ignore one of life's most touching aspects.

Therefore let us not envy the rich, whose apparent splendor hides much inner grief; nor let us forget that the rags of poverty may hang upon the most sublime virtues of abnegation and self-sacrifice. Neither should we forget that it is through the work, privation and devotion of the humble and the meek of this world that humanity exists and is perpetuated.

46

Selfishness

Selfishness is the brother of pride, and proceeds from the same causes. It is amongst the soul's greatest ailments, and there is no greater obstacle to social improvement. It suffices, of itself, to paralyze and annul most of the individual's endeavors towards righteousness. The constant efforts of all friends of progress and believers in justice should combine against it.

Selfishness is a remnant of the inferior state through which we have passed; it is a survival of the wild individualism that characterizes the brute. But the human being is pre-eminently a sociable being; he is destined to live with his fellows and can do nothing without them. Abandoned to himself, he would be powerless to satisfy his needs, to develop his qualities.

After God, it is to society that the person is indebted for all the good things of life and the privileges of civilization. He enjoys it, but precisely this enjoyment, this participation in the fruits of the common work, impose on him the duty to co-operate in the work itself. He is bound to society by the close ties of solidarity; he belongs to society, and society to him. To remain inactive, non-producing and useless in the midst of universal work amounts to a moral violation, almost a theft; it is to profit by the work of others, to accept a loan and afterwards to refuse to repay it.

As we form an integral part of society, all that touches it, touches us as well. It is by the understanding that each has social obligations and of the law of solidarity, that individual selfishness may be estimated. He who is capable of living for his fellow-beings has no reason to fear the attacks of this scourge; he has within him an infallible criterion of conduct. He will do nothing without first ascertaining whether that which he contemplates will benefit his neighbors; whether it will be useful or detrimental to the social body of which he is a member. If his contemplated acts appear to be profitable to himself alone and damaging to others, he will know that they must be detrimental to all, and therefore scrupulously avoid them.

Avarice is one of the most repulsive forms of selfishness. It reveals the baseness of the soul, which after monopolizing wealth that belongs to the community does not even know how to enjoy it. The miser, by his lot of gold and his rapacity in acquisition, impoverishes his fellow-beings and remains poor himself, as this apparent wealth which he has amassed to no one's advantage is nothing but poverty – a relative poverty as pitiful as destitution, a just subject for universal reprobation.

No elevated sentiment, nothing that is inherently noble, can proceed from a miserly soul. The envy and cupidity that haunt the miser condemn him to a wretched present and a still unhappier future. Nothing can exceed his despair when, standing upon the other side of the grave, he witnesses the partition and dispersion of his treasures.

You who seek peace of heart, avoid of all things this low and contemptible vice! But do not fly to the opposite extreme! Do not squander. Learn to use your resources with wisdom and moderation.

Selfishness contains its own punishment. The egotist is conscious of none but himself in the world; all that is foreign to his interests is indifferent to him. His hours seem slow and dreary; he lingers in this life as well as in the next, in a permanent atmosphere of tediousness, for all people and all spirits avoid him.

Whereas he who cooperates with all his strength in the consolidation of the social edifice; he who lives in pleasant communion with his fellow-beings, sharing with them his brains and his wealth as he shares in theirs; he who gives forth the best that is in him; that person will experience happiness. His heart is set upon the observance of the law and upon the necessity of being a useful member of society. All that goes on in the world interests him. All that is great and beautiful touches him and moves him; His soul vibrates in unison with all enlightened and generous souls, and neither tediousness nor disillusionment obtains hold upon him.

Our duty is then not to hold ourselves distant, but to battle unremittingly in the cause of truth and righteousness. It is neither sitting nor lying that one must contemplate the spectacle of human life with its perpetual changes, but rather on one's feet, a pioneer, a soldier, ready to take part in all the great tasks, to pave the way, to fertilize the common heritage of humanity.

Although selfishness is to be found in all grades of society, this vice belongs rather to the rich than to the poor. Prosperity too often drains the wells of sympathy, while misfortune, by showing us the meaning of sorrow, teaches us to appreciate the sufferings of others. Does the rich person even know at what cost of sorrows and hard work the thousand things that constitute his luxury have been created?

We should never sit down to a well-served meal without thinking of those that hunger. This thought will incline us to be temperate and measured in our tastes and appetites. Consider the millions of people who are constantly exposed to summer heat and winter frosts, who for the sake of earning a meager salary take from the soil those things that are consumed at our banquets and adorn our houses. Let us remember that if our houses are brightly illuminated and our hearths warmly glow, it is because people, who resemble us and who, like us, are capable of love and suffering, are working beneath the surface of the Earth; far from blues skies and happy sunshine they spend their lives, pickaxe in hand, digging in the entrails of the Earth. Let us consider that these mirrors which reflect our gaze, that these crystal chandeliers which hang from our ceilings, and countless other luxuries, are produced by yet another legion of workers who live their lives in the suffocating heat of furnaces and foundries, spent for lack of fresh air, used up and exhausted before their time; people who have nothing better to anticipate than a sickly and barren old age for their reward! It is well, indeed, to bear in mind that all this comfort which we so contemptuously enjoy, has been purchased by the suffering of the poor, the working of the lowly. May this thought penetrates us and haunt us, till, like a flaming sword, it will drive out the selfishness from our hearts and will force us to concentrate our wealth, leisure and intelligence to the amelioration of the condition of those that are weak and ailing and poor!

For there can be no peace among people, no security and no social happiness, until selfishness shall have been banished; until all favoritism and shocking inequalities shall have disappeared; until every person shall participate, according to his work and merit, in the common welfare. There is no possible peace or harmony without justice. As long as the selfishness of some will nourish upon the tears and privations of others, as long as the requirements of the ego continue to stifle the voice of duty –hatred will remain on Earth, the clashes of interests will divide people, and the heart of society be ceaselessly rent by social discord.

Thanks to the knowledge of the future that we now possess, the notion of solidarity will finally prevail. The law of the return to the flesh, the necessity for reincarnation under lowly conditions, these will act upon our selfishness like so many pivots. In face of this prospect, our exaggerated self-love will be attenuated by a better appreciation of our situation and allotted place in the universe. Knowing ourselves connected to all souls, in solidarity with their advancement and happiness, we shall be more interested in their situation, their progress, and achievements. In the degree in which this sentiment spreads, will the world's social institutions and mutual comprehension improve; fraternity, this banal word repeated by so many mouths, will blossom in the hearts of people and become a living fact. We shall truly live in others, rejoicing in their happiness and lamenting with their grief. Then will there be no complaint without echo, no sorrow without consolation; then the great human family, peaceful, united and confident, will advance more rapidly towards its glorious destiny.

47

Charity

Unlike the exclusionism which decrees that, "Without the Church there is no salvation" – as though a purely human decree could dispose of human's immortal future – Allan Kardec has placed the following words on his books: *"Without Charity there is no Salvation."* Indeed, the spirits instruct us that charity is the supreme virtue and that it alone possesses the key to the high heavens.

With Christ, they bid us, "love thy neighbor as thyself," these words embracing all the commandments of the moral law.

But, it might be objected, people are not lovable. It is hard to feel charitably towards them, for within them there enters too much wickedness.

If we think thus, is it not because we too exclusively consider the worst side of their character, their faults, passions, and weaknesses, constantly forgetting that we ourselves are not devoid of the same imperfections, so that if they need our charity, we no less require their indulgence?

However, it is not evil alone that rules the world; there is good also in the human being; he has some good qualities and some virtues. And, above all, there is much suffering! If we would be charitable – and this we should be, both for our own sake and for that of the community – we must not dwell upon that which, concerning our neighbors, might induce us to slander and disparage them; rather let us look upon the person as our companion in suffering, as a brother soldier in the great battle of life. Let us consider the ills he must endure, no matter what his rank may be. Where is the person who does not harbor some wound in the depths of his soul? Who does not bear the weight of grief and bitterness? When we view our fellow-beings in this light, our ill will is soon converted into sympathy.

Many, for instance, are constantly recriminating against the coarseness and brutality of some of the working classes – against their covetousness and ceaseless claims. Do we reflect sufficiently on the bad examples by which they have been surrounded from childhood up? The necessities of life, the imperious necessities of each day, impose on them a hard and unremitting work. They have only small respite and little leisure in which to cultivate their minds. The blessings of study and the delights of art are alike denied them. What do they know of moral law, of destiny, of the forces of the universe? Few consoling rays slip into this darkness. For them, the fierce struggle against necessity is an uninterrupted combat. Unemployment, sickness, and the ensuing privation, are constantly threatening and worrying them. Who would not be embittered by so much misery? To accept all this with resignation real stoicism is required, as well as an innate force of character, the more admirable because it is instinctive rather than reasoned.

Instead of blaming these unfortunate brothers and sisters, we should strive to make their burden lighter, and do our utmost to effect a more equitable division of the treasures of both wealth and thought. It is hard to realize the good that a kind word, a little show of interest, a hearty handshake, does to these embittered persons. We are shocked by the vices of the poor, and yet what an excuse is there in the depths of his misery! But we want to ignore its virtues, which are much more astonishing, flourishing in the quagmire. How much hidden devotion does we not find among the poor; what a determined and constant struggle against adversity!

To think of the countless families that vegetate without support, and without help; of the children that lack their daily bread; of the many who shiver with cold and hunger, that exist, huddled in dark, damp cellars or dismal attics! What a noble role is that which falls to the woman of the people, of the mother! When the winter snows have fallen, when there is no fuel for the fire, no food for the table; when on the icy bed rags take the place of the blanket that was sold or bartered for bread! Is not her sacrifice complete, when you consider the heart that is breaking as, helpless, dry-breast and empty-handed, she witnesses the sufferings of her little ones? Should not the rich idler be ashamed to display his wealth among so much suffering? What an overwhelming responsibility for him, if, in his abundance, he neglects to assist those that are perishing of want!

Undoubtedly, mixed among the scenes of the life of the little ones, there are many repulsive things and much that is vile; complaints and blasphemies, drunkenness and abortion, unnatural parents and heartless children, all manner of hideousness intermingled; but always, beneath even these repugnant aspects, it is ever the human soul that is suffering; a kindred soul, one therefore still deserving of our interest and affection.

To remove such a soul from the mud; to comfort and enlighten it, to help it to climb, rung by rung, the ladder of rehabilitation, this is surely a noble task! Everything is purified in the fire of charity. This is the flame that blazed so gloriously in Christ, in St. Vincent of Paul, and all those who, in their immense love for the weak and the fallen, found the principle of their sublime abnegation.

Thus is it with all who are capable of much love and of much suffering. Pain is to them an initiation in the science of comforting and assisting others. Pain is to them as an initiation to the art of consoling and relieving others. They know how to rise above their own ills in order to see only those that afflict their fellow-beings, and for these alone seek a remedy. Hence the noble example given by those superior souls who, in the midst of their own dissolution and dreadful agony, can still find the hidden balm that can heal the wounds of the world's defeated ones.

Charity has other forms than solicitude for the unfortunate. Material charity, or benevolence, can be applied to a certain number of our fellow-beings, in the form of relief, support, and encouragement. Moral charity should be extended to all that dwell with us in this world. This does not consist in almsgiving, but in a universal kindliness which is extended to all people, to saint and sinner alike, and upon which our common communication is based. We can all practice it, however modest our condition may be.

True charity is patient and indulgent. It never disdains, nor crush anyone; it is tolerant, and if it seeks to dissuade, it is with gentleness, without hurting or rushing any preconceived notion.

This however, is a rare quality. A certain trace of vanity urges us to criticize the defects of others, while remaining blind to our own. Strange, that being ourselves so imperfect, we should still take pleasure in discovering a blemish in our neighbor. True moral superiority is never to be found without charity and modesty. We have no right to condemn in others the faults to which we ourselves lie open; and even if our moral elevation had freed us for ever, we should not forget that there was once a time when we too were struggling against vice and desire.

There are few people who have no bad habits to eradicate, no evil tendencies to correct. Let us not forget that we shall be judged by the standards that we apply to others. The opinions we form of them are almost invariably a reflection of our own nature. Let us then be quicker to excuse than to blame.

Nothing is more harmful to the soul's future than slander, that familiar bad-mouthing which feeds the majority of ordinary conversation. The echo of our speech reverberates in the beyond, the fumes of our malevolent thoughts shape themselves into a species of thick mist that envelops and obscures the spirit. Let us be aware of these criticisms, those unkind remarks, those sarcastic words that would poison our future. Let us flee from slanderer as we would the plague, let us retain on our lips every bitter remark which is about to escape them, for upon such things does our happiness depend.

The charitable individual performs his good deeds in secrecy, whereas the vain one loudly proclaims the little that he does. "Do not let not your left hand to know what your right hand is doing," so Jesus taught us. "He that proclaim the good he does already has received his reward!"

To give secretly, to be indifferent to the approbation of others, denotes a real superiority that places the giver above the fleeting judgment of people, seeking his justification in the life which is without end.

Under these conditions, ingratitude and injustice cannot reach the charitable person. It does good because it is its duty and without expecting any advantage. It seeks no reward; it trusts to eternal justice for the consequences that its deeds will bring about – or rather, it gives the matter no thought. Its generosity is without calculation. In order to oblige others it unhesitatingly deprives itself, and sees but small merit in giving forth out of its own superfluity. This is the reason why the poor man's money, the widow's mite, the crust of bread shared by the beggar with his unfortunate brother, are greater than the rich person's largess. The poor man, in his destitution, can still help the poorest. There are a thousand ways of being useful and helpful to others.

Gold does not dry all tears, nor can it heal all wounds; there are ills for which a sincere friendship, a loving sympathy and a tender heart can work more good than all the wealth of the world.

We must be generous towards those that have succumbed in the fight against their passions, and whom evil has attracted; generous to sinners, to criminals, to the insensitive. How are we to know through what cruel tests these souls have passed, what sufferings they underwent before they failed? Had they received that precious knowledge of the superior laws, which sustains in the hour of peril? Ignorant, uncertain, swayed by all the external breezes, could they resist and conquer? Let us recollect that responsibility is proportionate to knowledge, and that much will be required of him who has the truth.

Let us be pitiful for the lonely, to the weak, the afflicted, for all those who are hurt in body or soul. Let us seek the environments where sorrows abound, where hearts are broken, where existences dry up in despair and neglect and despair. Let us descend into those abysses of misery to offer a vivifying consolation, a stirring exhortation, and strive to kindle a ray of that hope which is the sun of the unfortunate. Let us do our utmost to rescue some victim that we may purify and place beyond the reach of harm, thus showing one soul the road of redemption. It is only through devotion and affection that we will prevent social cataclysms, by extinguishing the hatred that is brewing at the heart of the disinherited.

All that people endeavor for his fellow-being, imprints itself in the great fluidic book whose pages are unrolling in space – the luminous pages upon which our actions, our sentiments and our thoughts are inscribed. These debts will be abundantly repaid in the world to come.

Nothing is lost, or ever forgotten. The bonds that unite the souls for all time are woven of past kindnesses. Eternal wisdom has ordained all things for the soul's good. Good works performed here below become a source of infinite future blessing to the doer.

Perfection in the human being is comprised in two words: Charity and Truth. Charity is the supreme virtue; it is of divine essence. It shines upon all worlds, it warms souls like a look, like a smile of the Lord. Its results outstrip those of knowledge or genius. Those do not go without some pride. They are contested, doubted sometimes; but charity always sweet and benevolent, softens the hardest hearts and disarms the wicked ones by its unfaltering love.

48

Patience and Goodness

If pride is the progenitor of many vices, charity is the mother of many virtues. Patience, mildness, moderation of thought and speech, are all derived from charity. It is easy for the charitable person to be patient and mild, and to forgive his offender; mercy is the companion of goodness. A lofty soul cannot experience hatred or harbor vengeance. It soars far above base rancor; it views all things from a high standpoint. Comprehending that the wrongs of people arise from their ignorance, it conceives neither bitterness nor resentment, for it knows that in the forgiving and the forgiveness of the wrongs committed against it, lies the annihilation of every cause of discord, in the future of this world as well as in the Eternity of Space.

Charity, sweetness, and the forgiveness of offence make us invulnerable to the assaults of perfidy and baseness. They ensure our progressive detachment from the vanities of this world and accustom us to direct our gaze toward those things that are beyond the reach of disappointment.

Forgiveness is the duty of the soul that aspires to the high heavens. How frequently have we not ourselves stood in need of forgiveness, how often have we not needed it? We must forgive if we would be forgiven. We cannot hope to obtain that which we refuse to others. If we would seek revenge, let it be in the doing of kind deeds. The good returned for evil disarms the enemy. His hatred is converted into surprise, and surprise into admiration; by awakening his somnolent conscience this lesson may produce a deep impression upon him. Thus shall we perchance, through enlightenment, have saved a soul from perversity.

The only evils which we are bound publicly to denounce and combat are those that might be injurious to humanity. When they take the shape of hypocrisy, duplicity and falsehood, it becomes our duty to unmask them, because others might suffer; but it is well that we keep silence on what affects only our own interests or our self-esteem.

Revenge in all its aspects, be it by duel or war, is a vestige of primitive barbarism, a remnant of an unenlightened and savage epoch. Whosoever has caught a glimpse of that marvelously sequential chain of the superior laws, and among them of the principle of justice whose effects are transmitted to the end of time, could never dream of revenge.

To take vengeance is to make two faults, two crimes, of one; it is to become as guilty as the offender. When outrage or injustice strike us, let us impose silence on our wounded dignity, let us think of those who, in the obscure past we ourselves must have offended, outraged, robbed, and that this slender is offered as the necessary reparation. Above all, let us not lose sight of our journey's end, which such episodes might incline us to forget. On no account must we stray from that narrow but certain path, or hearken to the desire which would tempt us to descend the dangerous slopes of animosity; but let us climb them rather with a redoubling courage. Vengeance is a folly that would shake the fruits from over the same ground. Perhaps, some day in another world, we shall bless those who have shown themselves merciless and hard-hearted, those who first despoiled, then handed us the cup of bitterness to drink. We will bless them, for out of their iniquities will come forth our spiritual happiness. They thought to hurt us, and they quickened our progress. They tormented us, and it gave us the opportunity uncomplainingly to endure, to forgive and to forget!

Patience is the virtue which enables us quietly to submit; not because we are either placid or indifferent, but because we have learned to seek beyond the boundaries of the present those further consolations which render the tribulations of this life secondary and futile.

Patience conduces to kindliness. Souls, like mirrors, reflect the image of the sentiments with which they have been imbued. Sympathy inspires sympathy, and indifference generates sourness.

Let us learn, when it seems necessary, to reprimand with kindness, to discuss without heat, to judge of all things with benevolence and moderation.

We must constantly be on our guard against anger, which awakens the brutal instincts, those legacies of a dark past that civilization and progress are striving to eradicate. The beast still partially survives in every person; this beast we must subdue by force of our will if we do not want to become transformed into wild beasts. Anger arouses these slumbering instincts, then all dignity, all reason, all respect for oneself vanish. Anger blinds us, makes us lose consciousness of our actions and, in its fury, can lead us to crime.

Self-possession is an attribute of wisdom, just as anger is the token of a backward character. He who is prone to anger must keep careful watch over himself, especially over his excessive sense of personality; he must refrain from speech or action so long as he feels himself to be under the influence of this sinister passion.

Let us endeavor to acquire goodness, that ineffable quality, the halo of old age, whose soft warm rays attract every living thing, which makes of the heart that possesses it a shrine at which the poorest pledge their faith and allegiance.

Indulgence, sympathy and kindness cast a peaceful spell upon people, drawing them to us and inclining them to listen to our good advice; whereas severity repels and moves them away. Goodness thus lends us a sort of spiritual authority over the soul which we may endeavor to touch and set aright. Let us then make of it the torch, by which we may hope to kindle, no matter how feebly, even the most obscure intelligences; a heavy undertaking surely, but all things are possible to love.

49

Love

Love is the divine gravitation of souls and worlds, the heavenly power that interconnects the diverse universe, impregnating and ruling its many parts; love is the countenance of God.

Glorify not, by such a title, that passion which is the offshoot of carnal desire; for it is but the shadow, the gross caricature of love. Love is the superlative sentiment in which are dissolved and blended all of the heart's best qualities; in which goodness, charity and mildness are intermingled. It is the blossoming in the soul of a force that draws us above matter, to divine heights, even to the divine heights; which unites us to all beings, and evokes within us that inner happiness that so far surpasses any possible material delight.

To love, is to live in all and for all; it is to subordinate self to death, to martyrdom – whatsoever the cause that impelled this love. If you want to know what love is, meditate upon those sublime figures who have illuminated the somber pages of humanity's history; above all upon that Christ for whom love was all the morality and all religion. Did He not say ... "Love your enemy, do good to those that persecute you[109] ...?

---

[109] See chapter VI.

In thus exhorting us, Christ does not require from us an affection that cannot be in our hearts, but proposed to us to refrain from hatred, to shun reprisal and to endeavor to help those who have persecuted us, if the opportunity is presented to us.

A species of misanthropy, of moral lassitude, seems to withhold some of the good spirits from active cooperation with their fellow-beings. It is necessary to react against this tendency of isolation by recalling the affection and many kindly deeds of which one has been the recipient. The individual who is estranged from his fellow-beings, without ties of family or country, is a useless and unhappy being. His faculties diminish, his strength diminishes, and his sadness invades him. He achieves nothing single-handed. This shows us that it is wholesome to live among people, and above all among companions. Good humor is the health of the soul. Let us then throw our hearts wide open to all strong and wholesome impressions. Above all, let us love, that we too may be loved!

If our sympathy should be extended to every living being, animal or man, even to the unknown tribes of the great human race, what a deep and unswerving affection do we not then owe our immediate family! To the father who guided us in our youth, who worked long that our path might be smoother! To the mother who has borne us, nourished us, whose tender eyes witnessed our first steps, and who soothed our early pains! What loving care is due to them now that they are grown old! What gratitude and what fondness, in return for that which they so freely expended upon us!

To our country likewise do we owe our heart's blood. Is not our fatherland the collector and transmitter of the legacy of the many generations that have worked and died to build up this civilization whose advantages we inherit at our birth? Custodian of the accumulated intellectual treasures of the ages, it watches over their preservation and expansion, and, like a generous mother, transmits them to its children. Of this sacred patrimony of art and science, laws and institutions, liberty and order – in short, of all the immense funds that have been contributed by the minds and hands of our ancestors, of all that constitutes the wealth, greatness and genius of a nation – have we not a share? Let us then endeavor to make the services we render our country worthy of the benefits that it has bestowed upon us. Were it not for this country and all that accrues from it, we should still be savages.

May we likewise venerate the memory of those who gave up their lives to increase this patrimony; of the heroes who fought for it in perilous times; of all those who, incessantly even to their dying breath, have proclaimed truth and upheld righteousness – finally transmitting, gloriously with their blood, the liberty and progress which now are ours.

Deep as the sea, infinite as the heavens, love encompasses all things; for love proceeds from God. As the sun shines upon living beings and warms all nature, so does the divine love vivify all souls; its rays enter even into the darkness of our egoism and kindle flickering lights in the shadows of every human heart. All beings were created for love. The atoms of spirituality, the germs of righteousness that are in them, will some day open up and ceaselessly blossom until such time as they are united by one great communion of affection into one universal brotherhood.

You who read these pages, whosoever you may be, rest assured that some day we shall meet; either in this world, or in the course of some ultimate existence upon one of the more advanced planets, or yet in the immensity of space – be this as it may, we, at all events, are assuredly destined to meet, to influence one another righteously, to help each other scale the universal heights. Children of God, members of the great spiritual family, bearing on our brows the sign of immortality; we are destined to know one another and to be united in the holy harmony of law, far from the passions and deceitful mirages of the world. While waiting for this day my thought goes out towards you, my brother, as a pledge of true affection. May it support you in your decisions; may it comfort you in your pains; may it raise you in your failures; may it unite with the prayer, imploring our common Father to help us to attain a better future.

50

Resignation in Adversity

Suffering is a law of our world. In all conditions, at all times, in all climates, the human being has suffered and sorrowed. In spite of social progress, millions of human beings are still bowed beneath the burden of suffering. The higher classes are not beyond its jurisdiction. Sensitiveness, which among the cultivated spirits is quicker and more acute, engenders keener impressions. The rich person, as well as the poor, suffers both in flesh and spirit. From all parts of the Earth the human complaints ascends into space.

Even in the midst of abundance, a sense of depression, a vague sadness overcomes the sensitive soul. It realizes that happiness on this Earth is not to be, that at best only some evanescent shreds of it can be grasped. The spirit aspires to a purer life and a better world, some intuition whispering that this world is not the end of all things. For him who is imbued with the philosophy of the spirits this intuition becomes a certainty. He knows where he goes, he comprehends the reason for his afflictions and the cause of his suffering. Beyond the shadows and sorrows of the Earth, he perceives the dawn of another life.

In order to weigh the blessings and the ills of this life, in order to ascertain what is truly happiness and what is unhappiness, one must rise above the narrow circle of terrestrial existence. The knowledge of the future life, and of the destiny which there awaits us, enables us to measure the consequences of our acts and their influence upon our future.

Seen in this light the unhappiness of a human being will no longer consists in suffering, in the loss of friends, in privation or distress; contrarily it will be all that degrades or lowers him, all that hinders his progress. To him who merely considers the present moment, unhappiness may indeed consist in poverty, infirmity, and sickness. To the transcendent spirit who can impartially view passing events from its lofty standpoint, unhappiness will arise from a love of pleasure, from pride and all other concomitants of a useless and possible guilty life. One cannot judge of a thing unless one can foresee its every ultimate consequence; therefore none can comprehend life if he knows neither its object nor its laws. Trial, by purifying the soul, prepares it for its elevation and happiness, whereas the pleasures, riches and passions of this world weaken the spirit and expose it to bitter disappointment in the future life. Hence, he who suffers in spirit and flesh, he who is crushed by adversity, is entitled to hope and may lift a confident gaze to heaven, for he is paying his debt to destiny and is conquering freedom; but he who rejoices in sensuality forges his own chains and accumulates new responsibilities which will lay a heavy burden on his future days.

Pain, in its multiple aspects, is the supreme remedy for the infirmities and imperfections of the soul. Without pain there is no possible salvation. As organic disease is frequently the result of our excesses, so do the moral trials that we endure arise from our past misdemeanors. Sooner or later these faults fall down on us, accompanied by their logical consequence. Such is the decree of justice, and it is in keeping with ethical harmony. Let us learn to accept its ordinances as we swallow bitter medicine, or submit to the painful surgeries that will restore our bodily vigor and health. Even if we are visited by sorrow, humiliation and total ruin, we must undergo them patiently. The worker ploughs the ground that it may yield a golden crop; in like manner shall our torn hearts give forth an abundant moral harvest.

The action of pain has the effect of separating from us that which is evil and impure; the gross appetites, vices and desires, all which proceeds from the earth and must return to the earth. Adversity is the great school, the laboratory of the golden transmutation. Through its teachings, evil passions are gradually changed into generous deeds and love of good. Nothing is ever lost; but the transformation is slow and difficult. Suffering, the constant warning against evil tendencies, and self-sacrifice, can alone accomplish it, but thanks to these, the soul acquires both wisdom and experience. From a green and acid fruit, through the regenerating dews of trial and the warm rays of divine love, it has changed at last into a ripe and perfect fruit, ready to go to the higher worlds.

Our ignorance of the universal laws is alone responsible for the impatience we manifest towards suffering. If we could understand how necessary is this suffering to our own advancement, if we could learn to love its very bitterness – then we would cease to consider it a burden in our existence. Nevertheless we all dread pain; the necessity for which only becomes evident when we have left the world, its domain. It fulfills, notwithstanding, an inestimable function, bringing to light these seeds of love, pity and tenderness. Those who have never experienced suffering, lack their highest attribute; barely has the surface of their soul been touched. In them there can be no depth, either of mind or heart. Never having suffered, they perforce remain cold and indifferent to the sufferings of others.

In our blindness, we dare to complain that our life is obscure, monotonous or sad; but if we lift our eyes above the Earth's low-lying horizons we would thus distinguish this life's real purpose, we would discover that such existences are precious and indispensable to subdue the proud spirit. If we were noble in spirit we would submit to that moral discipline, without which there is no possible progress.

Free to act as we wish, exempt from evils and worries, we let the impetuosity of our passions prevail; finally we discover, to our dismay, that far from improving, we have only added to our past faults new ones. Under the stress of suffering, when leading humble lives, we acquire the patience and meditation, the peace of mind that enable us to hear the voice of reason – that voice which is whispering to us from above.

In the crucible of pain great souls are formed. We have seen people who smilingly drain their cup of bitterness – a noble example to those who are carried away by the torment of the passions. Trial is a necessary reparation, and knowing it to be such many among us have chosen it of their own free will. Let us think upon this when hesitating, may the example of great suffering borne with touching resignation, impart to us also the strength to remain true to ourselves and to those virile resolutions which we made before returning into the flesh.

The new faith has resolved the problem of purification through suffering. Spirit voices have whispered brave counsel in times of trouble. Some, who have endured every possible earthly anguish, come and tell us:

> I have suffered and have been happy only through my suffering. Pain has redeemed many years of luxury and indolence. Suffering has taught me to meditate and to

pray. When I lived in the whirl of pleasure never once did a salutary thought enter my soul; never did a prayer rise to my lips! Blessed be my trials, since they have finally shown me the path that leads to wisdom and truth.[110]

Such is the work assigned to suffering! Is it not the greatest that can be accomplished for humanity? It is carried on in silence and secrecy, but its results are incomparable. It detaches the soul from all that is low, material and transitory, and uplifts and directs it towards the future, to those higher realms. It talks to the soul of God and of His eternal laws. It is doubtless a fine thing to come to a glorious end, to die young and like a hero. History will record your name, and the generations will honor your memory. But a long life of pain, of ills patiently endured, is far more fruitful to the progress of the spirit. History will not say anything of it, undoubtedly. These obscure and silent lives – lives of quiet struggle and meditation – are entered only in the annals of human oblivion, but those that have led them find their reward in the spiritual light. Pain softens the heart and kindles the embers of the spirit. Pain is the chisel that shapes the marble rendering it harmonious and delicate in contour, and finally making it shine with its most perfect beauty. A long and continuous labor of sacrifice accomplishes greater results than any single sublime deed.

Then take heart, you humble ones who are enduring many ills! And you also, whom the world condescendingly pities for your backwardness and poor mental endowments! Learn that among you there are great minds that wanted to be born ungifted; resigning, for a time, their brilliant capabilities, aptitudes and talents, that they might thereby be humble. Over many intellects has the expiatory veil been drawn, but at death this veil falls and

---

110 A mediumistic communication, received by the author.

those that were disdained because of their ignorance shall then eclipse the proud who repulsed them. Nobody should be disdained. Beneath weak and humble appearances, or foolish and idiotic, great minds hidden under the veil of the flesh, for they are atoning some heavy past.

Ah you who lead lives sad and lonely, soaked with tears, sanctified by duty; lives of struggle and self-sacrifice, abounding in renunciation for the sake of family, friends and weaklings; lives full of untold abnegation and beautiful devotion; far more meritorious than any related in the pageantry of history, such lives are the most glorious by far of the rungs in the soul's ladder of immortal happiness! Indeed it is thanks to you, O humble lives, replete with ceaseless struggle and searing humiliation, that this soul has become so complete, so pure, and so transcendent! You alone, in the anxieties of every day bitterness and repeated sacrifice, are teaching it to appreciate patience, constancy and the dazzling beauty of virtue. To you will the soul be indebted for that glittering aureole which, in the immense vista of the future that stretches beyond this tiny life, will crown the brow of him that has suffered, struggled and vanquished!

Of all the cruel trials which fall to our lot here below, there is none greater than the loss of our loved ones, when they disappear, carried away one after the other by death. Little by little solitude gradually surrounds us and more complete becomes the isolation and silence that enshroud us.

The successive departures of all those we love are as many solemn warnings; they show us the puerility of our material preoccupations, of our earthly ambitions, while inviting us to prepare for the great journey.

The loss of a mother is beyond repair; what a terrible sense of void overwhelms us when this best of all friends sinks into the grave; when those dear eyes are forever closed; when those lips are grown cold that so often and so gently caressed our forehead! A mother's love! Is there anything purer or more unselfish? Is it not like a reflection of God's love?

The death of our children is likewise a source of bitter sorrow. What father or mother could be indifferent to the loss of their children? It is in these dark hours that spiritual philosophy comes to our assistance. It argues with our despair, bidding us to reflect that premature death is a blessing for the spirit that leaves earthly danger and temptation behind it. This so brief life appears to us as an inscrutable mystery; yet it had its reason. The spirit that had been entrusted to our loving care was here to complete that which it could not fulfill in a previous incarnation. These things we look upon from human standpoint, thence we err. Likewise will the earthly sojourn of these little ones have been of benefit to us. Thanks to them, we shall have experienced the holy sentiments of paternity and those other hitherto unknown and ineffable thoughts, whose influence softens and ennobles the heart. Through them there will have been created ties strong enough to bind us to that unseen hereafter which is to unite us all. And herein lies the beauty of the doctrine of the spirits, which shows us that these beings are not lost to us forever. For a while they leave us, but we are destined to rejoin them.

They leave us! Not so – our separation is but apparent. These beloved spirits – father, mother, and children – are ever near us. Their fluid, their thought, surround us, their love watches over us. Sometimes even, are we able to communicate with them, to receive their words of comfort and their advices. Their affection for us has never disappeared; death has but made it deeper and clearer. They exhort us to set aside the vain regret and sterile sorrow, which they are unhappy to witness. They beseech us to work courageously and persistently at our self-improvement, that we may the sooner rejoin and unite with them in the spiritual life.

It is our duty to battle against adversity. To give in, to silently succumb, to resign oneself without effort to the onslaughts of life, is to play the coward's part. The difficulties we have to overcome should stimulate and develop our intelligence. However, when every effort has proved vain, when we are at last brought face to face with the inevitable, then is the time that we must summon resignation to our side. There is no power that can avert from us the consequences of our past. To rebel against the moral laws would be as senseless as to pit ourselves against the law of attraction or gravitation. The insane individual might struggle against the immutable laws of nature, whereas the judicious individual discovers in his trials a means of self-improvement and of strengthening his virile faculties. An intrepid spirit accepts the evils of fate, but by his intellect he rises superior to them, and makes of them a stepping-stone to virtue.

The deepest and most harrowing affliction, when accepted with that humility in which both heart and reason consent, usually indicates the end of our evils, the acquittal of the last fraction of our debt. This is the decisive moment when it is important to remain firm, to appeal to all our resolve and moral energy, so that we may emerge victorious from our trial and reap the benefits of our victory.

⁓

How often, in our troubled hours, will the thought of death comes to visit us? To desire death is not wrong; but death only becomes really desirable when we have triumphed over all of our temptations. What is the use of desiring death if being not still released from our vices we must again return to purify ourselves by painful reincarnation? Our shortcomings stick to us like the tunic of the centaur; repentance and atonement can alone rid us of them.

Pain always reigns supreme over the world – nevertheless, if we look closely into it, we may see with what wisdom and what foresight the divine will has attenuated the effects of it. From stage to stage, nature ever tends to a less savage and violent order of things. In the early days of our planet, suffering was the being's sole stimulator and only school. Little by little, suffering is growing less and those dread ills of plague, leprosy and famine are decreasing. Our times are already less harsh than those of the past. The human being has subdued the elements, lessened distances and conquered the Earth. Slavery is no more. Everything evolves and progresses. Slowly but surely, the world, even nature itself, are improving. Let us then place our faith in the power that directs the universe. Our limited intellect could hardly comprehend the totality of its intentions. God alone has an exact notion of that rhythmic cadence, that necessary alternation of life and death, of night and day, of joy and sorrow, out of which the happiness and the elevation of His creatures are finally evolved. Let us leave it to God to appoint the hour of our departure, and let us learn to await it with neither fear nor desire.

Finally, the road of tests is traveled, and the righteous person feels that he is approaching his term. The things of this Earth daily pale to his vision. The sun seems dim, the flowers colorless, and the road full of stones. With a confident heart he sees death drawing near; for will this death not be the calm that succeeds the storm, the haven, safe from the leaping waves?

How noble is the vision of a resigned spirit that is preparing to depart from this Earth after a life of suffering! The soul casts a last long glance over its past; again it sees – but dimly, as immersed in shadow – the contempt it has endured, the tears that it has swallowed, the groans it has muffled, the sufferings it has uncomplainingly withstood. Gently it feels the bonds being cast asunder, which enchained it to this world of trouble. It is about to leave behind it this body of clay – and also, far behind – all material servitude. What could it fear? Has it not given proofs of abnegation; sacrificed its own interests to truth and to duty? Has it not drained to the dregs the cup of mortification?

It likewise sees what awaits it. The fluidic images of its acts of sacrifice and of renunciation, and of its generous thoughts, have preceded it, strewing the path of its ascent with shining landmarks. These are the treasures of the new life.

All this is apparent, and the gaze of this departing spirit is directed still higher; there where none may approach but whose forehead is pure and whose heart is glowing with love and faith.

At this sight the spirit is overcome with a divine gladness; almost does it grieve that its sufferings were not greater. A last prayer, which is like a cry of joy, escapes from the depths of its being and mounts towards its Father and Beloved Master. The echoes of space reiterate this cry of deliverance to which are added the accents of the happy spirits who assembled to receive it.

51

Prayer

Prayer should be an intimate overflowing of the soul to God; a solemn conversation, a meditation, ever useful, often fruitful. It is the supreme resource of the afflicted and of those that are faint at heart. In hours of depression, of dark despair, who has not found in prayer some measure of calmness, of comfort, some balm for his wounds? A mystic communion is established between the suffering spirit and the power it invokes. The soul lays here its anguish, its weaknesses; it begs for strength, help and indulgence. Then, in the sanctuary of conscience a mystic voice replies; the voice of Him, from whom proceeds the strength for the struggles of this world, the balm for our wounds, the light that dispels the night of our uncertainties. And this voice comforts, persuades, uplifts; it fills us with courage, submission and stoical resignation. Then we arise, feeling less sad and less depressed; a celestial beam has shone upon our soul, causing a tiny seed of hope to germinate therein.

There are some who scorn prayer, deeming it commonplace and ridiculous. Either they have never prayed, or have not known how to pray. Of course – if by prayer they mean the mechanically muttered paternosters, recitations as vain as they are interminable and all such numbered speeches mumbled by the lips but in which the heart plays no part – there may be some truth in their criticism; but this is not to pray! To lower prayer to formulas which one measures the lengthy of it becomes a profanation, almost a sacrilege.

Prayer is uplifting above all earthly things, an ardent call, an impulse, a beat of the wing, a determined flight towards those regions where the rumors and febrile agitation of a material world do not enter; wherein the being may find the inspiration it craves. The stronger its impulse, the sincerer its appeal, the more distinct and the clearer will be the revelation of the harmonies, the voices, the purity of the higher worlds. Prayer is like a window opening upon the unseen, into infinitude, through which the soul perceives a thousand sublime and consoling impressions. With these it becomes impregnated, intoxicated, and from them as from a fluidic bath, it emerges invigorated and regenerated.

In these conversations of the soul with the Supreme Power let no studied thoughts or words be used. The language of prayer varies according to the needs and to the state of mind of him who prays. It may be a cry, a moan, an outpouring, a song of love, a tribute of adoration; an introspection, a self-examination held under the eye of God; or again, it may be only a simple thought, a memory, a heavenward glance.

There is no hour for prayer. It is well, no doubt, to lift one's heart towards God at the beginning and at the close of day; but if you do not feel disposed to pray, do not pray. But again, when your heart is touched or swayed by some deep impulse – be it by the edge of the great waters, by the light of day or beneath the starry vaults of night; when surrounded by fields and leafy groves, or alone in the silence of the forest – little matters how or when, the cause is a holy one that inclines the knee to bend, brings a tear to the eye and fetches from the heart an anthem of love, a cry of worship addressed to that Eternal Power which guides your steps even upon the edge of the abysses.

It would be a mistake to suppose that we might obtain everything through prayer or that its efficacy is great enough to turn from us those trials that are inseparable from life. The law of immutable justice could not be swayed to suit our whims. Some pray for riches, oblivious of the fact that to be wealthy would be a misfortune for them, giving a free flight to their passions. Others want to remove the evils, which are sometimes the necessary condition of their progress. Removing them would render their lives sterile. On the other hand, how could God satisfy all the desires that people pray for? Most people are unable to discern what would be suitable, and most profitable to them.

In his daily prayer to the Eternal, the wise person asks not that his fate be a happy one; he does not beg to be spared pain, disillusion or adversity. That which he does pray for, is to know the Law that he may better observe it; that which he craves is help from above, the guidance of good spirits, so that he may more worthily bear himself in the hour of suffering. And the good spirits listen to his call, but they do not attempt to deflect the course of justice or to obstruct the execution of the divine decrees. Pitiful towards human suffering, which they too have known and endured, they bring to their earthly brothers and sisters the inspiration which will fortify them against material influence; they favor all noble and salutary thoughts, all the wholesome impulses of the heart which, while uplifting the person, likewise preserve him from the snares and traps of the flesh. The wise person's prayer, uttered at a moment of deep meditation which precludes all self-preoccupation, awakens in him that intuition of duty, that high sense of righteousness and justice which will carry him through the perplexities of life, and will attune him to an intimate communion with the great universal harmony.

But the sovereign power does not only represent justice; it is also goodness – helpful, immense and infinite. Why then should we not obtain by our prayers all that mercy can reconcile with justice? In our hours of distress we may always ask for support. God alone knows what is best for us, and failing to satisfy our demands, God will at least send us fluidic assistance and resignation.

When a stone strikes the water, its surface is made to vibrate in concentric undulations. So, likewise is the universal fluid set to vibrating by our thoughts and prayers; but with this difference, the vibrations of the water are limited, whereas those of the universal fluid follow one another ad infinitum. All beings and all worlds are steeped in this element, just as we are in the Earth's atmosphere. It results from it that our thought, when impelled by a sufficient impulse and speeded by a sufficient will-force, has the power to impress other, perhaps incalculably distant, souls. A fluidic current is thus established which enables the advanced spirits to influence us and to answer our summons, even from the far depths of space.

A similar action may be exerted by us upon suffering spirits; prayer exercising an influence such as that of magnetism. It penetrates the dense, dark fluids that surround the troubled spirits, and lessens their sadness and dismay. It is the luminous arrow piercing their darkness; it is the melodious vibration which expands and rejoices the oppressed spirit. What comfort it must convey to such spirits to feel that they are not forsaken – to know that some human being still cares for them! Sounds, at once mighty and gentle, arise like a chant through space, and resound the more intensely as the lips from which they proceed are the more loving. They reach them and greatly are they touched thereby. That distant, friendly voice is bringing them peace, hope and courage. Could we but estimate the effect produced upon these unhappy spirits by an ardent prayer projected by a generous and energetic effort of our will, our voices would be unceasingly raised on behalf of the dispossessed and forsaken creatures of space – those whom no one remembers and who are, for the time being, steeped in the gloomiest despondency.

To pray for unhappy souls – to pray with fervor and love – is one of the most efficacious forms of charity, one which all may practice; for any one can facilitate the spirit's release and shorten the period of perturbation through which it passes after death – effecting this, by a wave of warm thought, by a kindly and affectionate remembrance. Prayer facilitates the disintegration of the body; it assists the spirit to free itself from the gross fluids that unite it to matter. Under the influence of the magnetic waves projected by a powerful will, torpor ceases, the spirit again becomes conscious of itself and regains its self-possession.

Prayer for others, for friends, for the sick and the unhappy, when it proceeds from a well-intentioned heart and a sincere faith, may also be of good effect. Even when the laws of destiny are opposed to the accomplishment of its object, even when the trial must be undergone to the bitter end, prayer is never useless. The salubrious fluids with which it is charged accumulate to overflow at death into the perispirit of the being prayed for.

"Gather you together to pray,"[111] was the apostle's injunction. United prayer is like a sheaf of wills, of beams, of harmonies, of perfumes which ascend with multiplied power towards its object. It may acquire an irresistible force, one capable of uplifting and

---

111 Acts XII, v.12.

upheaving the fluidic masses. What a lever it is for the earnest soul who imparts, by a mighty impulse, all the greatness, purity and elevation it possesses! When the spirit is in this mood thoughts gush forth, like an impetuous torrent, in great and mighty emanations. The soul has been seen, when engaged in prayer, to free itself from the body and, with vivid ecstasy, to follow the burning thought which it had cast as a forerunner into space. The human being has within him an incomparable motor from which he knows how to obtain but a trifling energy. In order to operate this motor two things are necessary: faith and will.

Prayer, thus considered, loses all mystic semblance. Its object is to obtain neither favor nor indulgence, but spiritual elevation and communication with the superior fluidic and moral powers. Prayer is a thought tending towards righteousness; a luminous thread which connects the dark worlds with the divine, the incarnated spirits with the free and radiant souls. To disdain prayer is to despise the one force that interposes itself between us and the clash of material interests and passions; which lifts us above transitory things into that which is fixed, permanent and immutable in the universe.

Instead of rejecting prayer because of the abuses committed in its name, is it not better to use it with wisdom and discretion? At the end of each day, before seeking our rest, let us look into ourselves and carefully scrutinize our actions; unreservedly condemning those that were bad, so as to prevent their repetition, and rejoicing over whatever good and useful things we may have done. Let us ask the Supreme Wisdom to help us realize, within and around us, a moral and perfect beauty. Let us lift up our thoughts far above the Earth, so that our spirit may speed, joyously and lovingly, towards the Eternal One. From this elevation it will return to the Earth, with courage and boundless patience, which will lighten its burden of duty and its labor of perfection.

If in our powerlessness to express our sentiments we feel the need of a text, let us say:

> Lord, Thou who art great, Thou who art all; let fall upon me – who am so small and who only am because it is Your will that I should be – a ray of Your light. Ordain that, penetrated by Your love, righteousness should seem easy and evil abhorrent; that, animated by the desire to please You, my spirit may overcome all obstacles to the triumph of truth over error, of fraternal love over selfishness; ordain that in each fellow-struggler I should recognize a brother, just as You see a child in each of the beings which emanate from You but to return to You. Grant me to love the work, which is the duty of all that dwell upon Earth. By the light of that torch, which You have placed in my hand, enlighten me as to those imperfections that delay my progress, both in this world and in the next.[112]

Let us unite our voices to the voices of space – wherein everything is worshipping and everything is rejoicing with the joy of life; from the mote dancing in the sunbeam to the great star that is afloat in the ether. The worship of the beings forms a prodigious volume of harmony that fills space and ascends to the Maker of all things. It is the anthem of the children to their Father; the homage rendered by the creatures to their Creator. Question nature in the radiance of sunny skies, in the stillness of starry nights; hearken to the great voice of the sea, to the sounds that arise from the desert's arid

---

[112] An extemporary prayer dictated, by the intermediary of spirit-rapping, by the spirit of Jerome of Prague to a workers' reunion, at Le Mans.

bosom and from the cool depths of the woods; to the mysterious murmurs that proceed from beneath the foliage, that allow themselves to be heard in mountain gorges, that are exhaled by valley and plain, that escape from mountain heights and that extend over the entire universe. From every hand, if you listen devoutly, you may hear that wonderful hymn of praise that the Earth is singing to the Great Spirit. Still more solemn is the prayer of the worlds of space; the grave, deep chant which causes the immensity to vibrate and of which the spirits alone can comprehend the sublime meaning.

52

Work, Sobriety and Continence

Work is the law of the inhabitants of this world, and of those of space. From the most rudimentary types to the angelic spirits who hold watch over the destiny of the worlds, each has his allotted task, his part in the great concert of the universe.

Painful and difficult for the inferior beings, work becomes lighter as life becomes more refined; it is a fount of joy for the advanced spirit, who, insensible to material attractions, is exclusively occupied in high studies.

It is by work that the individual overcomes the blind forces of nature and to ward off privation; it is by work that civilizations have evolved, and science and comfort have been popularized.

Work has been the individual's badge of honor and emblem of dignity. The idler, who unproductively enjoys the fruit of the labor of others, is only a parasite. As long as the human being attends to his duty, his passions remain quiescent. Idleness, on the contrary, releases them and provides them with a broad field of action.

Work, likewise, is a great comforter and a wholesome antidote to our cares and worries; it appeases the anguish of the spirit and stimulates the intellect. There is no mental suffering, no disappointment, no disillusion but that finds a palliative in work; there are no vicissitudes of fortune that can resist its constant action.

He who works has ever a refuge at hand in uncertain times and a true friend in adversity; to him life can never become and aimless thing. How sad is the lot of the worker who has been condemned by infirmity to passive inaction, especially of one who has discovered the nobility and blessedness of work; who he sees the general interest, the good of all, and wishes to contribute to it; there could hardly be a more bitter trial for such a being.

Such is the position in space of the spirit who has failed his duty and wasted his life. Comprehending only too late the innate nobility of work and the baseness of idleness, he suffers in as much as he cannot execute that which his soul desires and conceives.

Work is the communion of beings. Through it we are drawn closer together, we learn to assist one another, to unite; from this to fraternity there is but a step. Ancient Rome dishonored work by leaving it to her slaves. Hence Rome's moral sterility, corruption, and her heartless creed.

The present day has achieved a different conception of life. The fullness of life is sought in prolific and regenerating work. Spiritual philosophy also broadens this conception by showing us that the principle of all progress and elevation lies in the law of work, and by demonstrating that the scope of this law extends over the entire universe of worlds and beings. That is why we feel justified to say: "Awake, all you whose latent faculties and forces lie dormant! Arise and set you to work! Work, till the earth, and cause your factories to resound with the clang of hammer upon anvil, and with the steam whistle's strident call! Shake yourself in the great beehive of the world, for your task is both vast and holy. Your work concerns humanity, life, glory, and peace. And, you workers of thought, scrutinize the great problems, study nature, disseminate science broadcast among the multitudes, let your words be heartening and inspiring! From world's end to world's end again, may we all of us unite in mighty endeavor, each striving his uttermost; thus shall we contribute to enrich the kingdom of the human being, be it of matter, intellect or spirit."

⁓

The first requisite of him who desires to possess a clear conscience, a robust mentality and a well-balanced mind, is to be both moderate and chaste. Overindulgence in eating upsets body and mind, while over-drinking entails the loss of all dignity and the over-stepping of all bounds; a frequent repetition of either inevitably leads to sickness and infirmity and eventually to a miserable dotage.

Grant to the body that which it requires in order to remain a useful servant, and nothing more; this is the wise person's rule. To reduce the sum of its material needs, to subdue the senses and master the base appetites, is to shake off the yoke of the inferior forces, to prepare the spirit's emancipation. To have few needs is likewise a form of wealth.

Sobriety and continence go hand in hand. The pleasures of the flesh soften and enervate; they deflect us from the way of wisdom. Voluptuousness is a sea in which the human being's best qualities are engulfed. Far from satisfying us, it does nothing but poke our desires. As soon as we let it penetrate in us, it is a flood which invades us, absorbs us, and which extinguishes all that there is in our being of lights, of generous flames; at first a moderate visitor, it ends by mastering and utterly possessing us, body and soul.

Avoid the corrosive pleasures by which youth is deteriorated and life is poisoned or exhausted. In youth, choose a companion early and be faithful to her. Make yourself a family; it is the natural framework of an honest and regular existence. The love of wife and children, the blessed influences of home, are the sweetest antidote against every form of unrighteousness. Surrounded by these dear ones, our sense of responsibility, dignity and self-respect are necessarily enlarged, and we awaken to a better understanding of our duties. From this wholesome life we likewise glean new strength. How to dare to make acts of which we would have to blush under the glance of our wife and our children? To learn how to direct others, it is to learn how to direct oneself; it is to become wise and prudent and to avoid all that might tarnish our life.

It is wrong to live for self alone. To give up one's life to others; to see oneself reproduced in the children one has brought up to be useful men and women and zealous servants in the cause of good; to die after imparting to them a deep sense of their duty and a broad insight into their ultimate destiny; this is truly a well-filled life.

If there are exceptions to this rule, it is in favor of those who have valued humanity above family, and who for its sake have undertaken some higher mission and must therefore single handed face the vicissitudes of life, ascending in loneliness the arduous path; consecrating all their time, all their faculties and all their soul to some end, which the world cannot perceive, but of which they themselves never lose sight.

Sobriety and continence, the subjugation of the instincts, do not imply, as a pleasure-seeking person, a disregard for the natural laws or a contempt for this life; quite the contrary, they denote in him who practices them a profound acquaintance with the higher laws and an enlightened intuition of the future. The voluptuous whom death severs from all he loves is consumed by vain desire. He haunts the house of vice and such earthly associations that reminds him of his former way of life. Thus does he ever more firmly rivet his material chain, going ever further from the source of pure happiness and pledging himself ever deeper to darkness and bestiality.

To place one's happiness in carnal enjoyment is to deprive oneself, for a long interim, of the peace which is the heritage of the superior spirits. Purity alone can give his peace, as we learn even in this life. Our passions and desires give birth to images – phantoms that pursue us even in our sleep and disturb our visions – while, far from lying pleasures, the spirit can meditate, can gain strength and learn to appreciate delicate sensations. Then will its vision ascend towards eternity. Already detached from low-lived lust, it experiences no regret on abandoning its exhausted physical body.

Let us often meditate, and let us seek to apply this Eastern adage: *"To be strong, to be happy – be pure!"*

53

Study

Study is the source of much enjoyment, both pleasing and elevating. It helps us to forget the sordid troubles and cares of the world. A book is a faithful friend who stands by us in good and bad times. We naturally refer to the serious and useful book that comforts and sustains, not to the frivolous novel whose highest aim is amusement and which but too often misleads the reader. The true character of the good book is not sufficiently penetrated. It is like a voice that speaks to us through time, telling us of the works and achievements of those that preceded us over life's rough thoroughfare, and that died striving to make it smoother to our thankless feet.

Is it not one of the few felicities of this world to be able to communicate by thought with the great minds of all ages and countries? The finest minds of every age have poured into their books the very quintessence of their hearts and intellects; our facility of communion with them is one of the greatest boons of civilization. They take us by the hand and lead us through the labyrinth of history; they are our guides in the highest realms of science, literature and art. As we scan these sacred archives, human's greatest treasure, we feel less insignificant and are proud to belong to the race that has produced such genius. The radiance, of their thought illuminates and warms our minds.

We must then learn to read good books and to keep close contact with the elite spirits. Let us carefully reject the filthy books whose only mission is to pamper vulgar appetites. Above all we must be on our guard against that loose literature, the fruit of sensualism, which taints both mind and morality.

There are many who assert their fondness for study while deploring their lack of leisure. They seem, however, to have time enough to devote to recreation and frivolity. We are told that books are expensive; but in truth the money squandered on worthless pleasure would purchase a handsome library. The study of nature, moreover, which is the most helpful and comforting of all research, we may have for nothing.

Human science is both changeable and fallible, which the science of nature is not, for nature never contradicts itself; in our hours of doubt and uncertainty we cannot do better than turn to it. It will greet us like a mother smiling upon us and taking us to its bosom. The language of nature is simple and direct, its truths are artless and unadorned; it is strange that so few of us seem capable of hearkening to and comprehending them. The human being carries with him, even into the depths of solitude, his discontent and unrest, which are stronger than nature's quiet voice. If we would discern that latent revelation which lies at the core of things, we must first put down the turmoil raised by the delusions and noisy discussions of the human beings; we must meditate and instill peace within and about us. Then the public echoes die away, the soul retreats within itself and regains its relinquished touch with nature and its eternal laws, and becomes fitted to commune with the Supreme Reason.

If the study of nature strengthens and uplifts the mind, what then can we say of the vision of heaven?

When peaceful night unfolds its spangled dome, and when the starry procession begins; when the diffused and trembling light of the nebulous and stellar clusters disseminated in the remoteness of space descends upon us, a mysterious influence surrounds us and we are overcome by a deep religious feeling. How remote, at this hour, seem our trivial perplexities! How overwhelming that sense of the incommensurable that seizes upon us and forces us to our knees! What a flood of mute adoration gushes from our heart!

The Earth's frail skiff is afloat upon the waters of immensity; on which it glides, impelled by the mighty sun. Everywhere, beneath and above, are stretched tremendous depths that no brain can grasp, no eye can scan and remain untroubled. Everywhere likewise, at immense distances, are worlds and still other worlds; floating islands rocked upon a sea of ether. The eye cannot count them, but the mind, drawn by their subtle refulgence, wonders at them, and wondering, loves.

Their subtle radiations attract him. Great Jupiter, and you, Saturn, belted with your luminous scarf and crowned by nine golden moons[113]; giant suns of many-hued radiance, spheres unnumbered in the endless depths of space; we salute you all! Worlds that shine so far above our humble heads, what marvels do you conceal? We would like to know you, and would like to see your people, what strange cities and civilizations your mighty spheres may sustain. Some secret intuition whispers that you may be the abiding place of that happiness which, here below, we seek in vain.

---

113 N.T.: Saturn has 62 confirmed moons of which 9 are waiting to be officially named. (2017- Caltech.edu)

But why doubt or fear? Are these worlds not our legacy? Are we not destined to explore and inhabit them? Shall we not cruise among those stellar archipelagoes and discover their furthermost mystery? No limit can be affixed to our travels, our ambition and progress; if only we be careful to attune our will to the divine laws, and by our actions to acquire the true fullness of life, together with the divine happiness this entails.

54

Education

It is through education that the successive generations are transformed and improved. A new society requires new people, hence is the child's education of paramount importance.

It does not suffice that a child should acquire the elements of science. To learn to govern and conduct oneself as befits a reasonable and conscious being is quite as necessary as to learn to read, write and calculate; for only thus can one enter life prepared, not only for the material but above all for the moral struggles. One endeavors to develop the child's intellectual faculties and brilliant parts, but not his virtues. At school or at home, little effort is made to enlighten the child as to its duties and ultimate destiny. Wherefore, lacking the fundamental principles and ignoring the real object of his existence, the person finds himself, from his entrance into public life, exposed to the snares and temptations of a dissolute and corrupt society.

Even in secondary schools an indigestible conglomeration of facts and notions, names and dates, stifles the minds of the students without any attention being paid to their moral instruction. School morality, which is deprived of effective direction and without a universal purpose, cannot be otherwise than sterile of result and incapable of supplying youth with a strong moral fiber.

The education given by religious establishments is equally puerile. Within their walls the child is exposed to all manner of superstition and fanaticism, imbued with false notions concerning this world and the next.

A good moral education is rarely the work of a schoolmaster. To awaken in the child the first aspirations to good, to redress a difficult character, it is necessary at the same time perseverance, firmness, and affection, which only a parent can impart to his child. If the parents cannot succeed in this, how should the master, whose hands are already so full!

Education is not, however, as difficult a task as at first appears; it requires no very profound insight and may be undertaken by anyone acquainted with the inner nature and ultimate moral effects of what he teaches. Let us bear in mind that these spirits have come to us that we might assist them to overcome their imperfections, and prepare them for the duties of life. When we marry we tacitly accept this mission; let us achieve it with love, but with a love free from weakness, because the outraged affection is full with danger. From the cradle we should study the child's tendencies, tendencies that it has brought with it from anterior existences; applying ourselves to develop those that are good and to eliminate the others. Neither should the child be too much indulged, so that soon accustomed to disappointment it may learn that that terrestrial life is arduous, that each of us must learn to rely only on ourselves, on our work, from which all dignity and all independence proceed. Let us not try to divert them from the course of the eternal laws. There are stones in everyone's way which only wisdom alone can teach us to avoid them. Education should not be mercenary, wherefore entrust not your children to other hands, unless you are absolutely constrained; What does it matter to a nurse that a child speaks or walks before another? She lacks the maternal love and pride that cause a mother to exult at her darling's first steps! She loves, hence neither pain nor fatigue dismay her; do the same for the souls of your children. Have more solicitude for her than for the body. For the body will soon be exhausted and ready for the charnel house, whereas the immortal spirit, pure and resplendent, thanks to the care that has been given upon it as well as to its own progress and merit, will endure time without end to bless and to love you.

Education, based on an exact conception of life, would change the face of the world. Let us suppose every family to be initiated in the spiritualist beliefs which are founded upon facts, and their children to be brought up on these, while the neutral schools would inculcate the principles of science, and in a wonderfully short space of time would the influence of this double current become manifest.

All moral wrongs arise from a faulty education, to reform, to place it on new basis, would be productive of unspeakable good. Let us by all means instruct youth and enlighten its mind, but first let us appeal to the heart, pointing out its imperfections and their remedy. We must bear in mind that the highest science is that of self-improvement.

55

Social Problems

Social problems are a present cause of much anxiety. It has become evident that the march of civilization, the enormous increase of production and wealth and the development of education, have not been able to eliminate pauperism, nor have they cured the ills that overwhelmed the masses. Generosity and humanitarianism are not, however, extinct. Latent in the hearts of the people there lies an instinctive longing for justice, which is like the vague premonition of a better state of things to come. It is generally admitted that a more equitable distribution of wealth and position is necessary: hence a thousand theories and a thousand divergent systems, all designed to increase the welfare of the poorer classes, or at least to ensure to all people the bare necessities of life.

But the application of these theories demands, on the one hand, much skill and patience, and on the other that spirit of self-denial which is so rarely met with. Instead of a mutual good-will, which by bringing people together would enable them to resolve the most serious problems, it is violently and with threats that the poor person demands his seat at the social banquet; bitterly likewise does the rich person entrench himself within his selfishness and refuse to relinquish the least portion of his wealth to the needy. As a result, the gap widens, and misunderstandings, hatred and covetousness increase.

The state of war, or of armed peace, which weighs upon the nations, contributes to these hostile sentiments. The different governments are setting a lamentable example and assume a heavy responsibility in thus developing the warlike instincts to the detriment of peaceful and fruitful enterprise. How then can we hope to reconcile the clashing classes, to appease evil passions, to resolve intricate questions of common welfare – when all incites to violence and when the strength of mighty nations is expended upon a mission of destruction?[114]

Of the systems advanced by the socialists to bring about a practical organization of labor and a wise division of wealth, the best known are cooperation, based upon the workers' association; some go as far as to recommend communism. The partial application of these theories has so far produced but slight results. It is true that in order to live united and to participate in any enterprise in which many interests are combined, qualities, which have become rare, are required. Nor is the cause of present evils, or their remedy, to be found where they are generally sought. Vainly does the human being elaborate ingenious combinations. Theories follow upon theories and institutions follow upon institutions, but the human being is still unhappy, because he is still wicked. The root of evil lies within us, in our passions and in our errors. This is what we should seek to alter. To improve society, the individual must first be improved. That this may come to pass, a knowledge of the higher laws of progress and solidarity, a revelation of our inner

---

[114] While deploring the evils caused by war, we must not therefore lapse into an enervating state of peace at all costs. In order to ensure the moral and material integrity of France we still recognize the necessity for an army which the progress of civilization will some day utilize, let us hope, for higher works; such as those of general peace and welfare.

nature and ultimate destiny are requisite; these, spiritual philosophy alone can give us.

This thought may perchance seem strange! To pretend that this much-disdained Spiritism could affect the destiny of nations, that it could supply the key to social problems, is far indeed to modern reasoning. However, one will be forced to recognize that the opinions and the beliefs have a considerable influence on the shape of societies.

The social life of the Middle Ages was an exact reflex of the Catholic conceptions. Modern society, under the spell of materialism, perceives little in the universe beyond the petty rivalry of people and the battle for life; that terrific struggle in which all instincts and all passions are unleashed. This threatens to transform our world into some blind and preposterous machine by which people's life will be ground to dust, in which the human being himself will represent only some tiny and transitory component, evolved out of that nothingness back into which he will soon be whirled. Such a conception of life would soon put an end to all notion of solidarity.

How utterly does our point of view change, how soon is our entire attitude modified, when a new ideal comes to enlighten our mind and amend our ways. Once convinced that this life is only an isolated link in the chain of our lives, an opportunity granted us of progress and purification, we will attach less importance to transitory events. As soon as it is established that every human being must be born many times over in this world, undergoing all manner of social conditions – the obscure and sorrowful existences occurring far more frequently, and ill-applied wealth ever entailing crushing consequences – then will every one comprehend that in striving to ameliorate the condition of the poor, the lowly, the ailing, he is likewise working for himself, since he is bound to return to this Earth, and that there are nine chances to one of his being born to poverty.

In the light of this revelation, fraternity and solidarity become obvious necessities – such things are privileges, favors and titles being henceforth opposed to reason; nobility of acts and thoughts take the place of those or parchment.

Thus viewed, the social question takes on a different aspect. Concessions from one class to another become a matter of course, and all antagonism between labor and capital comes at once to an end. The truth once grasped, people would finally understand that the interest of the one is the interest of all, and that no one individual may be the prey of his fellows. Hence justice in distribution, and with justice instead of hateful rivalries, mutual trust, reciprocal esteem and affection would spring up; in a word the realization of the law of fraternity will become the only one among people.

This is the remedy of spiritual philosophy, applied to social evils. If the few gleams of truth that lay hidden under the obscure and incomprehensible dogmas have in the past inspired so many noble deeds, what should we not expect from a conception of life based upon facts, which teaches the individual that he is united to all beings; that, like them, he is bound to mount ever higher through progress and the working of profound and wise laws, until he and they attain to perfection.

Such an ideal is great enough to move any earnest soul to the utmost heights of enthusiasm, and to bring forth unparalleled results; its qualities of love, fraternity and unselfishness would not only suffice to create a new social order, but one that would totally surpass the he most sublime acts of antiquity.

The social question not only relates to the contentions of the different classes, but it is likewise concerned with the social status of woman. Woman has ever been sacrificed, and it would be just to allow her to exercise her natural rights, as well as to give her a more dignified position. This would consolidate family ties and make them still more holy; for woman, indeed, is the soul of the home, and the representative of peace and mildness in humanity. Freed from the trammels of superstition, if her voice could be heard in the councils of the nations and her influence could be felt, then the scourge of war would soon disappear.

Spiritual philosophy, by showing that the body is a borrowed form and that the principle of life is contained in the soul, establishes the equality of the sexes as concerns rights and merits. Spiritists grant to woman her full dues, both at their meetings and in their labors; in the latter, indeed, her influence is preponderant, as the delicacy of her nervous system peculiarly designs her for a medium.

The spirits affirm that by choosing incarnation in the feminine sex, a spirit can more rapidly progress from life to life to perfection, because woman more readily acquires the sovereign virtues of patience, gentleness and kindness; while in man the intellect seems to predominate, a woman's heart is greater and deeper.

Woman's social sphere is generally restricted, and sometimes she is treated like a slave; thence she becomes greater in the spiritual life, for insomuch as a being has been sacrificed and belittled here below, the greater will be its merit before Eternal Justice. This argument, however, cannot be advanced by those who desire to maintain woman in subjection, for it would be iniquitous under the pretext of a future happiness to perpetuate a present social wrong. Our duty is to work with our utmost strength for the realization on Earth of God's will. Woman's education and rehabilitation, the abolition of pauperism, ignorance and war, the fusion of classes into one brotherhood, the distribution of property, all these reforms are a part of the divine plan which is none other than the law of progress.

But of one thing we must not lose sight: the inevitable law can bestow upon a human being only such a degree of happiness as that being's personality merits. In worlds like ours poverty could not altogether disappear, since it is a necessary condition of the spirit, which must be purified through work and suffering. Poverty is the school of patience and resignation, just as wealth is the test of charity and abnegation.

Our institutions may change in form, but they can never rid us of those evils that are inherent in our imperfect nature. The happiness of the human being does not depend upon political changes, revolutions or any other social modifications. So long as society remains corrupt, even so will its institutions be, no matter how many changes may intervene. The only remedy lies in that moral transformation to which the higher teaching shows us the way. If the human being would only devote to this task a little of that passionate interest which he devotes to politics, if he would only pluck from his heart the root of his ailment, then would social iniquity soon cease to exist.

56

The Moral Law

In the preceding pages we have explained all that the spirits have revealed concerning the moral law. In this revelation lies the real grandeur of Spiritism, prefaced by phenomena that are to it as the rind is to the fruit – inseparable in gestation but of very different value.

Scientific research must inevitably lead to philosophical study, whose apex is attained in that morality which recapitulates, completes, and expounds all the ethics of the past to finally become the universal morality, the source of all wisdom and virtue, but whose experience and practice are acquired only after many existences.

The comprehension and realization of the moral law is the soul's most necessary and valuable attainment. It enables us to estimate our inner resources, and to dispose of them for our greater good. Our passions are forces, dangerous when we are their slaves, useful and beneficent when they are under our control. To dominate passion is to become great – to be dominated by it is to remain small and contemptible.

Reader, if you aspire to be liberated from earthly ills and to be no longer subjected to painful reincarnation, write within yourself this moral law and practice it. Allow to the material person only that which is indispensable, for he is a transitory being which death will dissolve; but carefully tend the spiritual being which will live forever. Detach yourself from perishable things – riches and worldly pleasures, which are but smoke – eternal only, are the good, the pure, the true!

Preserve your soul without stain, and your conscience without reproach. Every evil thought or deed will attract to yourself the impurity that lurks without; each endeavor and each effort towards righteousness adds to your strength and brings yourself into communion with the higher powers. Develop within yourself that inner life which connects yourself with the unseen world and with the entirety of nature – for this is the source of our true power, and of that exquisite happiness which will ever increase as the impressions of external things weaken with the coming of old age, and with our detachment from earthly matter. In your hours of meditation, lend ear to the harmony that surges from the depths of your being, like an echo from some half-forgotten dream-world: an echo that breathes of great moral struggles and of noble deeds performed. In these exquisitely mysterious sensations, in these inspirations, of which the wicked and sensuous have no inkling, recognize the prelude to the free life of space: a foretaste of that happiness which is the heritage of every righteous, good and dauntless spirit.

Recapitulation

To enhance the clearness of this study, we will recapitulate the essential principles of the Philosophy of the Spirits.

I -   A divine intelligence governs the worlds. With it is identified the Law: immanent, eternal, and ordaining – to which all beings and all creatures are submitted.

II - As the individual, beneath his material, incessantly renewed, envelope, preserves his spiritual identity – that indestructible self, that conscience by which he recognizes and regains possession of himself – thus does nature, beneath its changeable aspect, possess and reflect itself in a living unity which is the Self. The self of the universe is God: the Supreme Unity in whom all beings meet and utterly harmonize; the great focus of all light and perfection, which radiates and emits to the furthest world its Justice, Wisdom and Love!

III - Everything in the universe evolves and tends towards a higher state. Everything is transformed and perfected. Out of the depths of the abyss springs life; at first unformed, uncertain, animating forms innumerable, gradually more and more perfect, and finally evolving the human being, in whom it acquires conscience, reason and volition, and constitutes the soul or spirit.

IV - The soul is immortal. A coronation and synthesis of the lower forces of nature, it contains, in embryo, all the highest faculties which through its work and efforts it is destined to develop by incarnation in material worlds, ascending, degree by degree, through successive existences, to perfection.

The soul has two envelops: the one temporary, the earthly body, an instrument of work and trial which disintegrates at death; the other permanent, the fluidic body, from which it is inseparable and which progresses and is purified with it.

V - The earthly life is a school, a means of education and of improvement through work, study and suffering. There is neither eternal happiness nor eternal misery. Recompense and retribution consist in the extension or diminution of our faculties and of our field of perception, and depend upon the good or bad use we have made of our free will, and upon which aspirations or inclinations we have encouraged within us. Free and responsible, the soul contains the law of its own destiny; in the present it reaps the consequences of its past, and sows the joys and sorrows of its future. This life is the heritage of our preceding lives and the basis of those to come.

The soul is enlightened, and its intellectual and moral growth are proportionate to the distance it has traveled, and to the impulse it imparts to its actions in the sense of righteousness and truth.

VI - A close solidarity unites all spirits, who, all, are identical in origin and ultimate destiny, but different as regards their temporary condition – some being free in space, and the others confined within a perishable envelope – but all alternate from one condition to the other; death being but a period of rest between two earthly lives. Coming from God, their common Father, all spirits are brothers and sisters and, when united, form one great family. A perpetual intercommunion and a continual interchange connect the dead with the living.

VII - The spirits are classified in space by the density of their fluidic bodies, which itself is governed by their degree of advancement and purification. Their position is determined by precise laws; these laws plays, in the moral kingdom, a similar mission to those of attraction and gravitation in the physical domain. In this world justice rules as imperiously as gravity in the world of matter. A dense fluidic atmosphere that weighs them down towards the inferior worlds, in which they must incarnate in order to divest themselves of their imperfections, surrounds guilty and wicked spirits. The virtuous soul, encased in a subtle, ethereal body, participates in the sublimated sensations of spiritual life and rises towards brighter worlds, where matter has less sway, and where harmony and happiness prevail. The soul, in its superior and perfect state, collaborates with God and co-operates in the formation of the worlds, directing their evolution and watching over the progress of the many races, and the fulfillment of eternal laws.

VIII - Righteousness is the supreme law of the universe, and the object of the evolution of beings. Evil has no existence of its own, it is merely an effect of contrast. It is the state of inferiority, the transitory condition, which all beings experience during their ascent towards a better condition.

IX - The education of the soul being the very object of existence, it is important to summarize the precepts in a few words:

> *To repress all gross desires and material inclinations, and to cultivate, in their place, elevated and intellectual tastes. To strive, to struggle, and if needs be, to sacrifice self, to the advancement of humanity and worlds. To initiate in our brothers and sisters the transcendent beauty of Truth and Righteousness. To love truth and justice, and to practice good will and charity towards all; this is the key to future happiness, this is Duty.*

Conclusion

At all times rays of divine truth have shone upon humanity; every religion has had its share in them, but human passions and material interests quickly veiled or distorted these teachings; then followed dogmatism, religious persecution and all manner of abuses, and thus the human being relapsed into indifference and skepticism. The tide of materialism has overflowed all, relaxing the character and undermining the conscience.

Then, one day, the voice of the spirits, the voice of the dead, caused itself to be heard; truth started forth from the shade and revealed itself, more dazzlingly beautiful than ever before, and the voice cried: "Die, that you may be born again; profit by that rebirth that you may grow better and progress through struggle and suffering!" And death has ceased to be a thing of dread, since behind it we can perceive the resurrection. Thus, Spiritism was born. Being at once an experimental, philosophical, and ethical science, it imparts to us a general conception of the world and of life, which is based upon reason, upon the observation of facts and causes; a broader, completer and more enlightened conception than those that have preceded it.

Spiritism illuminates the past, casting a bright stream of light upon the ancient spiritualist doctrines, and reconciling apparently contradictory systems. It opens new vistas to humanity. By initiating the person into the mysteries of the future life and of the unseen world, it reveals to him his true position in the universe; it acquaints him with his dual corporeal and spiritual nature, which commands infinite horizons.

Of all systems, it alone can furnish objective proof of the being's survival, and indicate the means by which we can communicate with those we mistakenly call "the dead". Thanks to Spiritism we can indeed communicate with those we love here below, and whom we though we had lost forever; we are enabled to receive their teachings and counsels. Spiritism likewise teaches us to develop the scope of these communications by practice.

Spiritism reveals to us the moral law, and makes our duty manifest to us: its tendency is to unite humanity more closely through brotherhood, solidarity, and the community of views. It indicates to all a more worthy and higher purpose. With it comes a new conviction in prayer, an impulse to love and to work for others, to enrich heart and mind.

The doctrine of the spirits, which appeared upon humanity in the middle of the nineteenth century, has already been spread over the whole surface of the globe. Many prejudices, interests, and misapprehensions still retard its march, but it can afford to be patient, for the future belongs to it. It is strong, constant and tolerant of human's prejudices; progressive likewise, thriving on science and freedom; disinterested, with no higher aim than the happiness of humanity; to all it brings peace and confidence, imparting firmness in the hour of trial. Many religions and many philosophies have succeeded one another in the world's past, but never have more powerful appeals in favor of Almighty Goodness resounded in the heart of humanity, never has it been presented with a more rational, ethical and comforting doctrine. Thanks to this doctrine the period of vague hopes and uncertain aspirations is at an end. It is no longer a question of the dreams of a sickly mysticism, or the myths born of superstitious beliefs; it is reality itself which has cast aside the veil; it is in all verity, the genuine affirmation of departed spirits, momentarily returned to instruct us. Victorious over death, in translucent light they soar far above this world, which they still follow and direct in its perpetual mutations.

Enlightened by these spirits, certain of our duty and destiny, we resolutely follow in the traced path. Truly has our life assumed a different aspect! It is no longer the narrow, dark and lonely circuit which most people thought they saw. For us, this circle widens to the point of embracing the past and the future, which it connects to the present, to form a permanent, indissoluble unity. Nothing dies. Life simply alternates in form. The grave returns us to the cradle, but both voices proclaim immortality.

Perpetuity of existence, eternal solidarity of the generations, equality, ascension and universal progression – such are the tenets of the new faith, and these tenets are grounded upon the rock of experimental method.

Can the antagonists of this doctrine offer more to humanity? Is it that they can better soothe their sorrow, heal their wounds, proffer sweeter assurances or greater certitude? If so, let them speak and produce some proof to substantiate their assertions. Should they, however, still persist in a denial which the facts disprove; if the best they can offer instead of that which they so groundlessly deny, be either hell or annihilation, then we surely have every right to reject their anathemas and their sophistry.

Come to quench your thirst at this heavenly spring, all of you who suffer, all of you who thirst for truth; for into your soul will it pour its refreshing and regenerating waters. Refreshed by her, you can better face life's ordeals and be prepared more worthily to live and die.

Assiduously study the phenomena upon which these teachings are based, but do not make a play of it. Remember that to communicate with the dead is a serious matter and that it is no slight thing to receive from them the solution of great problems. Consider that these matters are destined to work the most astounding moral revolution that history has yet recorded, opening up to all the ignored perspective of the lives to come. That which was only a hypothesis for the thousand generations, for the immense majority of those that preceded you, for you is become a certainty. Surely such a revelation is deserving of all your attention and respect; use then wisely for your own good, as well as for that of your fellow being.

With this understanding the superior spirits will lend assistance to you; but should you attempt to use Spiritism frivolously, know that you would become the inevitable prey of lying spirits, the victim of their snares and mystifications.

And you, friend and brother, who, recognizing their full value, which received these truths in your heart; bear from me one last appeal, one final exhortation!

Remember that life is short. During this time, strive to acquire what you came to seek in this world: true perfection. May your spiritual being come out more pure than it has entered! Beware of the snares of the flesh; Think that the earth is a battlefield, where matter and the senses are perpetually assaulting the spirit. Against your base desires strive unweariyingly; strive with heart and mind to correct your faults; soften your character, and strengthen your will. Let your thought transcend the vulgarities of this world; and open for yourself loopholes which can command a glimpse of God's heaven.

Recollect that everything that is material is invariably ephemeral. Like the ocean waves, generations roll by, empires crumble, worlds even perish and suns are dissolved: everything disappears, everything vanishes. But there are three things which come from God and which like God are eternal, three things that shine above the shimmering of human glories, and these three are: Wisdom, Virtue and Love! Conquer them by your efforts, and having once acquired them you will rise above what is momentary and transitory, to enter into possession of that which is eternal.

Biography of Léon Denis

Léon Denis was born in a village called Foug, located in the surroundings of Tours, in France, on January 1st, 1846, of a humble family. Very early in life out of necessity, he did manual works and had to carry the heavy responsibilities of his family. From his first steps into this world, he sensed that invisible friends assisted him. Instead of participating in plays relating to his youth, he tried to instruct himself as intensely as possible. He read serious works, thus striving through his own efforts, to develop his intelligence, and became a serious and competent self-didactic.

At the age of 18, he started working as a sales representative, and because of this he traveled frequently. He loved music, and whenever he had a chance, he would attend operas or concerts. He played well-known arias at the piano and also some accords that he himself composed. He did not smoke, and was almost exclusively a vegetarian, nor did he indulge in fermented drinks. He found water to be his ideal drink.

It was his habit to review books with interest, of those displayed in the bookstores, and at the age of 18, by "chance" his eyes glanced at a work with an unusual title: The Spirits' Book by Allan Kardec. Having in his possession the amount needed to purchase the book, he bought it and rushed to his home immediately surrendering eagerly to the reading.

Denis commented after reading it: "I found in this book the clear solution, complete and logical, to a universal problem. My conviction became strong and sound. The Spiritist Theory dissipated my indifference and my doubts."

The year of 1882 marked, in reality, the beginning of an apostolate, during which he had to face successive obstacles, such as: the materialism and the positivism that viewed Spiritism ironically and with amusement, and also, the believers of other faiths who did not hesitate to align themselves with the atheists in order to ridicule and weaken Leon Denis. Denis, however as a heroic paragon, had no fear of facing the storm. The good spirits were placed at his side to encourage and to exhort him in the battle. "Courage, friend," the spirit of Joan of Arc told him, "we will always be with you to sustain and inspire you. You will never be alone. In time, the means will be provided to you, so that you can fulfill your task."

On November 2nd, 1882, on the day of the commemoration of the dead, an event of capital importance occurred in Denis's life: for the first time, the spirit who would be his guide, his best friend, his spiritual father, Jerome of Prague, manifested himself saying: "Go, my son, follow the open road before your eyes. I will walk behind you to sustain you."

By 1910, Léon Denis' vision was weakening day by day. The surgery to which he had submitted two years prior had not resulted in any improvement, but he calmly and with resignation withstood the implacable march of that illness that had persecuted him since his youth. He accepted everything stoically and with resignation. He was never heard complaining. Though, one can well imagine how immense his suffering must have been. In spite of this, he kept up with a voluminous amount of correspondence. He was never upset, loved his youth and possessed a happy soul. He was an enemy of sadness. Physical illness represented a smaller interference to him than the anguish he felt for the fact that he would no longer be capable of writing. Various secretaries substituted him in at this work; however, the greater difficulty for Denis consisted in reviewing and correcting the new edition of his books and of his writings. Thanks, however, to his incomparable memory and orderly spirit, he overcame all those setbacks, without the need to call on his friends for assistance.

After World War I, he studied and learned Braille, which allowed him to put on the paper the elements of chapters and articles that came into his mind, because at this time in life, he was practically blind.

It was a Tuesday, in March of 1927, at about 1:00 pm, that Denis breathed with great difficulty. Pneumonia had attacked him once again. Life seemed to abandon him, but his state of lucidity was perfect. His last words, pronounced with extraordinary calm, in spite of the great difficulty, were spoken to his assistant, Georgette: "It is necessary to finish, to summarize and to conclude." He was referring to the foreword of the new biographical edition of Kardec. At this exact moment, he completely lacked the energy to articulate another word. At 9:00 pm his spirit flew away. His countenance seemed as if he was still in a state of ecstasy.

The funeral services took place on April 16th, 1927. At his request, the funeral was very simple and without the participation or pronouncement of any confessional Church. He was buried in La Salle's cemetery, in the French city of Tours.

Among the great apostles of Spiritism, the extraordinary powerful presence of Léon Denis deserves a very distinctive place, particularly, in view of having been the logical follower of Allan Kardec's work. We can be sure that it constituted an extremely difficult task to write about Denis' life, given the magnitude of his mission on earth. It is difficult to determine what to point out first, whether it be his incredible personality, the good sense of reasoning with which he was endowed, his commitment to work, his dedication to his fellow beings or the fervent love he consecrated to the ideals that he embraced.

Léon Denis was the consolidator of Spiritism. He was not just the substitute and continuator of Allan Kardec, as is generally supposed. Denis had a mission practically as significant as the one of the Codifier. To him, was assigned the development of the doctrinaire studies, to proceed with the mediumistic research, to propel the Spiritist Movement in France and all over the world, to deepen the moral aspect of the Doctrine and above all, to consolidate it in the first decades of the Century. In that new Bible, (Spiritism) the role of Kardec is that of the wise person and the role of Denis is that of the philosopher. Léon Denis was nominated the Apostle of Spiritism, due to his magnificent work, and the words written and spoken on behalf of the new Doctrine. He can also be denominated its consolidator, the Philosopher of Spiritism. Possessing accentuated moral qualities, he dedicated his entire existence to the defense of the postulates that Kardec had transmitted in the books of the spiritist Pentateuch. The moral aspect (religious) of the Doctrine, the superior principles of life, the instruction, and the family, deserved his extreme cares, and, for that reason, his life of probation, work example, perseverance and faith, is a journey of light to every spiritist; we will declare further more: for all the individuals of goodwill of all eras. With these words of confidence and faith, Denis himself, summarized the mission that he had come to accomplish in favor of a noble cause: "I have consecrated this existence to the service of a Great cause, Spiritism or Modern Spiritualism that will certainly be the universal faith, and the religion of the future."

His bibliography is quite extensive and composed of monumental works that enrich the spiritualist libraries. It is due to him that the Spiritists have been blessed with the unique opportunity to see the enlarged new angles of the Spiritist Doctrine's philosophical aspect, because, his works generally focused on the numerous problems that occur to humanity, and also to the perpetually disturbing subject of the survival of the human soul in its laborious evolutionary process. Léon Denis was immortalized in the gigantic task of dissecting problems related to the afflictions that attack the incarnate beings, supplying valuable information which in essence throws new light on the problem of the terrestrial tribulations. He left behind the concepts that until then had prevailed, to present it engulfed in the light of highly comforting teachings, which resulted from the inexhaustible sources of the Doctrine of the Spirits.

Being devoted to the profound study of Spiritism, in its triple aspect, incorporating science, philosophy and religion, he took a long time with greater persistence in its philosophical aspect. Together with his serious studies in that field, he also made a valuable contribution, in dealing and studying historical subjects, supplying important subsidies clarifying the Celtic origins of France and concerning the dramatic episode of the martyrdom of Joan of Arc, the great French medium. His studies didn't stop there. He worried excessively about the origins of Christianity and its evolutionary process through the times.

Among his multiple occupations, he was honorary president of the Spiritist French Union, honorary member of the International Spiritist Federation, president of the International

Spiritist Congress, realized in Paris, in 1925. He also had the opportunity of directing for many years, an experimental group on Spiritism, in the French city of Tours.

His performance in the heart of Spiritism was more diverse than those developed by Allan Kardec. While the Codifier exercised his noble activities in the French capital, Léon Denis carried out his dignifying task in the countryside of France. His unusual intellectual capacity and his clarity in transcendental matters, led the Spiritist Movement in France, and in the rest of the world, to gravitate toward the city of Tours. After Allan Kardec's death, that city became the point of convergence of all who wanted to make contact with Spiritism, and receive illumination, because, undeniably, the Pleiades of Spirits that had as task, the success of the process of revelation of Spiritism, gave to the great apostle all the necessary support so that the new doctrine could be rooted firmly in a wide and unrestricted way.

While Kardec stood out as a personality of universal proportion, who made his name in the Academic World, before he became devoted to the spiritist research and to codify Spiritism, Léon Denis was an autodidactic who received his schooling in obscurity and in material poverty, to appear suddenly in the intellectual scene and to impose himself as a lecturer and a famous writer, becoming an exponential representative in the field of the doctrinaire dissemination of Spiritism. Denis possessed a robust intelligence; he was a great speaker and writer, enjoying an appreciable degree of intuition. Referring to him, one of his contemporaries Gabriel Gobron, wrote: "He met true victories and those who had the rare happiness of hearing him speak in a group attendance of two or three thousand people, know perfectly well, how charming and convincing his speeches were."

Denis never studied in an accredited academy; however, he developed in the practical school of life. He experienced his own pain and that of others. He was not well paid, having to undergo heroic deprivations, which taught him wisdom. For this reason, he used to say: "The ones that have not experienced those lessons usually ignore one of the most moving sides of life ". With the resources of his uncommon intelligence he could have been spared from poverty, but he preferred to live within it, as in his opinion it was difficult to accumulate selfishly for himself, that which he had received to be distributed among his fellow beings.

In a well-advanced age, blind, and with a relatively weak constitution, he still lived full of tribulations. Nothing, however, changed his way of proceeding. In spite of all those adverse conditions, he received everyone with deference. From the first hours of the morning he dictated letters to his secretary, answering voluminous correspondence, replying to the pleading of countless societies that he had founded or of which he had been named honorary president. Whenever he visited, he was always designated a place of greatest prominence, a mark achieved at the price of deep dedication, perseverance and untiring work in goodness.

MAIN WORKS OF LÉON DENIS:

"Christianity and Spiritism;
"Here and Hereafter;
"Spirits and Mediums;
"Joan of Arc;
"In the Invisible;
"The Beyond and the Survival of the Being;
"Spiritism and the Catholic Clergy;

"Spiritism in the Art;
"The Celtic Genius and the Invisible World;
"The Great Enigma;
"The Invisible World and the War;
"The Reason of Life;
"Life and Destiny;
"Progress;
"Experimental tests of the Survival;
"Socialism and Spiritism."

Made in the USA
Middletown, DE
03 March 2017